W9-BWR-156

Communities within Cities

To Fran and Tonwen

Communities within Cities
an Urban Social Geography

Wayne K. D. Davies and David T. Herbert

Belhaven Press
London

*Co-published in the Americas by Halsted Press, an imprint of
John Wiley & Sons, Inc., New York*

Belhaven Press
(a division of Pinter Publishers)
25 Floral Street, Covent Garden, London, WC2E 9DS, United Kingdom

First published in 1993

Co-published in the Americas by Halsted Press, an imprint of
John Wiley & Sons, Inc., 605 Third Avenue, New York, NY 10158-0012

W. K. D. Davies and D. T. Herbert are hereby identified as the authors of this work as provided under Section 77 of the Copyright, Designs and Patents Act, 1988.

British Library Cataloguing in Publication Data

A CIP catalogue record for this book is available from the British Library

ISBN   1 85293 155 8 (hb)
          1 85293 153 1 (pb)

Library of Congress Cataloging-in-Publication Data

A CIP catalog record for this title is available from the Library of Congress

ISBN   0-470-2202-28 (hb in the Americas only)
          0-470-2202-36 (pbk in the Americas only)

Typeset by Saxon Graphics Ltd., Derby
Printed and bound in Great Britain by SRP Ltd., Exeter

Contents

Preface

This book was conceived as a study of the social geography of communities within cities. As such it was intended to concentrate on the relevance of **place** to the broader ideas which have come to be known as the **community question**. In fact, although the implicit belief in the value of community as place is a theme which runs through the text, a broad interdisciplinary perspective has been developed which allows this focus to be seen in the context of the many other ways of interpreting and analysing community. The extant literature on community is very large and remains both vibrant and innovative; community as an urban reality is an integral part of a great deal of contemporary policy formation and implementation at both national and local levels, and has increasingly become a base for informal collective action within cities. This text has tried to reach out and evaluate all of these issues with a concern both for the key conceptual issues related to the idea of community and the need to consider the ways in which the plethora of recent empirical research advances our understanding of urban life. To claim a comprehensive analysis of community would be far too ambitious, although the need to direct substantial works to that theme has motivated this book. The selectivities and omissions reflect both the interests and biases of the authors and the constraints of space.

The book was made possible by two awards. Wayne Davies (normally a member of the Geography department) obtained a Fellowship in the Humanities Institute at the University of Calgary in 1991–2 which allowed a reduction in teaching commitments and time to research and write for this text. David Herbert was a recipient of the prestigious Killam Visiting Scholarship of the University of Calgary which allowed him to spent a semester at Calgary in a teaching and research capacity. These two awards from the University of Calgary are gratefully acknowledged. David Herbert is normally based at the University of Swansea and in 1990 Wayne Davies was made an Honorary Fellow of that University. International collaboration is well represented in this text, though both authors originate from the famed communities of Industrial South Wales and Wayne Davies's parents once lived in the pioneering neighbourhood of Bird's Hill in Letchworth.

Many other people have helped in various ways in the preparation of this book and we express our gratitude to them. At Calgary, Cindy, Ivan, Rhiannon and Kara helped with the word-processing and proof-reading of the text and references; at Swansea similar help was given by Lynn, Yvonne, Duncan and Nia. Our thanks must also go to our close mutual friend Guy Lewis who provided the cartographic and illustrative material in his usual helpful way; also to Iwan Saunders who did nothing specific but did help. The Departments of Geography at Calgary and Swansea provided the helpful environments for our academic literary efforts, and our colleagues in both places are acknowledged.

Calgary and Swansea
August, 1992

List of Figures

List of Tables

1

Alternative Perspectives on Community Studies

Introduction

Community is one of several similar words in the English language, such as communication and communal, which are derived from the same basic root: one that implies some kind of association, perhaps even sharing and participation in common relationships. Throughout history humans have always been part of groups we loosely call communities, in which *associations*, however weak, bind people together. These bonds come from a variety of characteristics: such as shared origins, perhaps based on kinship, tribe, history or place; similar features or activities such as economies, interactions or social structures; or similar attitudes linked to common values, behaviours and purposes. Not all have to be present at the same time. However, the common-sense meaning of the term 'community' is derived from these shared characteristics that bind people together. Frequently, but certainly not always, the associations take place in some *defined area*. Hence community can have a spatial or territorial context, a common territory or place that often reinforces the interactions, provides a psychological association and enhances its character. Community is also related to the term 'neighbourhood' for which it is sometimes used as a synonym. However, usually neighbourhood is much more restricted in spatial dimensions. It relates to the area around a residence within which people engage in neighbouring, which is usually viewed as a set of informal, face-to-face interactions based on residential proximity. It is this locational element that provided the initial rationale for the interest of human geographers in the topic, although the spatial dimensions of the common structures and networks as well as the way it produces the distinctiveness of places provide a more recent motivation. Community is best considered as a collective noun that stands for a variety of related, overlapping ideas that need to be clearly distinguished if we are to understand all of its ramifications.

The task of understanding the richness of the concepts embedded in the term 'community' is made more difficult because the term has holistic associations. Although most humans feel the need to belong to some mutually supportive network of relationships that are readily available, these go beyond primary group ties, neighbouring or gossip networks. In Keller's (1988, 169) words:

> Community ... must include something larger and grander — a collective framework; participation in a common enterprise; a sense of social solidarity that transcends individuals and private networks; and most especially a sense of mutual obligation and responsibility for social survival. That was certainly the sense in which community was featured by the great political theorists — from Plato... to Rousseau.

Moreover the term is not emotionally negative. Raymond Williams (1976, 66) argued in his book *Keywords* that community generally has positive connotations. Many of the contributors to a recent collection of philosophical essays on the concept (Rouner 1991) stressed the beneficial value of 'community' in combating the isolation and self-centredness of so much of modern life. Others would agree with Keller (1988, 181) that there are also 'the dangers of bigotry and Babbitry in small circumstances'. Yet the term often produces opposite attitudes. Many see 'community' in the same type of context as 'motherhood'. It conjures up positive feelings of belonging for some: even caring, sharing, safety, loyalty, rootedness and solidarity. These qualities contrast with opposing characteristics, which can best be summarized in the term 'individualism', namely, loneliness, selfishness and indifference to one's neighbours. However, not all share an intrinsically positive attitude towards community. Life in many communities frequently entails the loss of personal freedom because of persuasive intrusiveness and adherence to group mores. It can even be coercive if group norms are imposed upon individuals and the freedom to leave the community is withheld. This seems to be the case in many cults where the individual is reduced to an automaton subservient to the leader, or in repressive communalistic societies where the collective purpose is considered to be more important than the individual. Then individualism may be seen as positive, providing people with personal liberty.

Despite western society's achievement of some of the highest levels of personal freedom and the opportunity to pursue individual interests, many still express dissatisfaction with our society, particularly its individualism, its emotional coldness and competition. Some critics of the present hark back to the imagined satisfactions found in some bucolic, pastoral community of harmony and togetherness. Few choose to remember the reality of most historic rural communities: that of unremitting toil, the constant threat of starvation and depredation by outsiders, internal rivalries, frequent backbiting and a persuasive intrusiveness. Indeed it is salutary to remember that many of those who wrote about the idyllic bliss of some communal rural past frequently had more in common with the élite that controlled the system, rather than the people who really experienced it. Throughout history critics have proposed new forms of communities as solutions to the perceived ills of their period, as seen in utopian experiments (Mumford 1922).

Others have rejected their contemporary world in the search for a community ideal. History is replete with many examples of failed community experiments at the settlement level which failed to solve the negative features of closed communities. Yet the survival and growth of agriculturally based communities that have a religious cohesion must be noted, such as the German-speaking Hutterite colonies in western Canada (Peters 1987), still based on the sixteenth-century teachings of their founder, or the strength of the almost socialistic Israeli kibbutz movement (Blasi 1986). These provide evidence of long-lasting settlements with high levels of sharing and communal control. Such settlements contrast with the thousands of more ephemeral hippy or cult communes that sprang up in the 1960s. Many other attempts to search for ways of combating the problems of isolation and self-interest in contemporary society can be recognized, from the communist attempt to build a better society in the Soviet Union and eastern Europe, to returns to belief systems based on other-worldly considerations, such as Muslim Traditionalism or Born-Again Christianity. Despite their many differences, both return the individual to a subservience to God. Far more people in the western world seek communities of more intimate relationships through membership in a church, some shared spiritual experience based on belief in some other world and shared moral ideals. Others have created communities based on their similar ethnic origin. Sometimes the concentration is an involuntary one, forced upon the groups by barriers in the host society. In other cases it may be a voluntary one, due to a strong desire to be among people of similar origins, to adhere to a different lifestyle, perhaps reinforced by religious beliefs. These ethnic enclaves are paralleled by the rapid growth of what can be called 'lifestyle communities', by people with a different set of values or attitudes, organized as a commune. Examples range from Bagwan Rajneesh's cult community in Antelope (Oregon) to the gay community in cities such as San Francisco, where many, though far from all, are concentrated in the Castro and

Lower Haight areas (Fitzgerald 1981). Another example of the development of communities in recent years has been the rapid growth of community or neighbourhood organizations in residential areas, especially in suburban areas in North America. Many provide local services, provide a defence against change, or are designed to counteract some of the perceived problems of an individualistic society.

Apart from all the locality-based associations described earlier our modern settlements have literally thousands of formal and informal groups, clubs, societies and organizations that cater to specific interests: groups devoted to flower-arranging, Bible meetings, kung-fu, or stamp-collecting — the list is endless!! Clearly we live in what can best be described as an *associated society*. This huge range of available options might lead to the view that our society is a paradise for individuals seeking personal fulfilment. Obviously it is not. A world full of associations is not enough to solve the *Angst* of modern or postmodern life. The problem seems to be that most contemporary associations are only partial ones, related to the specific purpose of the interest group or the service provided. As such they fail to provide the emotional identity and unconditional support that seems so desirable to many who espouse the community ideal. So the holistic community ideal cannot be achieved by mere association, the joining of a group to fulfil some needs or pursue some interests. Many will argue that the holistic ideal is an impossible dream. It is one that can be achieved only by giving up many of the freedoms so perilously won by our predecessors, and is based on some quite untenable views about the extent of harmony, trust and equality of previous communities. Nevertheless we should not deny the utility of the community approach in helping to find solutions to some of our contemporary problems. Before this can be dealt with in detail, we need to clarify the meaning of the term and direct more precisely the aim of this study.

Alternative Approaches to Community Study

Ambiguity and elusiveness in meaning seem to be gross understatements when one attempts to understand the many different ways in which the word 'community' has been used — whether by academics or in popular parlance — and this explains why so much confusion exists over its use. Hundreds of books and thousands of articles have been written on the topic within a number of different disciplinary areas. It seems that the term has been used in five different contexts, namely, community as association; as a community-of-interest area; as territorial units, whole or part; as ideal or utopia: as places or areas in cities.

Community as an Association

At its simplest level, the word 'community' is often used as a synonym for membership in some interest group, institution, or workplace. Individuals are often described as members of a school or university 'community'. Clearly the basic idea here is that the individual members have an *association* with one another: they meet, combine or interact to fulfil some common purpose, or share some common interest (Hiller 1941). No territorial basis is necessary, except that the members are located in earth space and the relationships may be conditioned by area. For example, the informal interrelationships between people whose residences are located in close proximity are usually described as 'neighbouring'. Most associations, however, do not necessarily require any territorial base. Studies of interaction, of communities as associations or networks, are becoming the focus of a new branch of knowledge called 'social networks', or more recently as 'social structures'.

Community-of-Interest Areas

Geographers have been active in analysing this type of community for many years (Dickinson

1947). It follows from the recognition that people in many rural areas are bound together by their linkages (particularly shopping or commuting ties) to a nodal centre, a town or city. These provide the workplaces, stores, markets, entertainment centres or social facilities for people from the surrounding areas. This community is still an association in one sense — the people in the area are bound together by their common ties to the node or central place. However, in this case a region of dependence around the town or city is defined — an area usually known as a 'community-of-interest' region or hinterland. Many different data sources have been used, such as the use of daily shopping or commuting trips, whilst sophisticated techniques, such as multivariate methods (Davies 1981; 1984) or theoretical models have been used to define the regions.

Communities as Territorial Units: Whole or Partial

The most general use of the term 'community' lies in its application to a complete settlement, to any town or village. Community studies, therefore, provide empirical investigations and descriptions of the way of life of people in particular settlements or localities. Literally thousands of studies, from primitive hunting and gathering groups to villages and small towns in the western and underdeveloped world, have provided the basis for an extensive literature in anthropology, sociology, and to a lesser, but still important extent, in geography. Most were of relatively small places, the size of area that could be studied by a single researcher or small research team. The origin of these studies can be traced back to the turn of the century and is based on two traditions. The stronger lay in the development of a more scientific approach in the emerging field of anthropology in the 1930s, in which the emphasis was first placed upon primitive societies, and was later applied by sociologists to larger settlements in modern and industrial societies, such as Warner (1941) in the United States, Lewis

(1986) in Wales, or Stacey (1961) in Banbury, England. The second tradition of interest in this type of community study grew from a different intellectual source, namely, that of the local region or *pays* approach in human geography. French geographers at the turn of the century had developed a far more humanistic approach to the description of local areas than the environmental or deterministic emphasis of their contemporary German counterparts, primarily because of their strong links with history. Paul Vidal de la Blache and his students pioneered the study of these *pays*, or small, distinctive rural areas. By integrating the physical and human characteristics of these areas that had combined to form a distinctive *genre de vie*, regional geographers provided vivid descriptions of many localities, often recognizable rural communities in France. It is important to note that the values, meanings, customs and heritage accounted for as much of the distinctiveness of areas as the physical endowment, although in subsequent decades the dependence on statistical description meant that these qualitative and intangible features were gradually dropped. These studies are usually called 'regional' rather than 'community studies' and they often parallel the later work of many anthropologists or sociologists — although it must be understood that they were carried out on a different scale and with more interest in economic issues than landscape description.

In some cases, especially in isolated mining towns and fishing villages, the similarity of occupation and isolation often led to much local interaction, and a social solidarity that was best seen in co-operative behaviour in the face of common deprivation and daily danger in the workplace. The result was a strong and frequently reinforced sense of community. However, the change to a service economy and the welfare state reduced the number of these distinctive settlements and the degree of common feeling. By the 1960s there was widespread disillusionment with community and small-scale regional studies. Most social scientists became more interested in the systematic studies of processes linked to separate social phenomena. Yet in the last resort the application of the methods of social anthropology that were honed in primitive societies to modern settlements failed to resolve problems caused by the implicit assumptions of *community wholeness, the holistic community*. The concept of 'wholeness' refers to the ability of the community group to maintain themselves economically, biologically, and culturally: basically to eat, to reproduce and to transmit its culture (its way of doing things, its view of the world) to successive generations (Arensberg and Kimball 1965, 17).

Historically, the most basic form of the holistic community was the three-generational hunting and gathering group. It needed the experience and memory of the old, and the reproductive and hunting capacity of the young adults, to guarantee their own survival and to ensure the time-consuming nurturing of its young. Such groups were not usually permanently located in one place, except in locations rich in renewable food stocks such as economies based on fishing. Instead they were nomadic, ranging over a territory. Today, most settlements are not microcosms of some larger society: they represent only a specialized part of it. Moreover, unlike many plant or animal communities, individual small settlements do not represent an enduring entity, with generational growth or maintenance and with enough relationships with the larger society of which it was a part, to throw light on these macro relationships. Nevertheless, considered as *partial entities*, local territorial communities can still be worthwhile units of analysis for several reasons.

1. They identify local patterns of life, local attitudes and problems that may be impossible to uncover by other methods.
2. They provide a valuable counterweight to the modern tendency to adopt the analytical approach of pursuing single patterns or relationships. By stressing the interrelationships between different features or elements in a settlement they show the horizontal linkages, rather than the vertical associations with the larger society.
3. They provide valuable case studies in illustrating the effect of national or higher scale societal changes upon the individual settlement, and in identifying problems that affect these areas.
4. New hypotheses and meanings may emerge from the participant-observation method that is employed to understand the perspective of the 'insiders' in place of that imposed by 'outsiders', as well as understandings that cannot be gained from detached observation.
5. Studies of small regions or settlements can still produce valuable insights into part of the way of life and functioning of society — although the crucial word here is 'part'.

Arensberg and Kimball (1965, 36–40) provided an extensive inventory of the variety of issues and questions that should be considered by community studies. Even if these represent a body of literature that is not easily integrated, it is one that has provided a wealth of insight into local culture and relationships.

Community as Ideal or Utopia

Related to the concept of a community as an association or territorial entity is the idea of the community as some sort of desired or ideal life. This is very much a value-laden interpretation, one linked to a quest for some new moral or spiritual associations entailing an intimate relationship with other human beings. These idealistic communities were frequently based on communal endeavour in a settlement separated from the rest of society. Plato's *Republic* and Thomas More's *Utopia* are the best known, although hundreds of theoretical suggestions have been made through the centuries (Negley 1977), together with practical experiments such as Robert Owen's New Harmony and New Lanark experiments. Mumford (1922) and Fishman (1977) are among many who have provided reviews of the range of utopian experiments, with the first two of these concentrating on the past and the twentieth centuries respectively. These have been extended by studies in individual countries, such as those by Armytage (1961) in England and have attempted to compare the character of individual utopias in a cross-cultural sense. Few of the ideal communities have been built and fewer have lasted for long. This has not discouraged new imitators — even in the present period. Their exponents believe that it is necessary to move away from the corruption and anonymity of modern life; only a separate settlement founded on new principles can provide the antidote to the perceived ills of our contemporary society.

Place Communities in Cities

The term 'community' is also frequently applied to areas within cities — districts that have particular characteristics that set them apart from the rest of the city. *The rest of this study concentrates on community in this interpretation of the word.* Since these place communities are obviously set within the larger built-up entity of a settlement, they are subsidiary to the city, and can be considered as subunits within the urban place. Although social commentators described the distinctive social areas in nineteenth-century cities (see Chapter 3), it was not until the work of the human ecologists at the University of Chicago in the 1920s that the study of these areas became a distinctive academic tradition. Robert Park and his associates (see Burgess 1925) coined the term 'natural area' for the distinctive subdivisions that could be identified in cities — areas that were homogeneous in one or more characteristics, whether social class or land use. In recent decades academics have avoided the term 'natural area', mainly because of its implicit association with the plant ecology principles that were used as generalizing processes by the Chicago School. The term 'residential mosaic' has been more in fashion, a term that also carries the implication that there are a series of

distinctive and perhaps overlapping social regions within the modern city. It is worth noting that there has always been confusion between the terms 'neighbourhood' and 'community'. The Chicago ecologists recognized that neighbourhoods nested within the larger communities (Hunter 1974, 7), although they never comprehensively dealt with the difference. Neighbourhoods are usually considered to be much smaller — as areas of a few houses, or at most a few blocks — defined as areas in which neighbours routinely interact (see Chapter 4). Unfortunately, the terms are often used interchangeably in popular parlance or as categories for various scales of social units in planning documents.

The rest of this book is devoted to an overview of the various ways that intra-urban communities can be studied. There are literally hundreds of books and thousands of articles on the topic. Most concentrate only on part of the community phenomena. If the multidimensional character of urban place communities is to be understood, these variations need to be defined in more detail. The study is divided into three broad sections. Chapter 2 continues the direction of this first chapter by setting the context for the rest of the book, not in terms of alternative definitions as in Chapter 1, but in exploring the relationships between western society and community. It demonstrates that the eclipse of community anticipated by Stein (1960) must be attributed to deeper causes than the developments of the past century. However, recent work has shown that individualism and the communications revolution has not destroyed place-based communities in cities, merely transformed them. The next three chapters review the concept of community from three different perspectives. Chapter 3 deals with what is described as their areal content, the approach often called 'ecological'. Chapter 4 discusses the interactions and organizations that are associated with concepts such as 'social networks'. Chapter 5 summarizes their cognitive and affective dimensions, which relate to 'sense-of-place' ideas and extend the symbolic-cultural approach of workers such as Hunter (1974). All three aspects are needed to understand the multiplicity of features that comprise the 'place community' concept within cities. Three essentially applied chapters follow. Chapter 6 summarizes the community development literature, illustrating the problems and potentialities of the various forms in which services have been provided to city areas. Chapter 7 concentrates on the results of this process, the way in which the provision of services for local areas in the city relates to communities. Chapter 8 shows how developers have attempted to create distinctive physical plans to define and enhance place communities in the city. Chapter 9 is a brief final chapter that summarizes the ideas developed and looks towards the future of communities. Two limits of the study are worth stressing. First, the focus of the study is upon the *western world*, particularly the English-speaking one, although occasional comments from other cultures are used to provide a context and comparison. Second, the study is an introductory *overview of the variety of alternative themes*. Space constraints mean that two themes of major interest in urban community studies are not covered in depth: the recent, government-inspired, inner-city community initiatives; and specific interest or biological communities, such as those based on ethnicity.

References

Arensberg, C. M. and Kimball, S. T., 1965, *Culture and community*, Harcourt and Brace, New York.

Armytage, W. H. G., 1961, *Heavens below: utopian experiments in England*, 1560–1960, Routledge and Kegan Paul, London.

Blasi, J. R., 1986, *The communal experiment of the kibbutz*, New Brunswick, New Jersey.

Burgess, E. W., 1925, The growth of the city, in Park, R. E. et al. (eds), *The city*, University of Chicago Press, 47–62.

Davies, Wayne K. D., 1981, Higher order factor analysis and functional regionalization, *Environment and Planning*, A, *12*, 685–701.

Davies, Wayne K. D., 1984, *Factorial ecology*, Gower, Aldershot, England.

Dickinson, R. E., 1947, *City, region and regionalism*, Routledge and Kegan Paul, London.

Fishman, Robert, 1977, *Urban utopias in the twentieth century*, New York.

Fitzgerald, Frances, 1981, *Cities on a hill*, Touchstone, Simon and Schuster, New York.

Hiller, E. T., 1941, The community as a social group, *American Sociological Review*, 6, 189–202.

Hunter, A. A., 1974, *Symbolic communities*, University of Chicago Press.

Keller, S., 1988, The American dream of community: an unfinished agenda, *Sociological Forum*, 3, 167–83.

Lewis, G. J., 1986, Welsh rural communities: retrospect and prospect, in Davies, W. K. D. (ed.), *Human geography from Wales, Part I, Cambria, 13*, 27–40.

Mumford, Lewis, 1922, *The story of utopias*, republished, 1962 edition, Viking, New York.

Negley, Glenn, 1977, *Utopian literature: a bibliography*, University of Kansas Press, Lawrence, Kansas.

Peters, K. A., 1987, *The dynamics of Hutterite society*, University of Alberta Press, Edmonton.

Rouner, L. S., 1991, *On community*, University of Notre Dame Press, Indiana.

Stacey, M., 1961, *Tradition and change: a study of Banbury*, Oxford University Press, England.

Stein, M. R., 1960, *The eclipse of community*, Princeton University Press, New Jersey.

Warner, J. Lloyd, 1941, *The social life of a modern community*, Yale University Press.

Williams, Raymond, 1976, *Keywords: a vocabulary of culture and society*, Fontana, London.

2

Community Studies: The Societal Context

Societal Types

It is difficult to separate the presence of communal action, or co-operative behaviour between individuals towards some group goal, from both the development of the human species as we know it, or from the development of the first cities and the major advances in both our material ability and knowledge. Yet group action is not unique to humans. Many mammals co-operate and bond together for particular purposes, although the grouping does seem to be largely instinctive, namely, some biological imprinting that conditions behaviour. Although biologists in recent years have discovered many examples of deliberate sharing between animals of the same species that are not related, and is based on choice rather than instinct, we still do not understand how humans managed to create a very different set of relationships that set them on the path to the cultivation of their greater intelligence and manipulative skills. What is apparent is that communal and co-operative action helped humans to transcend their individual limits — whether in hunting, in preserving security, nurturing their young, or ensuring the transmission of their culture. The last is a complex concept which can be expressed most simply as ways of seeing, acting in, and thinking about the world. This communal action is expressed in social organizations that take myriad different forms, and most authorities (for example, Barash 1986) believe that we do not have any underlying genetic propensity for any one structure.

For most of human history our species was based on small kinship groups organized by reciprocity and linked to hunting and gathering. Larger than a nuclear family, these groups can be considered the first communities because of their common ancestry and a social cohesion reinforced by occupance of a common territory and a shared life. Individuals were provided with what they needed, irrespective of their own contribution. We must not forget that there was a specialization in roles, whether raising children, building shelters, in particular parts of the hunt, or in the development of cave painting. Moreover, the scattered groups often migrated over large areas in response to changing food opportunities, although they came together at different times for major ceremonies or festivals. These meetings had their primary function in the maintenance of shared values, such as some religion or for the exchange of goods, rather than for the typical seasonal groupings of many other mammals: mating and the reproduction of the species. Once the collective of the groups becomes more than a simple aggregate of the individual groups, based on kinship, place or both, a larger social grouping or society can be identified. The societies in which the sedentary or mobile communities exist are characterized by a series of interrelationships that lead to shared values, dependencies and specializations, which, in turn, produce differentiation. The first human groups, therefore, whether based on place or kinship, *were society*; to all intents and purposes the communities, the local bands or settlements were the repetitive elements. With an increase in extra-community interrelationships and specializations they become individual entities within the larger framework we call society, therefore providing a disjunction between community and society and the loss of concern with place.

Few doubt that the subsequent development of civilization was based on a transformation of relationships from those dominated by reciprocity to those that are redistributive in economic terms, characterized by hierarchical rank divisions, high levels of specialization and, through the development of states and empires, by the subordination of individuals and local settlements to some higher authority. Hallpike's (1986) review of the social evolutionary process documents the multiplicity of forms and the absence of a single evolutionary path. The domestication of animals and plants generated huge surpluses, assuring food supply and allowing even greater numbers of specialists to be supported. They not only controlled society but also produced the material and intellectual advances to sustain and enhance it. Added to this was the development of a sedentary way of life in some areas, a major growth in the size of the population, and a greater ability at least partly to control the environment to yield even larger surpluses.

These sedentary societies appeared in many forms. Some societies were command economies with high degrees of central control, especially those which depended upon irrigation, where control over water supply determined productive levels. Others were far more loosely organized, with virtual independence for people in the individual settlements. Most territorial communities in such societies were socially homogeneous, although individuals were not equal: the communities were stratified and dominated by an individual or group and linked by primary ties of kinship. This created social obligations between individuals which were perpetuated by tradition, and in which rewards and behaviour were linked to the rank into which one was born. However, there was a social solidarity beyond the family which was reinforced by shared work practices and expressed in shared values and joint rituals. Hence most societies were dominated by a set of given or accepted relationships that are usually described as primordial, or having

mechanical solidarity in Durkheim's (1964) terms. They defined communities in which *ascriptive or assigned relationships* dominated — rather than those based on choice as in the modern world — producing seemingly permanent ties which were rarely the subject of personal manipulation or management. Some did manage to escape, although these exceptions were not the rule: most people were unable to transcend the bonds of family, status or ethnicity. These societal chains were even tighter in non-western societies. In Hindu society, for example, rank differences were enshrined as rigid caste divisions, and most individuals were unable to break out of their assigned roles. When the relationships were reinforced by other-worldly beliefs which put a premium upon maintaining harmony and order, the earthly bonds were made even more rigid. Perhaps it is little wonder that a philosophy of a reincarnation into different lives seemed such an attractive option for many in Asia.

Many of the associations between people in these historic societies were a product of residence in a common settlement or area. In such groups there were high degrees of local interaction because of the isolation of most individual settlements, primitive transport systems, and a largely self-sufficient local economy linked to the soil. The essential characteristics of these societies, often called folk or traditional, could be identified by the study of the individual, and essentially repetitive, settlements that composed them. In many cases the local communities *were* society — just as in the reciprocal hunting and gathering groups — for there were few additional features beyond the individual group. However, few were completely self-sufficient or self-contained. Dependencies on economic, religious or political organizations external to the individual settlements existed. A local community, therefore, was only a part of a larger societal grouping.

As larger political units emerged and more intense trading contacts dominated local economies, the residents of local settlements became increasingly governed by these outside forces. The élite abrogated control of the land, the primary source of wealth: a control often justified by the other-worldly authority claimed by priests. In European feudal society, the land, or rather the right to use it, was given to the peasants to till in return for a share of the harvest or the obligation to give service to the overlords. In return they either provided or claimed to provide military protection or participation in the necessary religious rites to propitiate the gods. In other societies — especially irrigation areas — the control over the production workers was much more direct. Yet in both cases a series of localized, reinforcing connections and mutually co-operative procedures in work created high levels of local group interaction. However, as society became more specialized, with local production designed for distant markets and control in economic and political terms being exercised from core regions, the self-sufficiency and independence of local areas decayed.

The result of these changes was what may be called *vertical linkages* binding the specialized elements and associations of settlements and people together, instead of *horizontal*, local associations based on coincidence of residence, work, place and religion. Political allegiances meant ties beyond the local unit. Religious organizations, such as the Roman Catholic church, often had hierarchical levels — parish priest, bishop, archbishop — linked to different degrees of authority. Individual societies could not be easily defined or understood by the example of a single settlement, one node in a repetitive sea of similar entities. Instead of the enduring, primary or primordial ties fixed by the circumstances of sex, birth, family and tribe found in traditional societies, the distribution of rewards and associations between people became less determinate and was based on *achieved not ascribed status*, on achievement in occupations, or on individual effort and choice. They represent *secondary*, not primary associations. Durkheim (1964) described these relationships as an 'organic solidarity'. The development of merchant and then industrial capitalism, together with the growth of the corporation and government bureaucracies, were among the forces that

accelerated these trends in the western world by breaking many of the bonds of blood and soil which integrated place-based communities. It will be shown that they are not the only ones. The result is that modern society is characterized by a multitude of pluralistic roles and impersonal behaviour, more frequently based on self-interest than communal goals. The point is made by those who have described the emergence of a post-modern or post-industrial society in recent years (Aggar 1991), in which individualism and self-interest are seen as two key characteristics. There are associations in the contemporary world which are based on some group or collective goal although most are not exclusive: membership is based on choice. Instead, contemporary society is characterized by a complexity and a fragmentation that would be bewildering to individuals from other ages where relationships and dependencies were usually known and given.

Many attempts have been made to summarize the differences in societal relationships which can be found in both the past and present. One of the most enduring is the dichotomy presented by Tonnies (1887) in his book *Gemeinschaft und Gesellschaft*. He used the term *Gemeinschaft*, or community, to describe the traditional societies dominated by communal relationships where there is co-operation to achieve common goals. This contrasted with twentieth-century western society, which he characterized as *Gesellschaft*, a society dominated by associations. It is often assumed that the terms are two polar opposites that summarize an inevitable progression from folk to contemporary society. Such an interpretation must be questioned on three grounds.

First, Tonnies did not make an exact equivalence between *Gemeinschaft* as 'folk' and *Gesellschaft* as 'modern' societies. They were really proposed as *ideal types*, describing end-members of a *range* along which all societies could be arranged. Although folk societies were closer to the former end of the scale and modern societies at the latter, there were *elements of both Gemeinschaft and Gesellschaft in most societies*. Some examples may clarify the point. In many traditional societies the élite were frequently motivated by self-interest, by the desire to increase their own wealth or power. Such motivations were often disguised as being in the group interest, such as the need to raise temple complexes to propitiate the gods or the need to conquer a 'threatening' neighbouring territory. By the same token many modern societies have co-operative retail stores, housing projects and self-help agencies in which people have voluntarily bound themselves together to achieve some collective or group ends.

Second, Schmalenbach (1977) has argued that the dualism is incomplete because it ignores the role of conscious action. *Gemeinschaft* should be regarded as a pre-conscious state, not the consequence of some deliberate purpose. Throughout most of history people lived together in a common life because they were born into a society which had established it and from which it was difficult to escape. By contrast the *Gesellschaft* society is one which requires a high level of conscious behaviour based on rationality. Individuals make selective choices or even liaisons with others to achieve goals, whether these be in the choice of jobs, shops or friends, leading to a societal fragmentation that is even greater if these choices are made in different locations. Yet the transition to *Gesellschaft*, or association by choice, is not inevitable. People can deliberately work together to build or enhance their community relationships rather than passing inevitably into *Gesellschaft*. Schmalenbach (1977) suggested the German word *bund* can succinctly describe such consciously created groups (Wilkenson 1989, 341) and these issues are described in Chapter 6.

Third, recent work on folk and pre-industrial societies has also demonstrated that they were rarely the integrated, harmonious units idealized by early commentators. Social historians (Laslett 1965) have shown that few villages were completely self-sufficient or isolated from the world outside: many people migrated between areas and rivalry and schisms were found in the smallest places.

The result of these reinterpretations of Tonnies' succinct dichotomy has been to extend its utility. No longer is it necessary to force the variety of societies of the past and present into two simple groups. Instead *each society can be thought of as possessing different degrees of Gemeinschaft and Gesellschaft*. However, the progression or balance between the two is not inevitable because *communities can be consciously created*, even though the increasing complexity of society provides more *Gesellschaft* forms. This is best seen by two comparisons with non-western societies.

The first example comes from modern Japan. Much has been made of the way in which most Japanese remain with the same companies throughout their working lives. These companies deliberately try to enhance company solidarity through company songs, activities and promotion schemes, welding an individual's identity to the company, the group. Similarly, work teams on production lines are encouraged to find ways of improving productivity, of contributing to the job beyond the immediate task. These examples demonstrate one overwhelming feature of Japanese society — the deliberate conformity to the group, one that is nurtured from birth through the shared intimacy of the family. Individuality is frowned upon. Certainly westerners may criticize the loss of personal freedom, although this misses the point: individualism is not an inevitable result of industrialization. The Japanese have shown there can be an alternative, even if it may be at the expense of something westerners value: their personal freedom.

The second example is a historic one. We tend to view Chinese society after Confucius as the epitome of group solidarity, with obedience to the family at the most basic level and to the maintenance of order in society at the state level through the supreme role given to the Emperor and his Mandarinate. Yet Schwartz (1991) has stressed that the family in Confucian times was not regarded as a self-sufficient, isolated community, but part of a larger socio-cultural order, and both the values of the family and the political order were being weakened by new forces at this time. The Analects of

Confucius were developed not simply as a set of rites and rituals but also as a reaction against the forces that were weakening families and the political order. This means the familial or the state *gemeinde* did not have 'any automatic power to internalize its own norms into members of the community.... It is only when good and wise individuals create the appropriate environment that realization of the ideals is possible on the popular level' (Schwartz 1991, 124). The Confucian family may be based on a natural order — one that is biologically derived — and may be deeper than the European tradition because it is linked to ancestor worship and maintained by cosmically ordered rituals. Yet the order it brought was not inevitable, rather it was created. Schwartz argued that Confucianism can be seen as a resistance to *Gesellschaft* tendencies in the state. The redemption of society at a family and state levels could occur only as a result of the moral cultivation of individuals, whether fathers, officials or emperors. Thus, moral and individual self-cultivation and the manner in which the roles are played, not the structures or offices themselves, held the key to success. So Confucianism could be regarded not as a simple natural order but as a society that was very much influenced by what Schwartz (1991, 125) described as 'not only an ethical individualism but also as a cosmic–religious–mystical individualism' because of its links to religion. Nevertheless, we must stress the individualism in Confucian society was an élitism, where only the few could develop their latent talents and mould society. It did not lead to the individualism of the west, with freedom and legal protection for each individual, or the replacement of a hierarchical order by a pluralism. It is to these western characteristics that we must turn.

Contemporary Societal Fragmentation

Contemporary western society is a pluralistic and fragmented one. Most behaviours are based on personal choice and individual roles within larger organizations, rather than central control or communal interaction. The resultant individualism is not anarchic and completely subject to individual whim. It has been derived from major changes in the encompassing society, ensuring that individuals and groups based in localities are subject to high degrees of macro-system dominance. Although the last section of this chapter will show that community linkages have been transformed, rather than lost, and there is an emerging recognition of the importance of place differences, as well as the need to cultivate them, the emergence of western society has also been associated with the diminution of local ties. Before describing the causal forces responsible, the primary consequences of these trends are summarized, rather than identifying lists of separate forces, such as those developed by previous workers (Warren 1978). Table 2.1 shows that *western societal fragmentation* can be described by three major forces, called *specialization, subordination* and *spatial flexibility*. These are reinforced and extended by *urbanization*. These elements summarize the fragmentation, and the substitution of vertical for horizontal linkages in modern society, which has so reduced the role of territorial communities in society.

Specialization

Much of the complexity of the contemporary world stems from its specialization, a characteristic that is found in a number of different aspects of society.

1. The most obvious is the extensive *division of labour:* the specialization of occupational roles, providing a multitude of specialized services or jobs, many producing parts of a complex good.
2. Paralleling this occupational complexity is the variety of *associations* which can be found in cities, linked to the fulfilment of many different goals, from coin-collecting to golfing.
3. The number of *interests* of people has exploded in our complex society, providing further divisions between individuals. Of

Table 2.1 Elements in social fragmentation

Societal Fragmentation due to			
A. **SPECIALIZATION**	**B.** **SUBORDINATION**	**C.** **SPATIAL FLEXI-BILITY**	**D.** **URBAN IMPACT**
Divisions of:	Dependence on:	Accessibility due to:	

1. Society
 	
  (a) Labour
  (b) Interests
  (c) Associations
  (d) Roles
  (e) Attitudes
  (f) Values
  (g) Lifestyles
	1. Society
	
	  (a) Owners by
	     Wage-earners
	  (b) Co-ordinators
	     of Workplaces
	  (c) Government
	     and Order
		1. New
		  Communication
		  Devices
			(a) Settlement Size
			    and Form
			(b) Social Mixing

2. Areas:
 	
  (a) Districts
  (b) Settlements
  (c) Regions
	2. Areas
	
	  (a) Core and
	    Periphery
	  (b) Regions
		2. Areal Separation:
		
		  (a) Locales of
		    Activities
		  (b) Actions from
		    Proximity	

Table 2.2 Alternative human attitudes to co-operation

Type	Human Nature	Goals	Attitudes to co-operatives	Attitudes to State
1. Individualists	Competitive	Self-Interest	Negative	Suspicious
2. Pluralists	Various	Better People	Encouragement	Too Remote
3. Collectivists	Subordinate to Economic Production	New Persons from Societal Transformation	Downplayed (Transitional only)	Totalitarian Control by Proletariat
4. Communitarians	Co-operative	Fraternity in New Society	Decentralization and Self-Reliance	Anti-Bureaucratic Control

Source: Summarized from discussion in Birchall 1988.

particular note are the attempts to differentiate people according to their *relative participation in the world at large* compared with local concerns, such as the cosmopolite-localite (Webber 1963).

4. Also, it can be argued that people fulfil different *roles* in varied ways during parts of the day: for example, as father, employee, interest group member, participant in political debate, etc.

5. In addition, it has been argued that there are very different *attitudes* towards associations and co-operation. A multitude of different views could be identified; however, since the issue of individualism and co-operation is essential to the discussion in this chapter it is worth summarizing the ideal types proposed by Birchall (1988) as a background to his study of housing co-operatives. He suggested there are four basic world-views which may be summarized as: Individualists; Pluralists; Collectivists; and Communitarians. The essential characteristics of each type are identified in Table 2.2 and provide a useful summary breakdown of alternative attitudes found in society, illustrating that one must accept the presence of many different views.

6. *Different values* may be adopted in these various roles: perhaps disciplinarian as father, obsequiousness as employee, co-operation in an interest group, critic in a political party. The familiar figure in the Old Testament, a tribal patriarch providing consistency and achieving dominance in all aspects of life, is rarely found today. Extended family linkages, several generations living under one roof or in close proximity, have been replaced by nuclear families, and increasingly by single mother and children groupings.

7. Finally, it is possible to see the presence of very different *lifestyles* in contemporary society. In most contemporary cities there is a greater tolerance of different lifestyles and orientations with fewer societal dictates. Enjoyment and consumption have as much value to many

people today as the work ethic of the past. Behaviour is not so determined by tradition and moral premise as by choice, thereby adding to the specialization of society.

One result of this specialization has been the creation of what Janowitz (1967) called *communities of limited liability*. Individuals give only part of their time and commitment to their communities, which were viewed primarily as interest groups. Nevertheless, the idea can be applied to the participation of people in their residential areas, ensuring that urban communities or neighbourhoods are also characterized by partial and more voluntaristic associations.

These societal specializations are paralleled at the *areal* level where land uses, settlements and regions also display high levels of differentiation and specialization. Most settlements in the western world display a segregation of land use that keeps many functions and people apart and is one that is deliberately planned. Residential areas are usually segregated from industrial areas, with commercial zones providing distinctive modes of concentration. Even within these land use types more specialized associations occur, with upper-income or class areas separated from low-income regions, although this is not a matter of legal zoning but a consequence of the relative purchasing power of various groups and the ability of the real estate market to perpetuate these divisions. Furthermore, few settlements are identical in their economic structure as quantitative studies of urban systems (Berry and Smith 1972; Davies 1984) have shown. A broad hierarchy of service centres by size is overlain by specializations based on different bundles of economic activity, such as industrial centre, military base, port, mining or government centre. The repetitive self-sufficiency of the pre-industrial world, with minor points of concentration of economic activity, has been replaced by a specialized, interconnected world with only a few pools of self-sufficiency.

Subordination

Emile Durkheim (1964) and Max Weber (1958a) were some of the first researchers to describe the way in which late nineteenth and early twentieth-century individuals and settlements, increasingly dependent upon a larger society, were subject to greater bureaucratic management and impersonal relationships. These conditions can all be summarized as various types of *subordination or dependency* which, like specialization, contribute to the fragmentation of society. Instead of the allegiance to a tribal or feudal leader, or at most a group of leaders, subordination in our society is multiple in nature. Few individuals today are independent, in the sense of being able to fulfil their own needs or derive them from a small local group. Instead, most people depend upon their wage labour; they are dependent upon the owners of their firm, or the managers of the institution. This dependency on the marketplace means that the 'work for wage' relationship is paramount and does not include many other obligations. With minor exceptions, such as sick leave etc., the inability to perform work leads to the loss of wages and eventually the loss of the job. Employers do not have the responsibility of caring for an employee and dependants as in other societies: although in a welfare state there is responsibility, it is administered by some level of government from tax contributions.

Within each workplace the specialization of production means that the scope for individual initiative and action is also limited: these actions are performed by the *co-ordinators*, or managers of the workplace. This leads to another level of subordination. Certainly the degree of local initiative does vary. Much of the success of Japanese post-war industrialization has been attributed to quality control or initiative groups, where workers were encouraged to help maintain quality and improve their production. The high levels of dependency in the workplace are duplicated by the fact that provision of many services, or the maintenance of order in society, is no longer the result of action or co-operation by members of a local residential area. Government employs the workers who provide the sewers and roads on which we depend for waste disposal and transport, the police force to maintain order, planners to organize and co-ordinate changes in land uses, as well as the taxation officials to obtain the money to support these activities. Although many of these dependencies are not new, in a specialized world they have mushroomed in numbers and created huge bureaucracies to administer the functions. Perhaps of crucial importance in this discussion is the fact that these functions are carried out by different people. This contrasts with the tribal chief of folk societies who performed many roles, either by himself or in co-operation with a council of elders. In contemporary society different people exercise the range of functions. They are supported by bureaucracies which appear impenetrable to the outsider, and which frequently operate on different principles and seem to work in different directions.

The impact of those functional dependencies is enlarged because of the different locations of the various parts due to the specialization of settlements. Many of the managers or administrators in modern society are concentrated in headquarter cities (Harper 1982) or political centres, which are often clustered in core regions of a nation. The single functional dependency of all peripheries upon an imperial capital found in so many pre-industrial empires is replaced by multiple and often conflicting relationships in a range of organizations. In addition they do not have the family loyalties or reciprocal allegiances found in competing groups in feudal societies, which helped reduce the alienation of the various ties. The result of these societal and areal dependencies is to increase further the degree of fragmentation in modern society.

Spatial Flexibility

The degree of specialization and subordination of individuals and settlements has been increased by the high degree of spatial flexibility that exists in our contemporary behaviour. One of the major forces for societal transformation has been the tremendous recent innovations in transportation and communication, and the affluence to use them. The result has been a drastic decline in the cost and time of transportation in the past thirty years. By means of fax, electronic mail and cellular phones based on satellites, communication between various parts of the world can be almost instantaneous. This has meant a decrease in the friction of space, increasing the number of alternative locational options for businesses and residences. Obviously there are still agglomeration economies which bind activities together; however, the consequence of these changes has been a unprecedented increase in spatial flexibility in our contemporary society. This has further weakened the bonds of local communities and increased societal fragmentation. Relationships can be maintained over greater distances, with greater degrees of intimacy, rather than being episodic and transitory as in the past.

The second contribution to spatial flexibility comes from two features of spatial separation. One is related to the specialization of regions, settlements and areas within cities. This means that people have to move between different areas to carry out many of their specialized functions. This is very different from the basic movements found in so many folk societies, from agricultural village centre to various fields and back. In aggregate, in the contemporary world, it has produced a seemingly chaotic series of movements between the areas where specialized activities are carried out. For example, an individual may go to work downtown, return home for a meal, take the children to a music lesson, go on to a store, return to pick up the children, take them home and then visit a bar to socialize with friends. Many of these movements may be habitual, for limited periods, although they can vary by the week, or season. Others may have coincident journeys, journeying to work in downtown or industrial areas at particular times, producing traffic jams and congestion. All these features add to the fragmentation of society. The his-

toric pre-industrial urban pattern in which most activities were based on the household in multi-purpose buildings or those in close proximity is no longer a feature of society. The computer age has meant that some people are able to run businesses from their own home but its importance in terms of total employment is still very limited.

A second feature that contributes to the high level of spatial flexibility in society is the new separation between action and location. Historically, behaviour or action depended upon local proximity: to plead a case with a tribal chief or feudal lord one had to be present. The invention of writing meant that many requests could be directly transmitted across distances, rather than through intermediaries carrying verbal messages. It also meant information was capable of being stored for use at a different time and for passing knowledge through the generations. Two obvious results were the development of more accurate and larger stores of information than was possible by memory. With the successive development of telegraph, radio, telephone, television, computers and fax messages, words and images could be passed between different locations. Now computer networks integrate the world — our so-called global community means that more and more actions can be initiated not only at a distance, but also immediately, if the communication devices are present. For Webber (1963, 1964) these changes created a *non-place urban realm*, where new 'communities of interest' (derived from the medieval political sense of 'realm'), could be maintained without the necessity of spatial juxtaposition. In the catch-phrase of the day *community without propinquity* (Webber 1964) had arrived. Obviously this is the extreme case and one must be careful not to exaggerate. Not all actions are carried out in this way. Most people still go to work, and interact with family and neighbours. Time, therefore, is partitioned into degrees of local or distant participation, rather than being either one or the other. Just as communities have elements of *Gemeinschaft and Gesellschaft*, so 'localism' and 'non-place urban realms' are best viewed as polar extremes.

Most people have various degrees of participation in their local and global areas, together with associations that apply on other levels, whether city, region, province, or nation.

Urbanization

Large, densely populated settlements are usually more specialized and ethnically complex than smaller places. Strong correlations between size and the number of organizational features have been reviewed in primitive societies (Hallpike 1986) and modern institutions (Strauss 1974), because of the need to provide social control. Hence an increase in the levels of big city urbanization, the *size effect*, can reinforce the specialization trends already described. One must be careful not to be too deterministic since Webber (1956) noted the way many eastern cities were more segmented, an agglomeration of village-like settlements, rather than the more integrated and specialized structures that were found in the west. By its very nature a large city adds to the number of contacts, producing an overload that leads people to retreat from casual relationships. This avoidance mechanism reduces the stress of dealing with strangers, although it internalizes the stress produced by the potential inability to share or engage in human contact (Barash 1986). The problem is intensified by the construction of suburbs, essentially *single family residential areas*, whose land use monotony may be relieved only by a few commercial or recreational areas. This means that many women who look after families are isolated in these areas, individually performing a variety of tasks, such as child-care and cooking, which were formerly the shared or co-operative tasks of extended families. The trend to dual-income earners has actually increased the pressures and stress on those families unable to afford child-care. Children have to be looked after, houses cleaned and meals cooked — often after exhausting days at work. The number and variety of *cultural groups* found in cities also increase the impact of the other trends, for the presence of unfamiliar customs or different

ways of life may increase the degree of alienation and separation among those unable to tolerate differences. Some of these groups may have extended families and collective arrangements that may provide evidence for higher degrees of co-operation between individuals, although it is not general, being restricted to the ethnic groups. The result of these three characteristics is an acceleration in the three major forces that have created societal fragmentation.

The consequence of these factors is that each community-of-interest area, or settlement, is part of a larger society. The integration of previous centuries in which people spent a great deal of their time in defined areas and in common tasks has decayed. Now *each territorial community is not the more or less self-sufficient entity that existed in the past, rather it is only a node within an increasingly complex macro-world system* (Wallerstein 1979). Inevitably the degree of local control and influence has diminished. Even if there is a conscious attempt to empower localities, the primary decisions on the economic enterprises in the urban unit are usually taken elsewhere, so the degree of local influence may be quite small. A primary question, therefore, is whether territorially-based communities have been obliterated or are simply transformed. Before this question can be properly answered we need to understand the major historical forces that have eclipsed our *traditional* community way of life in the west.

Explanations for Societal Fragmentation

The development of a modern western society in which relationships are dominated by self-interest, by individual rather than collective behaviour, is usually attributed to the changes in society, particularly the effects of the Industrial Revolution. Marx (1967 reprint) dissected the nature of capitalism and exposed the sinews of a new exploitation of the majority. Emile Durkheim (1964) and Max Weber (1958b reprint) described the growth of huge bureaucracies, the new cities and the pathologies of the emerging society. Simmel (Wolff 1950) concentrated on the growth of personal freedom and the loss of personal identity, and the Chicago School of Human Ecology (Park et al. 1925) discussed urban influences in the transformation of social relations and land uses.

> The Chicago School told us that certain critical events and values were systematically being bred out of our society: personal, warm ties between people, a sense of community, a sense of identity and co-operation with other people... in which cities were thought to be a mechanism to destroy people's capacity to relate to others in a positive, humanistic way. (Warren and Warren 1977, 2)

Louis Wirth (1938) claimed the new conditions of settlement size, density and heterogeneity which ushered in a specialized world had primary causal value, explaining why there were fewer intimate links between people and more formal controls — often through government action — to ensure orderly relationships between the new concentrations of people. Nevertheless, even a cursory review of history must reveal that the causes of these changes in western society cannot be exclusively laid at the door of increasing urbanization and accelerating industrialization. These were only the last stages of a western history of progression towards an increasing pluralism in alternatives and individual choice in western society which destroyed many of the older hierarchical orders and communal form. Hallpike's (1986, 370) summary of the principles of social evolution emphasized the inheritance of basic institutional and ideological principles. He cautiously suggested that the Chinese–European societal differences may be, in part, a product of the early sedentary nature of Chinese society with its development of large centralized states, unlike the long, pastoral and migratory traditions of the Indo-Europeans producing more individual behaviour. However, it is unlikely that a single causal mechanism exists: instead a multitude of forces has been influential, although priority can be given to five related forces or historical macro trends in western society.

1. the results of the seventeenth and eighteenth-century Enlightenment;
2. the individualism underlying much of Christian philosophy;
3. the dominance of capitalism, especially industrial capitalism;
4. the invention and use of new communication devices;
5. the philosophical position of active individualism.

Each of these forces has helped transform western society towards a more *Gesellschaft* rather than *Gemeinschaft* form, with control being found in an increasingly complex macro-societal framework. Nevertheless, the summary of these forces must not be allowed to disguise the fact that the sequence was never complete or inevitable. Within each of these forces the growth of individualism and the decrease in communal activity was often blocked or slowed down by opposite trends, ensuring there was no simple, linear and inevitable progression.

The Enlightenment: Growth of Independence and Rationality

Most authorities regard the fifth century BCE achievements of the Greeks as providing the mainspring of Western civilization (Mumford 1961). The period was one characterized by a veritable deluge of new ideas and a questioning of the nature of the universe. Although the flowering of these new ideas occupied barely a century, and the changes in thought were more often an ideal than values practised, they left an intellectual heritage based on the twin principles of rationality and democracy. The first lay in the assertion of the importance of man's individual will, the creation of knowledge through his own thought processes, rather than complete dependency upon some revealed truth handed down by some gods. The second was the ability of a group of citizens to exercise government for, and by themselves, in the city-state. This was a political form that devolved power from the previous centres, the political citadel and the temple, to the people — or rather some of people.

The break with the past in the Greek experiment was never complete. The gods remained an important force in Greek life. Conceptions of the world were still based on the view that man was simply revealing some divine purpose based on an integrated whole. Their democratic experiments were soon replaced by the rule of despots and later by imperial conquest — first by the Macedonians, Philip and then Alexander, and later by Rome. However, the ideals of political independence and rationality never died completely: they lay dormant and became the sparking plug for the Renaissance in western Europe — that classical rebirth which comprehensively questioned and eventually destroyed the collective bonds of the medieval society and in later centuries led to the Enlightenment.

Despite its classical underpinnings the Renaissance produced a revival of individuality in art, architecture, commerce and scientific thought. The emergence of scientific knowledge from the sixteenth century onwards created a knowledge very different in kind from the revealed truth of religious belief, and eventually provided such a powerful hand-maiden to industrial progress. Empiricism, the study of the world around through observation and common-sense interpretations, provided explanations based on the behaviour of individual entities. The analytical approach directed attention upon the isolation of things, not their holistic complexity. To some the knowledge was seen as a new revelation of God's will and mechanisms, although the new ideas and their spread via new inventions such as the printing press helped break the historic monopoly of the Catholic church. In other contexts, the centralization was enhanced initially. In political affairs, the increasingly absolutist monarchies of the new nation-states attempted to concentrate political power. Such trends were often challenged and eventually criticized in the work of seventeenth-century philosophers, such as Descartes and Locke.

In the political context of the English-speaking world, John Locke's rejection of the doctrine of the Divine Right of Kings was vital in the development of a new liberal and democratic tradition that helped destroy the old communal bonds. Locke maintained that man was subject to the role of Natural Law, viewed as 'God's Law made known by reason'. Since man had several natural rights — Life, Liberty and Property — Locke believed men only *entrusted* power to sovereigns. If these rights were ignored by rulers they could be replaced. These ideas certainly fuelled the political debate of the eighteenth century and were translated into the revolutions in America and France. However, Locke cannot be considered a modern democrat or liberal. Like the Classical Greeks his democracy was for a limited property-owning group. He believed working men should be excluded from full political responsibility. Their dependence on wage labour meant that they had little material interest in political association, in which the property-owners should engage to protect their property. Moreover, Locke regarded poverty as a sign of the moral failure of an individual — not a misfortune — believing that there was always work for the idle to do. This means Locke displayed few signs of any social compassion for the poorest individuals. Nevertheless, once the monopoly on political power had been breached by his type of logic, it was but a short step to extend these rights to all men and women. The theory of individual rights took another two and a half centuries to be put into general practice in the western world, although there have been many reversals.

More generally, it was Descartes' famous pronouncement *cogito ergo sum* (I think, therefore I am) which began that process of *disengaged reason* where man is no longer subject to cosmic forces, part of some divine order, or subject to its earthly representative, the monarch. Instead each person has an independent mind of his own. Until the Enlightenment humans were considered as part of the collective entity, subject to cosmic forces, whether single or multiple gods. The Cartesian revolution heralded a separation between humans and the rest of the cosmos. Individuals no longer automatically shared some identity with others or other living things, in the sense that they were all part of some general purpose of nature based on divine will. This produced the loss of the 'ultimate, all-embracing community, of groups that share the same beliefs. Instead, understanding or knowledge of others is reduced to behaviourism, based upon observations of what others do. For many centuries the loss was never absolute. An individual's lifestyle was often highly conditioned by societal orderings and/or moral attitudes linked to other-worldly spiritual beliefs that often stressed conformity to sets of particular values and behaviour. Many individuals did escape the confines of their local communities or larger societies — indeed, some of these created new ways of life or religions, whereas others were simply outlaws or hermits. Apart from these exceptions and societal upheavals, however, there was always the assertion of conformity, the re-establishment of the primacy of links to others — to the primordial society described previously. Even when ideas of equality did emerge, they often led to speedy repression, as can be seen by the ruthless crushing of those who expounded such views, such as the Levellers or Diggers of the English Civil War period (Hill 1975), whilst the 'liberty, equality and fraternity' banner of the French Revolution led to a blood-bath that made a mockery of these principles. In time the concept of individual rights gradually won the day, to become one of the cornerstones of our specialized western society.

Christianity

The second fundamental force that helped the rise of individualism in western society is the impact of Christianity, a tradition very different from the order-inducing religions of the Far East which are based on collective subordination to some cosmic harmony — not revelation for an individual. There may be a paradox here. Christianity is often regarded as one of the collective, binding forces of medieval west European society in which the organized Roman Catholic church played such a role.

Nevertheless, it can be argued that much of the Christian message represented both a trend to individuality and a force for societal fragmentation. The basis of this assertion lies in the crucial role that individual salvation plays in the Christian faith and the creation of a division between the secular and spiritual worlds of society, perhaps best expressed in the words attributed to Jesus: 'give to Caesar ... what belongs to Caesar, and to God, what belongs to God' (St Luke Chapter 20: J.B. Phillips 1972, 165). Dualism in the source of power and control occurred in other societies, such as pre-Inca civilizations. However, the eventual triumph of the division of secular and spiritual authority in Europe, rather than the constant or perhaps idealistic conception of the single order so typical in Asian civilizations, created tensions within the emerging western society. This eventually led to its greater fragmentation.

Christian belief was linked originally to what is now described as 'millenarianism', with the assumption of Christ's second coming and the creation of a moral and just society on earth. Through the work of St Augustine, especially in his 'City of God', the focus changed. The millennium was not to be achieved in this world: it would be created in the 'other world', the Christian heaven. Within the existing world, however, early Christians believed they should set up their own groups or communities, set apart from their surrounding world and united by ties of exclusive fellowship. As Seligman (1989, 16) observed: 'Cutting across existing solidarities of kith and kin, the message of the early church was one of social solidarity rooted only in a shared experience of the sacred.'

At first sight the creation of these new moral communities within the encompassing society, based on participation in the sharing of the Eucharist (the Christian communion) appears to provide evidence for the opposite of the individualist thesis. However, to achieve and extend this religion, the church, as an organization, created new structures of authority — priests and bishops — separate from the existing Roman imperial, and later feudal order. This led to a hierarchy of authority and a centralization in the Roman Catholic church, so different from the individualistic tendencies of other early Christian groups, such as the Celtic church in Britain. Also important is the fact that the Catholic church grew to monopolize all the contact between communicants and the transcendental order, leading to the separation of church and state in western society. Certainly there were many attempts to combine the secular and spiritual orders by secular-minded Popes and Holy Roman Emperors alike. Power was not something that medieval European leaders wanted to share. Nevertheless, the recurring theme in west European history is that of a separation of authority, a frequent rivalry between Pope and Emperor. This contrasts with the persistent merging of the two orders in the imperial Chinese dynasties, leading to the reinforcement of imperial order based on the maintenance of harmony between the cosmos and earth after periods of warring regional states (Wheatley 1971).

Also important was the way in which the individuality of the Christian message was subverted to the authority of the church. The Roman Catholic church tried to monopolize all contact between the secular and sacred worlds. The major rites of the religion had to be carried out in defined places, consecrated churches, with authorized priests, supported by tithes based on parishes. A straitjacket was put on independent thought. The church monopoly was often challenged, such as by the Cathars in thirteenth-century southern France, leading to bloody repression. However, the Catholic monopoly was finally broken in the sixteenth century by the Reformation. This began with the simple desire to root out the corruption of the organized church and a questioning of the need for priestly interpretation and organization of the faith. In part the changes brought a revival of the primitive Christian message — that of unifying the realm of faith with the material world. Individuals flocked to form new Protestant associations: communities or groups of religious people, practising in their everyday lives the moral precepts of God. These new Christian communities were not

ordained by some priestly authority; they were based on a consensual concept of voluntary membership. Participants were not united through the mysticism of the sacraments and led by a priestly class, but through a covenant voluntarily made by participants. This meant a rejection of the 'top–down' principles of administration in favour of a grass-roots or 'bottom–up' approach, with the eventual divergence of opinions.

Many nation-states attempted to use the new church as buttresses or justifications for their power, in part to combine secular and religious authority or at least to dominate the latter — as in the Church of England. Elsewhere individual groups — the Calvinists in Geneva, the Anabaptists in Munster, and the Pilgrims in New England — attempted to create new societies in their settlements based on their opinion of Christian precepts. At a state or city level the fusion of secular and spiritual authority in these new settlements did not last for long in the western world. There were too many individual antagonisms and personal views of what the moral code was supposed to be, rejecting the coercion to particular beliefs and behaviour. Religious and secular power finally diverged. Within the Protestant groups there has been a constant creation of new sects, further emphasizing the divisive and individualistic trends that characterize western religion. Certainly Christians have founded and maintained their own associations — their religious communities — within this world. In addition, there are examples of agricultural village groups, such as the Amish and Hutterites (Peters 1987), which have maintained much of their religious identity throughout the centuries, first by migration to Russia and then to the United States and Canada. Similarly many new sects, some Christian, some secular, others a mixture of world religions, have established their own exclusive settlements to practise their own beliefs, as separate from the world as possible. However fascinating these examples may be, they represent minor aberrations in the total settlement pattern. Returning to the main theme, it seems that the important consequence of Christianity for modern western society has been the creation of separate lines of authority and a constantly increasing series of alternative, yet related, beliefs. These have contributed to the *fission of local communities*, not fusion by religious ties, at the local and state level.

The growth of Protestantism in the western world did more than foster factionalism in society. In New England the attempts to create a Christian paradise foundered on the rocks of new community-based intolerances. Nevertheless it provided emerging American society with a greater degree of self-reliance and a firm belief in individual participation in governance. More generally, its emphasis upon personal behaviour and moral example has been credited with a new work ethic (Tawney 1936) which greatly increased the productivity of western society. Moreover, like Christianity in general, there was also a basic moral imperative to care for the less economically fortunate. Although this traditional Christian advocacy was often more obvious in the breach than in the practice, the revival of this message and the Protestant clarion call for self-reliance and improvement, not charity, is important. In the context of community action it explains the 'settlement movement' in many late nineteenth-century inner-city slums as beacons of hope designed to improve the quality of life (see Chapter 6).

Dominance of Capitalism

The third force contributing to the fragmentation of western society is often considered to be the major one, yet its success may not have been possible without the previous individualistic and liberalizing trends. As an economic mechanism it is based on the exchange of all goods, services and needs in the market-place. Here an exchange based on prices occurs, one determined by supply and demand and by the production and trade for profit. At its heart is the individual self-interest of entrepreneurs who invest in production and trade to obtain a profit, a margin over production costs. This leads to the provision of greater and greater

production, for they are not subject to the dictates of a small élite. This profit can be spent in conspicuous consumption or can be reinvested to provide more goods and greater profit. Obviously there are limits to the cycle of reinvestment, linked to debt crises and the saturation of markets, although temporary solutions to these problems can be obtained through the discovery of new markets or investment in other circuits of capital (Harvey 1985). The key to this system is its competitive nature: between the individuals who have money to invest — the capitalists — who compete to produce or trade goods; between the buyers, the consumers who compete to satisfy their needs; and between the suppliers, such as those providing labour or goods. Its consequence has been an unprecedented acceleration in the production of goods and services.

At its most basic level — for example, local food markets — the capitalist system is an ancient form of exchange. However, in most historic societies there were major barriers to its growth to include the exchange of all or most goods and services. Many goods were not *commodified*, to use Wallerstein's (1979) phrase: they were not subject to exchange by markets. Instead other means of exchange operate, such as redistribution by rank or barter. In addition, there were major barriers to the freedom of markets. Monopolies granted by the élite reserved certain production or trade activities for individuals or groups. Societal constraints, such as the Christian abhorrence of usury — that is, deriving profit from money-lending — restricted the opportunity for many Christians to make profits on lending money, allowing Jews to fill the niche.

The growth of production and trade during the early medieval period was intimately linked to the expansion of the capitalist system in trade and production. However, the constraints of the church, of feudal obligations, and feudal extraction provided important limits. In the city-states of Italy, and in the virtually independent trading-centres of the Hansa merchants, many grew wealthy from the growing profits of the application of the capitalist system to trade. Through the invention of accounting, money drafts, etc. they laid down the framework of a fully developed capitalist system. Many of the capitalist *nouveaux riches* converted their profits to land and became feudal lords in their own right, for social status was still inextricably bound up with landed estates. In the merchant cities the wealthy often became part of a new oligarchy, holding political as well as economic power. However, the fundamental change lay in the enlargement of a new merchant class who helped finance the needs and wars of the feudal lords and, in return, received privileges to make them more and more independent. Certainly the burgesses of the towns created their own associations — the guilds — to protect their own interests, although the importance of these changes for our thesis was the creation of another source of fragmentation in western society. The guilds formed an alternative source of power to the traditional feudal authority based on rural estates.

The history of western Europe from the sixteenth to nineteenth centuries in often seen in terms of three revolutions: commercial, agricultural and industrial (Blaudel 1981; Viljoen 1974). In each the capitalist system advanced, linked to expansions in trade, agriculture and industry respectively, creating increases in production and exchange, and new profits for the people able to invest successfully in these activities. It is not without significance that these economic revolutions had most importance in those regions less subject to the imposition of monopolies and extractive behaviour by exploitive monarchies, as much as the Protestant work ethic or available resources. By the nineteenth century the production and distribution of most goods and services in the western world became subject to the marketplace. Self-sufficiency was increasingly rare. Communal activity declined except for its revival in the nineteenth-century co-operative movement. This new economic system combined with the increased use of fossil energy and a mechanization of activities to produce an explosion in the production and exchange of goods. In addition there was an expansion in the number and variety of goods, derived from

trade with distant countries and from the new industrial processes and inventions. The growth process frequently fed upon itself: the use of steam engines increased the demand for coal and for steel rails; this, in turn, made the transport of goods cheaper, which helped increase both demand and the supply of resources from more distant areas. The parallel growth of engineering knowledge improved the efficiency and power of engines, which led to a further speeding up of communication and decreased costs in the means of production. Through the colonization of new lands, the commercial and industrial revolution was spread across the globe to create the real beginnings of a world industrial-commercial economy in place of the scattered trade links of previous centuries.

In socio-economic terms the spread of capitalism allowed the successful investors of capital to obtain huge rewards, the majority were reduced to dependence upon their wage labour. Most workers remained at the mercy of large organizations that grew up to control trade and manufacturing, frequently moving to, and labouring in, noisy and unhealthy factories or mines under squalid conditions. Although many of the working class may have been released from an essentially subsistence agriculture, it is worth noting that seventeenth and eighteenth-century industrialization had frequently led to the organization or outputting of production to rural areas, so local rural communities survived in a new economic form (Vance 1977). The country had been industrialized, but not urbanized. The big nineteenth-century change lay in the urbanization of production in large new factories. This new industrialization, combined with the concentration of people into cities, broke many of the old co-operative ties, creating a huge new under-class, a 'reserve army' in Marxist terms, which struggled to survive in the competitive life of the new industrial-commercial cities. For these groups it can be argued that the new individualism and greater choice meant little: they lacked the purchasing power or political clout to influence their lives to any great extent. For Marxists, therefore, a new societal determinism was created. Although man was no longer subservient to the plans or the whims of the gods, he still had limited personal room for manoeuvre. New chains had been created, embedded in the new ensemble of social relations. These were economic dependencies, based on the workers' subservience to the market-place and the capitalist search for profit. The motive force of the new system was not the old, traditional domination of feudal society by a political élite: in capitalism, the capitalists provided the 'hidden hands' that controlled the system. Economic conditions, therefore, were considered to have determined societal relationships.

This is hardly the place to delve into the detailed effects of capitalism on society and its geographical consequences for cities and communities (Harvey 1973; 1985; Dear and Scott 1981). However, two issues are important. First, capitalism did not create poverty and extremes of wealth: in historic feudal societies many people existed at subsistence levels. Now there are more sources of power in society. Second, capitalism helped to destroy many of the co-operative and communal associations in the preceding society, especially work practices in agricultural pursuits and the care of the least able. The inevitable reaction against the squalor of living conditions and the degradation of individuals took place with the growth of socialist and communist movements. Eventually governments took over a large number of functions, from the provision of adequate sewers, water supply and roads, to education and social welfare. Co-operation between the wage labourers created working men's associations and unions dedicated to improving both wages and working conditions. Marxists still argue that these are but palliatives; capitalism's social conscience, as expressed in democratic socialism, is seen as simply a means of maximizing extraction from the working class. For Marxists, only a communist dictatorship of the proletariat can deliver equality for individuals. It is difficult to judge the real effects of attempts to introduce this type of system. Although communist governments in China have certainly eradicated

widespread impoverishment and many of the old social divisions, and can claim increased production, it has been achieved by coercion as much as by voluntary effort and co-operation. In eastern Europe the same totalitarianism has been rapidly rejected from 1989 onwards. Most now believe that inefficiency, environmental degradation and sheer bureaucratic ineptitude produced a less wealthy society than would have been achieved if a liberal market-based democracy had been created after World War II.

Communication Changes

The fourth major force that has helped the fragmentation of society is associated with the communication revolution, particularly those technological changes beginning in the last century which reduced the extent and proportion of interaction based in small local areas. Steam trains and ships drastically reduced travel times across the globe, a process speeded up by the growing use of internal combustion and jet engines in the last fifty years. However, it has been the growth of first radio and telephones, then television, and finally electronic data networks which have provided the possibility of almost instant communication between people living in various parts of the globe. These contacts are not simply place to place, the tied associations of the morse code and telegraph linkages. With the development of radio came the spatial contact fields in which all can share in messages emanating from some centre; place is replaced by space. Certainly the ability to use these machines is related to the ability to have access to and pay for these devices; however, in the western world the majority now have this capability. People can speak to one another or send images across the world at the dial of a telephone or fax machine rather than having to wait for a letter. Satellite technology and cellular phones perpetuate the space-contact fields pioneered by radio and reduce the importance of places. This growing engagement in national or global linkages means an individual may not know his neighbour. Why should he? What do two people located in adjoining residences have in common in a specialist world? In an interaction sense these changes have diminished the importance of local contacts in favour of distant ones. Paradoxically, short distances have become longer in an effective sense, because there are no reasons to bridge the gap: people are too busy interacting in their chosen workplaces, their recreational areas, or tuning into world events to be concerned about other events in their immediate area. The relationships in the American television drama *Dallas* or the British *Coronation Street* are more real for many people than potential associations with residents living in close proximity. Plato's idea that reality is seen as flickering images in a cave seems to have been brought to life — although in rather more comfortable circumstances!

Active Philosophical Individualism

Much of the recent acceleration in individualism and loss of community feeling must also be attributed to a persuasive contemporary philosophical position linked to 'individualism' or a 'focus on self'. Although in part it may be considered to be the derivative of the ideas discussed in the first section, some recent developments mean it deserves a separate treatment for it has implications for community development. This position has produced a series of characteristics that have been heavily criticized in recent years, such as 'hedonism or permissiveness' (Bell 1978), 'narcissism' (Lasch 1979), 'the closing of the minds' (Bloom 1987), or 'the atomism of the self-absorbed world' (Taylor 1991). In the political sphere Galbraith (1992) has coined the term 'culture of contentment' to describe the persistent contemporary vote for conservative or centre parties which will protect the lifestyle of the comfortable and successful, rather than being more concerned for the less able, the motivation for so much radical legislation during other periods in this century. Much of this criticism can be linked to older concerns about human frailties, such as the selfishness

or self-indulgence criticized in the Christian Bible, or the self-absorption expressed in the ancient Greek story of Narcissus. Even so, the modern fulminations against this emphasis on 'self' go much further: they are associated with dismay at the moral laxity of modern life, its subjectivity and lack of respect for others, and what appears to be an irresponsible, anarchic individualism. Older lifestyles, linked to moralities based on the principle of responsibilities to others, or derived from spiritual guidance, seem to have decayed. The decline of interest in the great achievements of our civilization is paralleled by the rise of the self-indulgent and ephemeral pop culture of the present. In the context of the concerns of this chapter the consequence is an even greater fragmentation of society, for in the last resort it seems acceptable that each person is not simply a member of a group, but a self-absorbed individual with distinctive attitudes and values. Of course, it could be argued that this has always been true. Each human has always been distinct, not a biologically self-programmed automaton that either fulfils some assigned role in a collective community, such as an ant colony, or clusters for mutual protection, as in a herd of caribou. What is different about the contemporary fascination with 'self' is the widespread acceptance of the primacy of this individualistic position as an acceptable moral position — as basic as the democratic right to vote. This is of quite recent general acceptance and goes beyond the post-Cartesian identification of self. Since it has implications for the development of communities we need to know how this position evolved.

The contemporary fascination with 'self' can be seen to be the derivative of all the trends described previously, as well as the specific contribution of Jacques Rousseau who built upon the ideas of personal freedom to espouse the concept of self-determining freedom for individuals. The Canadian philosopher and political theorist Charles Taylor (1989; 1991) proposed that the German philosopher Herder articulated a crucial addition: that each of us has a distinctive way of being human, of achieving personal self-fulfilment. This means a person is not given — in the sense of either being a product of God or some cosmic plan, or determined by the conditions of society, as in the Marxist belief system. Rather a person should be seen as *a result of personal achievement, not as a given*, a view accepted by a large number of our contemporaries. Taylor maintains this view leads to an important consequence, namely: 'a new importance to being true to myself. If I am not, I miss the point of my life, I miss what is being human for me' (Taylor 1991, 29).

The attitude has an extension. If a person does not develop his or her life to the fullest, then something vital is missing, part of our humanness is gone, leading to a loss for the individual as well as society as a whole. The contemporary individualism has been called 'authenticity', defined as 'my finding the design of my life myself, against the demands of external conformity' (Taylor 1991, 67). This is more than just a passive position. Each one of us seems to have, or rather believe in, a new compulsion or duty to achieve this fulfilment. It is the widespread acceptance of this need to act on this philosophical belief that is so different today, and explains the use of the term 'active philosophical individualism' as a title for this section.

The gradual development of the individualism that is at the core of this philosophical position, separate from the confines of collective binds — whether of God or secular norms — has not led to universal acceptance. Taylor (1991) observes that for Kafka it led to fear and abhorrence of the 'spiritual isolation of the self' in the modern state. By contrast Sartre and the existentialists (Warnock 1965; Passmore 1968) created a particular variant that expressed joy in the revolt against the bindings of authority and the belief in one's own values as a justification for action. The recent social commentators on contemporary standards noted above provide an almost universal condemnation in a set of weighty tomes, from those thundering against the specifics of moral laxity, to those which see the trends heralding the decline of civilization (Bloom 1987). Nevertheless,

despite the variety of critics, this focus on 'self' is attractive to many members of our already fragmented society even if they do not accept the claims of the existentialists. Indeed the contemporary individualism is difficult to counter in our western society where it is assumed that we are all equal — not an attitude that was common through history. Two derivatives of the contemporary concern for equality is the modern passion with equity for an increasing number of different groups, and the attitude that each group or person's opinions and values must be treated with respect. This makes challenge and debate difficult. An individual can always retreat into a subjectivist position and claim primacy for his or her own attitude, values and actions. One cannot be too critical of the growing acceptance of this position: in contemporary parlance it is the situation in which the 'me generation are doing their own thing'. After all, the development of individual freedoms and search for profit has produced many advantages: not only an explosion of wealth for the majority, but also the release of many more from unquestioned authority structures based on older dominances, or values other than mutual respect.

There are still many criticisms of this contemporary fascination with 'self' and the opportunities for real freedom. For example, Marxists claim the freedom for individual action is illusory. Most individuals are not free: they are bound to lifestyles determined by their dependence upon wage-labour which conditions most of their existence. However, the communist experiment in freeing people from the 'slavery of capitalism' led to the extinction of other freedoms. For other critics, the problems are much wider and cannot be solved by changing the market mechanism or returning to other-worldly values. In the *Malaise of modernity* Charles Taylor (1991) maintained that contemporary authenticity should not be dismissed as some 'facile relativism'. The irresponsible individualisms so heavily criticized at the present are simply the debased forms of what Taylor claims to be an acceptable moral position in which the 'development of the self' can be considered as a primary objective. Taylor sees the challenge as using the advantages of 'authenticity' to increase societal as well as personal fulfilment, rather than a retreat to older forms or allowing the idea of self-determining freedom to be pushed to its limits in which no boundaries are recognized. He accepts that this is not easy, given two major features of our modern society. First, individualism has led to a 'loss of meaning or purpose' in life because of the discrediting of the older orders that had some moral purpose, whether religion or some future communist paradise. Second, there has been an 'eclipse of ends', due to the triumph of what Taylor calls 'instrumental reason' — the application of rationality in so many aspects of life. This has reduced the ability of an individual to influence events and created a feeling of powerlessness. He argues that these individualistic tendencies have not led to an increase in democratic action, rather the reverse. Contemporary society is characterized by a 'loss of political will', with a decline in levels of political participation due to our self-absorption and feeling of helplessness in the shadow of the big institutions that dominate our lives. This might have been anticipated. De Toqueville's eighteenth-century survey of the new phenomenon of democracy in America predicted that it would evolve into a fascination with what he described as 'life's little pleasures', producing a 'soft despotism' in which everything is run by various bureaucracies over which people have little control. It has proved to be a perceptive view of much of contemporary life.

Taylor sees the contemporary problem as retrieving the current situation, of establishing authenticity as a moral position, not destroying it as in the Marxist model, or retreating from it to some commune. This requires a struggle against what he calls the debased forms, the characteristics criticized by Lasch (1979) and Bloom (1987). It is argued:

> we ought to be trying to persuade people that self-fulfilment, so far from excluding unconditional relationships and moral demands beyond the self, actually requires these in some form... to shut out demands emanating beyond the self is

precisely to suppress the conditions of significance and hence to court trivialization. (Taylor 1991, 37–40)

A revived form of place community action may be *one of the ways* this can be achieved.

Such a brief review does scant justice to the multitude of influences that have created such a high degree of individualism in western society. Instead, the objective has been to provide a background to the community question: to focus the discussion by identifying the primary forces that have contributed to this transformation in the western world.

Changing Nature of Local Communities

This chapter has traced the major influences that seem to have led to the inexorable decline of place-based communities in contemporary western cities. Research seems to show that personal communities were being transformed, so that people were embedded in contact fields and social support systems which extended across the metropolitan area (Fischer 1976) and to global relationships (Webber 1964). Nevertheless, it has become obvious that these trends have not eradicated communities, merely transformed their nature. Wellman and his associates (1979; 1988) have produced perhaps the most ordered discussions of the changing nature of local community in cities with the triad of terms: *community lost*, *community saved*, and *community liberated*. Not surprisingly the relationships found in these various communities varied considerably and Wellman and Leighton (1979) described the differences in a comprehensive manner.

First, *community lost* represented the school of thought perhaps most easily linked with Louis Wirth (1938) and his 'urbanism as a way of life'. For supporters of this interpretation, larger, denser, and more heterogeneous cities led to the breakdown of 'locality-based or community' life. Local, face-to-face relationships associated with residence were replaced with secondary linkages based on workplace and interest groups. Ties to locality were eroded and individuals were assumed to be submerged in the general anonymity of urban life.

Second, *community saved* was the counter-argument that believed that neighbourhood and kinship networks continue to flourish in the city. Writers such as Jacobs (1961), Suttles (1968) and Fischer (1981) provided empirical examples of the continuing reality of localities and primary ties. Urban populations, by one means or another, were sifted and sorted out into the mosaic of more homogeneous residential areas where the communal desire for informal social control exerted itself. Although Wellman et al. argued that the community-saved school did demonstrate convincingly that primary relationships were not lost within the large city and that local communities had force, he failed to recognize explicitly that the whole urban system, including its local components, was undergoing an overarching process of change.

Third, a compromise position was termed *community liberated*, which affirmed the importance of community ties — mainly what we have described as interest associations — although it did not see them as necessarily tightly bounded and contained within territorial limits as in the past. In studies within East York (Toronto) Wellman showed his respondents were not 'encapsulated in decoupled little worlds' — the implicit assumption of many neighbourhood plans. Most have a variety of links within the larger web of the metropolitan area, and network analysis provides one way of investigating these linkages — although it must be admitted that some authorities prefer to use the term 'structural analysis' to identify this approach to interest communities. Wellman and Berkovitz (1988, 47) concluded: 'analysts have found abundant evidence of "community" by looking for it in networks rather than in neighborhoods'. In part this is playing with words and the different meanings of 'community'. By distinguishing between place-based communities and the spatial spread of communities as interest associations, the difference becomes clearer. Local associations certainly continued,

although they were maintained over larger areas. The result was the 'selective use of specialized, diversified, sparsely knit social nets to achieve a limited number of ends. The streets were deserted because the residents were driving to friends' homes or were on the telephone' (Wellman and Berkovitz 1988). These networks were proposed as the new spatially-dispersed interest communities. However, Wellman cautioned that none of the three alternatives fits very well: 'most networks contain kin and friends, local and long distance ties, clusters and isolates, multistranded and specialized ties' (Wellman and Berkovitz 1988, 174). The coexistence of Saved ties and Liberated friendship links was shown to make for low communal solidarity, although it provided his East York respondents with indirect access to a wide range of resources.

Fischer (1981; 1982), using studies in N. California, is another prominent researcher who showed that the extent to which individuals or households depend upon local communities for primary ties will vary with their own personal characteristics and changes over time. Also events and processes external to local community often activated locally based groups and gave the latter more meaning. Fischer went further, suggesting that urbanism does not produce estrangement of close associates or of proximate groups such as neighbours. It does, however, 'produce estrangement from, and even conflict with, the unknown, socially dissimilar and potentially threatening people and sub-cultures who make up the city — the inhabitants of the "world of strangers"' (Fischer 1981, 315). These sentiments are echoed elsewhere in the literature and give further credence to the continuation and even rise of localism in the social geography of the contemporary city. Three factors contribute to this trend.

First, as cities are perceived to be more dangerous places, many feel that local community has an enhanced value as a 'haven', a familiar territory which forms a buttress against the new and sometimes violent hazards of urban life. Indeed, 'places' are increasingly seen as the immediate social contexts of people's lives (Agnew and Duncan 1989) which are imbued with values, meanings, and experiences, thereby creating distinctive 'senses of place' (Chapter 4).

A second source of localism comes from the activism that has revived and even extended many of the local or grass-roots community organizations in many cities, especially in the United States. Community activists have tried to improve local social and economic conditions and to restore people power and pride in local areas, producing what one political scientist hoped would herald a new grass-roots democracy (Williams 1985). Linked to this is the continued influence of zoning ordinances, which Shlay and Rossi (1981) have claimed to be of greater concern to more people than any other statute. The zoning ordinance has a locality base; it is the mechanism by which local groups have been able to protect their residential neighbourhoods and affect local planning policy.

Third, a rather surprising new interest in community springs from the political economy approach of geographers normally associated with structuralist ideas, some of which are Marxist in nature. At first sight this is a contradictory source of ideas, since 'structuralists' (those seeking deep-seated societal explanations) have at times appeared to deny the value of local dimensions in what they have viewed as essentially macro explanations of societal differentiation and change. Although any brief attempt to summarize approaches within this essentially political economy perspective has to be sweeping in its generalizations, Bartelt et al. (1987) has provided a useful framework which picks up three themes in recent analyses of the political economy of cities.

1. Urban structure is a mirror of class, economic and political interests in which the urban landscape is a 'mosaic of financial interests', the outcome of investment decisions.
2. Evident patterns of segregation of classes and ethnic groups are products of the inequality of wages and the economic order. The city becomes the social arena within which the conflicts over consumption of land are played out.

3. Traditional approaches must be modified by an understanding of the ways in which economy is organized across space.

Bartelt et al. pointed out that the political economy of cities is more than a mixed bag of these different approaches: 'The most basic element of the political economic approach to urban structure is the general assertion that cities are what the larger economic order makes them' (Bartelt et al. 1987, 180). It is this last quotation which set the tone for the 'structuralist' literature during most of the 1970s and 1980s. Smith (1987) argued that the analysis of urban and regional restructuring was almost exclusively a Marxist preserve in this period; studies of de-industrialization, uneven development and disinvestment were dominated by theories based upon an economic system of accumulation and crisis — by a social world differentiated by class and the roles of the political sphere. However, the modifying effects of local spatial issues can be seen in the last of Bartelt's themes. This entailed both a move towards more empirical research and a greater willingness to recognize the 'active' roles which local as opposed to societal processes can play.

There are many *markers* of this change in thinking along political economy lines, of reactions to this shift and the development of a 'critical edge' which has crept into the ensuing debate. One of the important works was Massey's (1984) study entitled *The spatial divisions of labour*, in which she argued that geographical differentiation had been ignored in recent literature, so there needed to be a 'rediscovery of place': 'No two places are alike ... most people still live their lives locally, their consciousness is formed in a distinct geographical place' (Massey 1984, 117).

An additional focus for this new interest in local influences came from the British research initiative concerned with urban and regional restructuring (CURS). Although researchers such as Smith (1987) criticized its focus on specific localities and empirical fact-finding, at the expense of theoretical rigour, Cooke (1987) offered some defence against this criticism. He argued that what has been described as 'localities' research did not imply the neglect of process, and that explanation should not be bound by the limitations of Marxism. The critical perspective entering this debate is best exemplified by the 1987 volume of *Environment and Planning, Society and Space*, which contains a number of articles on this issue. David Harvey's (1987) contribution, 'Three myths in search of a reality in urban studies', is a rigorous defence of the Marxist position, arguing that whereas it is perfectly correct to claim that space, place, and particularity (of every sort) must have a stronger position in historical materialism, this does not mean an abandonment of universal statements and abstractions.

These arguments show that despite all the trends that seem to point to the destruction of local differentiation and interaction, the local community — especially within cities — still plays an important role in contemporary urban life. It has survived both general scepticism from social scientists and planners and some close research scrutiny. It emerges, if not completely unscathed and expressed in different ways, at least as a valid object for contemporary analysis. Perhaps in some ways the local place communities can be depicted as a fact in search of a theory or in others as a specific and selective means of understanding some aspects of urban life, rather than a blunt instrument which can be applied generally to all kinds of people in all kinds of places. Fischer (1982, 8) has crystallized the issue with his suggestion that 'different kinds of people, with different kinds of social preferences, tend to prefer different kinds of places'. Although this may be a trite statement, it is, nevertheless, accurate. One can come closer to the flexible nature of the meanings of local community in cities by repeating the point that the term is multi-dimensional, being composed of a variety of features. Unfortunately not all of the variety of features that contribute to a distinctive place community in a city are found in all places at the same time. Most individual manifestations, the features we describe as a distinctive community, are based on only some of the range of features that have been identified in various

areas. To understand more fully these place communities in the social mosaic of our western cities, we need to identify the different features which contribute to their varied character. This is the subject-matter of the next three chapters.

References

Aggar, B., 1991, Critical theory, poststructuralism, postmodernism: their sociological relevance, *Annual Review of Sociology*, 17, 105–31.

Agnew, J. R. and Duncan, J. S., 1989, *The power of place: bringing together geographical and sociological imaginations*, Unwin Hyman, Boston.

Barash, D., 1986, *The hare and the tortoise: culture, biology and human nature*, Viking Penguin, New York.

Bartelt, D., Elesh, D., Goldstein, I., Leon, G. and Yancey, W., 1987, Islands in the stream, neighbourhoods, and the political economy of the city, in I. Altman and A. W. Wandersman (eds), *Neighbourhood and community environments*, Plenum Press, New York, 163–89.

Bell, Daniel, 1978, *The cultural contradictions of capitalism*, Basic Books, New York.

Berry, B. J. L. and Smith, K., 1972, *The city classification handbook*, John Wiley, New York.

Birchall, J., 1988, *Building communities the co-operative way*, Routledge and Kegan Paul, London.

Blaudel, F., 1981, *Civilization and capitalism from 15–18th centuries*, translated by Sian Reynolds, William Collins, London.

Bloom, Alan, 1987, *The closing of the American mind*, Simon and Schuster, New York.

Cooke, P., 1987, Clinical inference and geographical theory, *Antipode*, 19, 69–98.

Davies, W. K. D., 1984, *Factorial ecology*, Gower Press, Aldershot, England.

Dear, M. and Scott, A. J., 1981, *Urbanization and urban planning in capitalist society*, Methuen, London.

Durkheim, E., 1964, *The division of labour in society*, new edition, Free Press, New York, original edition 1893.

Cranston, M., 1957, *Locke: a biography*, Longman, London.

Fischer, C. S., 1976, *The urban experience*, H. B. Ivon, New York.

Fischer, C. S., 1981, The public and private worlds of city life, *American Sociological Review*, 46, 306–16.

Fischer, C., 1982, *To dwell among friends*, University of Chicago Press.

Galbraith, J. K., 1992, *The culture of contentment*, Sinclair-Stevenson, London.

Hallpike, C. R., 1986, *The principles of social evolution*, Clarendon Press, Oxford, England.

Harper, R. A., 1982, *Modern metropolitan systems*, C. E. Merrill, Columbus, Ohio.

Harvey, D., 1973, *Social justice and the city*, Edward Arnold, London.

Harvey, D., 1985, *The urbanization of capital*, Basil Blackwell, Oxford.

Harvey, David, 1987, Three myths in search of a reality in urban studies, *Environment and Planning, Society and Space*, 5, 367–76.

Hill, C., 1975, *The world turned upside down: radical ideas during the English revolution*, Penguin, Harmondsworth, England.

Jacobs, Jane, 1961, *The life and death of great American cities*, Random House, New York.

Janowitz, Morris (ed.), 1967, *The community press in an urban setting*, University of Chicago Press.

Lasch, C., 1979, *The culture of narcissism*, Norton, New York.

Laslett, P., 1965, *The world we have lost*, Charles Scribner's Sons, New York.

Marx, K., 1967 reprint, *Capital*, three volumes, International Publishers, New York.

Massey, Doreen, 1984, *Spatial divisions of labour: social structure and the geography of production*, Macmillan, London.

Mumford, Lewis, 1961, *The city in history*, Harcourt Brace, New York.

Park, R. E. et al. (eds), 1925, *The city*, University of Chicago Press.

Passmore, J., 1968, *A hundred years of philosophy*, Penguin, London.

Peters, K. A., 1987, *The dynamics of Hutterite society*, University of Alberta Press, Canada.

Phillips, J. B., 1972, *The New Testament in modern English*, Macmillan Paperbacks, New York.

Shlay, A. B. and Rossi, P. H., 1981, Keeping up the neighbourhood: estimating net effects of zoning, *American Sociological Review*, 46, 703–19.

Schmalenbach, H., 1977, *On society and experience: selected papers*, translated from German and edited by G. Luschen and Gregory Stone, University of Chicago Press, Chicago.

Schwartz, B., 1991, Chinese culture and the concept of community, in L. S. Rouner (ed.), *On community*, University of Notre Dame Press, 117–129.

Seligman, Adam (ed.), 1989, *Order and transcendence*, E. J. Brill, Lieden, New York.

Smith, N., 1987, Rascal concepts, minimalising discussion and the politics of geography, *Environment and Planning, Society and Space*, 5, 377–83.

Stein, M. R., 1960, *The eclipse of community*, Princeton University Press, New Jersey.

Strauss, G., 1974, *Organizational behaviour*, University of Wisconsin Press, Madison.

Suttles, G., 1968, *The social order of the slum*, University of Chicago Press, Chicago.

Tawney, R. H., 1936, *Religion and the rise of capitalism*, reprinted 1962, P. Smith, Gloucester, Mass.

Taylor, C., 1989, *Sources of self*, Harvard University Press, Cambridge, Mass.

Taylor, C., 1991, *The malaise of modernity*, Anansi, Concord, Ontario.

Tonnies, Ferdinand, 1887, *Community and society*, new edition translated 1963 by C. P. Loomis, Harper and Row, New York.

Vance, J., 1977, *This scene of man*, Harpers College Press, USA.

Viljoen, S., 1974, *Economic systems in world history*, Longman, London.

Wallerstein, I. M., 1979, *The capitalist world economy*, Cambridge University Press, England.

Warnock, Mary, 1965, *The philosophy of Sartre*, Hutchinson's University Library, London.

Warren, R. B. and Warren, D. I., 1977, *The neighbourhood organizer's handbook*, University of Notre Dame Press, Indiana.

Warren, R., 1978, *The community in America*, Rand McNally, New York.

Webber, M., 1963, Order in diversity, in L. Wingo et al. (eds), *Cities and space*, Johns Hopkins University Press, Baltimore.

Webber, M., 1964, The urban place and non-place realm, in M. Webber, J. Dyckman et al. (eds), *Explorations into urban structure*, University of Pennsylvania Press, 79–138.

Weber, Max, 1958, *The Protestant ethic and the spirit of capitalism*, translated by Talcott Parsons, Charles Scribner's Sons, New York.

Weber, Max, 1958, *The city*, translated and edited by D. Martindale and G. Neuwirth, Free Press, New York.

Wellman, B. and Berkovitz, S., 1988, *Social structures*, Cambridge University Press.

Wellman, B. and Leighton, B., 1979, Networks, neighbours and communities, *Urban Affairs Quarterly*, 14, 363–90.

Wheatley, P., 1971, *The pivot of the four quarters*, Aldine, Chicago.

Wilkenson, K. P., 1989, The future for community development, in J. A. Christenson and J. W.

Robinson (eds), *Community development in perspective*, Iowa State Press, Ames, 337–54.

Williams, M. R., 1985, *Neighborhood organizations: seeds of a new urban life*, Greenwood Press, Westport, Connecticut.

Wirth, L., 1938, Urbanism as a way of life, *American Journal of Sociology*, 44, 8–20.

Wolff, K. H., 1950, *The sociology of Georg Simmel*, translated by H. H. Gerth and C. W. Mills, Free Press, New York.

3

Areal Content and Context

Introduction

Attempts to study the character of intra-urban community areas have faced the problems of all community studies: that of adequately defining and measuring the phenomena of interest. These problems are not easily resolved. Communities, considered as areas within cities, are collective entities that have a physical plan, particular land uses and facilities, such as shops and churches, and contain people with different characteristics such as gender, family, age, ethnicity, etc. When one adds the behaviour, interrelationships and organizations of these individuals, their personality types, and how they interpret and perceive these areas, it is clear that communities, considered as intra-urban areas, must be very complex in their character. This has led to many competing interpretations of their basic character. Table 3.1 uses seven selected examples from experts in the field to illustrate the range of these definitions .

At first sight this variety in definitions may lead to a feeling of despair about what constitutes the essential character of place communities and neighbourhoods. This variation and the resultant imprecision of these concepts have led some to abandon them and use different terms. For example, the term 'home area' was used by the British Community Attitudes Survey (HMSO 1969) in the research that preceded the reorganization of local government in 1972. Banerjee and Baer's (1984) comprehensive survey of the character and attitudes found in twenty-two selected districts of Los Angeles proposed the term *residential environments* to include the following features:

the land, facilities, services and social structure which supplements the home in providing for the satisfaction of individual and family needs, social interaction, personal development and political participation, and which delimit the territory appropriately included in the design of a residential environment. (Banerjee and Baer 1984, 33)

An important part of this definition is the idea that there is an area and set of functions outside the home which have a certain character and in which certain needs are met and can be planned for. This is close to the heart of the common-sense concept of the intra-urban community, although it must be noted that the definition is rather weak on what is now known as the cognitive-affective domains (see Chapter 5). Nevertheless, it is difficult to see the advantage of using alternative words or phrases, for they do little to help us in our understanding of the nature of these areas. Fortunately the problem of comprehension may not be as bad as it seems initially. Hillery's (1955) review of almost a hundred different definitions of community found three recurrent features: *area, common ties* and *social interaction*. These elements can be considered to provide the basic bedrock of what a community is supposed to be. However, to concentrate on the similarities alone is unwise. To do so is to lose the detail of the additional characteristics that the various authors thought were important. This illustrates a fundamental problem in the search for community character. Although the communality identified in the sets of definitions — namely some basic derived similarities — may produce clarity in the resultant generalization, it also produces an *overemphasis upon mini-*

Table 3.1 Selected definitions of neighbourhoods and communities

---

1) "Proximity and neighbourly contact are the basis for the simplest and most elementary form of association which we have in the organisation of city life. Local interests and associations breed local sentiment, and, under a system which makes residence the basis for participation in the government, the neighbourhood becomes the basis of political control ... it is the smallest local unit ... The neighbourhood exists without formal organisation" (R.E. Park 1925, 7).
[Elements: Proximity, Local Interests, Local Associations, Sentiment, Participation, Political Control]

2) "A neighbourhood is a distinct territorial group, distinct by virtue of the specific physical characteristics of the area and the specific social characteristics of the inhabitants" (R. Glass 1948, 18).
[Elements: Territorial Group, Physical Character, Social Character]

3) "The term neighbourhood ... refers to distinctive areas into which larger spatial units may be subdivided such as gold coast and slums ... middle class and working class areas. The distinctiveness of these areas stems from different sources whose independent contributions are difficult to assess: geographical boundaries, ethnic or cultural characteristics of the inhabitants, psychological unity among people who feel that they belong together, or concentrated use of an area's facilities for shopping, leisure, and learning ... Neighbourhoods containing all four elements are very rare in modern cities ... geographical and personal boundaries do not always coincide" (S. Keller 1968, 87).
[Elements: Boundaries, Social Character, Unity or Belonging, Local Facility Use]

4) "When community area boundaries were delimited ... the objective was to define a set of sub-areas of the city each of which could be regarded as having a history of its own as a community, a name, an awareness on the part of its inhabitants of community interests, and a set of local businesses and organisations orientated to the local community" (E. Kitagawa and K. Taeuber, 1963, xiii, Chicago Local Community Fact Book)
[Elements: Area, History, Name, Local Awareness, Local Organisations, Local Business]

5) "A community consists of a population carrying on a collective life through a set of institutional arrangements. Common interests and norms of conduct are implied in this definition" (U.S. National Research Council 1975, 2).
[Elements: Population, Collective Life, Organisation, Common Interests, Common Conduct]

6) "In last analysis each neighbourhood is what the inhabitants think it is. The only genuinely accurate delimitation of neighbourhood is done by people who live there, work there, retire there, and take pride in themselves as well as their community"
(U.S. National Commission on Neighbourhoods 1979, 7).
[Elements: Cognition, Residents, Workers, Retired, Self-Pride, Area Pride]

7) "Community is not a place, but it is a place-orientated process. It is not the sum of social relationships in a population but it contributes to the wholeness of local social life. A community is a process of inter-related actions through which residents express their shared interest in the local society" (Wilkenson 1989, 339).
[Elements: Place-oriented Process, Partial Social Relations; Shared Interest]

---

malist concepts. The use of some common features or elements of community character may exclude some vital or key ideas whose importance may not yet have been generally recognized.

Summarizing Community Character

Through time the number of different elements or features identified as being important to neighbourhood and community definition has increased substantially. Previous attempts by a large number of authors (such as Suttles 1972; Warren and Warren 1977; Williams 1985; and Rivlin 1987) are extended in Table 3.2 within the two broad categories of content and context (see Davies, 1992). Each of these were divided into three parts.

Content categories

Three separate *domains* of features are identified. A domain is considered to be a broad category of characteristics capable of being separated into several different parts, which can be defined as the individual elements or *dimensions*, many of which can be measured by individual *variables*.

Areal Content. This summarizes the physical or social differences in area which have traditionally been part of the 'ecological' approach, although the list needs to be expanded to include the environment and the morphology of areas, the man-made skeleton of cities. Many of these may be our common-sense interpretations of different features, such as the vegetation–climate differences in the environmental dimension. Others may be derived from individual indicators linked to census variables, such as the managerial occupation, income, university education variables, which are the traditional measure of the high status side of the economic status factorial dimension. A longer discussion of these issues is provided below.

Behaviour or Interaction. These dimensions consist of the behaviour between people or facilities, best seen in interaction between individuals who are neighbours, or in journeys to visit shops, as well as the interactions that take place in relation to political or informal organizations. Most of these dimensions are derived from questionnaire studies that measure the flows of interactions or from travel diaries in which people record all their movements, purchases and interactions. These interactional issues will be explored in detail in Chapter 5, leaving the discussion on organizations to Chapter 6.

Conceptual Identity. A third set of characteristics relates to the attitudes that people have to their areas, as seen in Park's 'sentiment' variable in Table 3.1, extended to the 'symbolic and sentiment' associations by Firey (1945; 1947), and subsequently to a variety of characteristics that will be described in detail in Chapter 4. It is becoming normal to divide the area into two subtypes: **the cognitive and affective domains**. The former deals with the identification and relationships of the physical features in the area, such as in Lynch's (1960) mental mapping approach, whereas the latter is concerned specifically with the meanings and attitudes that people have about the areas. Many of the dimensions cannot be observed directly, being derived from questionnaires designed to elicit peoples' attitudes to, and knowledge of, their surroundings.

Context categories

The specific contents of communities cannot be viewed as relating to a single place at one time. They must be placed in three contexts.

The Dynamic or Temporal domain relates to the changes that occur in all the dimensions described above through time. These are rarely discussed in the literature because most studies are analyses carried out during one period. Rivlin (1987) made it clear that the Dynamic issue must be considered a funda-

Table 3.2 Elements of Community Character

1. Domains	2. Major Dimensions	Subdivisions (a), (b), (c) etc.	3. Functions Performed	E. Externality or Spatial Scale
A. AREAL CONTENT	1. Area	(a) Size, (b) Distances, (c) Density		1. Household
	2. Environment	(a) Climate, (b) Landforms, (c) Plants etc.		2. Blockface
	3. Facilities	(a) Open spaces, (b) Shops, (c) Leisure Support, (d) Workplaces, (e) Homes, (f) Roads etc.	(Degree of Homogeneity)	3. Functional or Defined Area
	4. Morphology	(a) Design types: Styles, (b) Degree of decay		4. City Sector
	5. Social Variety	(a) Family status, Economic status, Ethnicity, Mobility, Impoverishment etc, (b) Personalities		5. City
				6. Region
				7. Nation etc.
B. BEHAVIOUR (INTERACTIONS)	1. Activity or Facility Use	(a) Shopping, (b) Recreation, (c) Workplace	1. Servicing Needs (Food, Shelter etc.)	INTERNAL VS EXTERNAL FLOWS
	2. Informal Interaction	(a) Neighbouring, (b) Friendship, (c) Family	2. Sociability, Emotional Support, Aid	
	3. Mutual Informal Co-operation (Supportive)	(a) Instrumental, (b) Informational	3. Mutual Aid (e.g. Surveillance) Knowledge of Area	
	4. Organisations (Formal)	(a) Community, (b) Church, (c) Festivals etc	4. Group Needs or Ordering	
	5. Political Participation	(a) Voting, (b) Meetings, (c) Officer	5. Representation, Influence	
	6. Supportive Milieu	(a) Charity, (b) Government	6. Needs Provision	
	7. Economic or Capital Flows		7. Accumulation/Outflow from Outside	
C. CONCEPTUAL IDENTITY i) PERCEPTION & COGNITION (Recognition of X, relating it to knowledge)	1. Place Identity	(a) Naming	1 & 2. Place Familiarity, & Use	INSIDERS VS OUTSIDERS (Resident or Workers)
	2. Cognitive Mapping	(a) Mapping, (b) Bounding		
	3. People Identity	(a) Ethnicity, (b) Dialect, (c) Gender, (d) Age, (e) Clothing, (f) Cosmetic Management	3. People Familiarity, Degree of Comfort	
	4. Symbolic Communication	(a) Symbolic Decoration, (b) Territory marking	4. Personalisation, Aesthetics Barriers, Defence	
ii) AFFECTIVE (Attitudes Motivation)	1. Symbolism of Place		1. Enhancement of Self	
	2. Sentiment & Attachment		2. Rootedness	
	3. Evaluation & Appraisal		3. Place Satisfaction, Appraisal	
	4. Nuisances - Annoyances		4. Dissatisfaction	
	5. Security - Safety		5. Fear or Threat	
	6. Empowerment		6. Degree of Control	
	7. Place Appearance		7. Social Malaise or Contentment	
	8. Latent Involvement/ Participation		8. Expected Mutual Aid	
	9. Aesthetics		9. Beauty or Order	
	10. Common Values		10. Interpersonal Influence, Cohesion	
	11. Empathy or Belonging		11. Common Feelings	
D. DYNAMIC CHANGE	1. Short Term			
	2. Episodic (Seasonal, Annual etc)			
	3. Long Term Events			

mental part of neighbourhood character, reinforcing the observation of Park (1925) that a 'common heritage' is an important aspect of community distinctiveness. Few studies of a quantitative nature have ever really tried to incorporate temporal issues. The one exception occurs when a temporal variable, such as 'length of residence', is included to explain the degree of neighbouring or 'place familiarity'.

Geographical Scale and Externality refers to the spatial issues, to the area that is occupied, and its relationships to areas around. It is the geographical space where the physical elements, relationships and attitudes are found and with which they have interaction, as well as that outside. In this discussion to date it has been assumed that there is a geographically definable area in which all or most of the elements can be found. This is not always true, for the definition of a community is a basic research task in inner-city space. For many of the Areal Content dimensions the issue may be quite straightforward for physically located phenomena are being examined. For the Behavioural dimensions the community may be identified by the extent of close interaction within a certain territory, although the connections outside the area are equally important. The degree of externality, therefore, is a vital source of variation. In the simplest sense one can simply measure contacts outside the area of interest, so that an *internal–external* dichotomy can be established. In the case of the cognitive and affective domains the division is probably best described as the *insider–outsider* dichotomy, although not all those outside will have similar attitudes and there will be varying opinions about the spatial extent of the community. Alternatively, one can specify various scales of aggregation of the data. Regional analysts have struggled with a similar dilemma in their regional descriptions, for again there is no simple hierarchy of phenomena. Haggett's (1967, 7) G scale and Doxiadis's Ekistics scale (1968) are more recent attempts to resolve the problem, whilst Galster (1986) has provided a more sophisticated 'realist' interpretation based on the perceptions of people who use the local space. A basic way of partly resolving this dilemma is to modify the suggestion put forward by Suttles (1972) by identifying five different scales: block-face; functional neighbourhood; community as defined by the city; sector, a broad part of the city such as a north-west segment; and the city itself. To this may be added regional, national and international scales, with subdivisions within these if necessary. All interactions could be aggregated at these various levels or simply portrayed spatially as contact fields to interpret the character of the spatial structure of the linkages, although the importance of non-place linkages must be remembered (see Chapter 2 for the discussion on the non-place realm concept).

The Surrounding Society must be viewed in its broadest sense, as the range of forces and factors that are found in the surrounding society and discussed in Chapter 2.

Table 3.2 summarizes the subdivisions with the various dimensions, and, where necessary, identifies the primary functions performed by these dimensions. Only the Areal Content and the three context domains will be dealt with in this chapter, the Behavioural and Conceptual Identity domains being the subject-matter of Chapters 4 and 5. All these elements seem to apply as much to neighbourhoods as place communities in cities, although an important difference can be identified. In general, neighbourhoods — with the exception of their use in 'neighbourhood unit plans' — are considered to be smaller. They define areas with people in close proximity, perhaps those within a block who 'neighbour' or interact in an informal fashion, whilst place communities are usually considered to consist of a larger area. Either they imply some common purpose, perhaps even a common identity among residents or outsiders, or they have been defined by city authorities for the delivery of certain functions. Two important caveats about the universality of the elements found in Table 3.2 must be made. First, it must not be assumed that all the features identified in Table 3.2 relate to the same area, in the sense that the community is always located in a common space. Some communities are areas that are bounded by strong distinctive barriers. Mostly, however, the individual elements that make a community distinctive are not coincident: they overlap with one another, although in some cases there may be a common core with a periphery defined by individual criteria. For example, even within an area of distinctive morphology or design there may be several foci of informal interaction and linkages outside the areal unit (Chapter 4), whilst people may have very different views on where the community begins and ends (see Chapter 5). As Wilkenson (1989, 339) put it, a community is not just, or necessarily, a place but is also a 'place-orientated process... of interrelated actions through which residents express their shared interest in the local society.' Second, not all of the elements have distinctiveness in each area, so their incidence is selective. The distinctiveness of particular communities may be due to a unique element, such as a high level of ethnicity, or a combination of several characteristics. Given the variety of elements that exist, it is hardly surprising that there are so many different types of communities. What Table 3.2 provides is the range of raw material from which communities can be fashioned. Although ideally, each of these dimensions needs to be explored in detail, few studies have been able to produce comprehensive analyses of the variety of elements found in what can be called the Areal Content of areas within the context of the community literature. Most community studies take the environmental issues for granted although it is clear that intra-urban areas can vary in their environmental character. Similarly, there are many schemes for classifying the land use patterns in cities, particularly the arrangement of commercial areas (Jones and Simmons 1987), whilst the morphological variations in the design of residential areas is the subject of a huge literature in which historical surveys by Mumford (1961) and Reps (1965) have stood the test of time. Space constraints mean that it is impossible to deal with these variations in detail here, although subsequent chapters deal with the major changes in community design (Chapter

8), and less fully with retail provision at the local level (Chapter 7). The rest of this chapter deals with the content area that has received the most attention in the study of communities within cities, namely their social character, identifying the methods applied to the task of describing areas, isolating the dimensions or sources of variation and their associated patterns, and the major factors that account for these variations. This is followed by consideration of the dynamics of social change within cities, the principal features that create change in the character of intra-urban areas over time. A final section describes the various typologies of intra-urban communities which have been isolated.

Measuring Social Structures

It is possible to identify a number of different phases of investigations dealing with the variations in the social structures of urban areas, the collective characteristics of people living in areas within cities. Although each of the five major phases follows the other in a temporal sequence, they never completely replace previous phases. In recent years the intellectual interest in studying urban social variations for their own sake becomes more important than the prescriptive approaches of the past designed to provide the background for policies that attempt to diminish this social problem.

Verbal Description

Throughout the centuries vivid summaries of the social characteristics of areas within cities can be gleaned from the work of social commentators, historians and particularly novelists. However, because these descriptions are the by-product of some other objective, they are rarely comprehensive. Nevertheless, tantalizing, yet all too brief vignettes of the differentiation of urban space can be found in the work of journalists such as Henry Mayhew, reformers such as Frederich Engels, and novelists such as Charles Dickens. The last in particular described in poignant detail the squalor of life for the working class in these cities, particularly in the many poor, crime-infested warrens, such as the Rookeries in London. There is little doubt that these portrayals helped inform the influential public and hastened the progress of reform that sought to eradicate these conditions. They did not provide the basis for a systematic literature, leading to precise measurements of the social differences between areas.

Statistical Description

The late nineteenth century saw a rapid growth in the analytical and quantified approaches to scientific knowledge. Although quantified information, both in raw numbers, and in ratios such as percentages, had been used by many social commentators, the work of Charles Booth in the last part of the nineteenth century can be said to have begun a new phase of investigation. His development of social survey methods, mapping techniques and statistical description made him a pioneer in many fields (Davies 1978b), although he may be best remembered for his seventeen volumes of description (Booth 1902) detailing the life of the working class in various trades, as well as in areas. From a community perspective it is not so much his survey methods that excite attention, as his attempts to measure and portray the conditions that he found. Booth and his employees used Board of Education records on schoolchildren to define the level of prosperity in each building in the urban area. This information was plotted on maps using a seven-point scale: lowest class; very poor; moderate poverty; poverty and comfort mixed; fairly comfortable; well-to-do; wealthy. The result was a detailed geographical portrayal of the social conditions of each area in London, not as an aggregate for an area, but on an individual building scale. It is hard to underestimate the importance of his work: it was the first time that such a detailed portrayal of the condition of life in each part of the city had

ever been produced. Indeed it is hard to imagine such a map being constructed today, given the sensitivity of both the population at large and city administrators to the publication of such information.

Booth recognized that the production of such detailed surveys of poverty was too time-consuming to be repeated easily. So he recommended a short-cut to this problem in his Presidential Address to the Royal Statistical Society (Booth 1894). He advocated the use of indicators taken from the Census of Population: indicators which should be measuring the same type of conditions. Each of these values was scaled from 0 to 100 to make them comparable and plotted on a graph in which the twenty-seven areas of London were arranged in order of their scores on the indicators. The importance of this study lay in three features. First, he had generalized the detailed variations in his street-by-street poverty maps to single values for each indicator in each area, producing a geographical aggregation of his data. Second, he observed that the various indicators displayed similar trends, implying that they were measuring aspects of a single dimension or source of social variation, which he called 'social condition'. Third, by adding the various indicators together for each area and dividing by the number of variables he obtained a summary 'index of social condition'. The result was a succinct portrayal, and indeed measurement of each area, one that went beyond the detail of individual variables. Booth concluded that he had produced 'an instrument' for the measurement of the social variation in cities, which could be applied to cities as diverse as Calcutta and New York. In doing so he maintained that the problem of what he called the *terra incognita* of cities could be resolved. Unfortunately, Booth's work was largely ignored by researchers interested in quantitative approaches.

The Urban Ecologists

Robert Park, and his principal co-workers Robert McKenzie and Ernest Burgess, also began their investigations into the spatial variation in intra-urban character because of their concern at the transformation of life in the cities: in the loss of personal interaction between people, and even the moral degradation produced by new influences such as dance halls! (Park 1925). Three interlinked approaches were used. One of the major tasks of the 'Chicago School' was to define these areas, and Burgess isolated seventy-five such communities in the 1920s. Others provided detailed studies of these distinctive communities, such as Wirth's (1928) study, *The ghetto*, or the formation of gangs, described the behaviour of groups and conditions of life. A second approach lay in the search for principles to describe social change in various areas of the city; also in their outline of an idealized model, really a typology or classification of city areas, based on their land use and social character. Previous investigators such as Engels (1845) had provided verbal descriptions of the spatial patterns of the new commercial–industrial cities. However, instead of single summaries, the urban ecologists linked such spatial patterns together as part of a more integrated, or at least an interrelated body of systematic inquiry using analogies from the field of plant ecology, such as the *invasion* of an area by social groups or land uses and the resultant *succession* of land use or social types. In addition, they proposed the concept of 'natural areas', maintaining that a natural order of distinctive areas could be found in most cities. The competitive sorting-out process produced by the operation of the land market through thousands of individual decisions by residents, landlords, developers and city officials created broadly homogeneous areas of land use and social character, paralleling the natural areas that were being mapped in the plant and animal kingdoms. The third distinctive feature lay in the attempts to provide spatial summaries of these trends, although these go beyond the ecological school. Burgess (1925) is famous for his concentric zone model which produced the fivefold division of intra-urban space shown in Figure 3.1. Subsequent investigators criticized the concentric zonation, replacing this pattern with sectoral formulations that stressed the sectoral pattern of land uses (Hoyt 1939), or the complex multi-nuclei nature of cities formed by the creation of spatial separate nuclei of land use in particular areas and their subsequent expansion and coalescence (Harris and Ullman 1945). By contrast Firey (1945, 1947) criticized the emphasis on observable land uses and economic criteria describing the importance of the social valuation of space (see Chapter 5). Many texts have summarized the contribution of this school of thought and its deficiencies (Johnston 1971). In the context of this chapter the absence of a theoretical base and rigorous measurement techniques are of note.

Social Area Analysis

The publication of Shevky and Bell's *Social area analysis* in 1955 had a profound effect upon the study of urban social differentiation. It was the first study in the field to provide a theoretical backing for the choice of variables which were considered as indexing three basic constructs or fundamental components of variation. The model specified constructs called Social Rank, Urbanization (Family Status) and Segregation (Ethnicity). Each of these were indexed by three variables, which were then used to produce a classification of each census tract in the study area. Although the importance of this work in the history of ideas cannot be challenged, subsequent criticism has reduced the utility of this breakthrough. First, the urban relevance of a theory of 'increasing scale' in society has been criticized, for the theory was derived from an anthropological work on the traditional:modern transition in East Africa. Second, the logical sequence of the stages must be questioned, because each successive phase is not a necessary outcome. There are major jumps in logic. Moreover, it is difficult to see why 'migration' is not derived as an additional construct, or fundamental source of variation. Third, the measurement technique used to combine the variables depended on some rather crude ratio measures, scaling each construct along the 0–100 scale. Although this

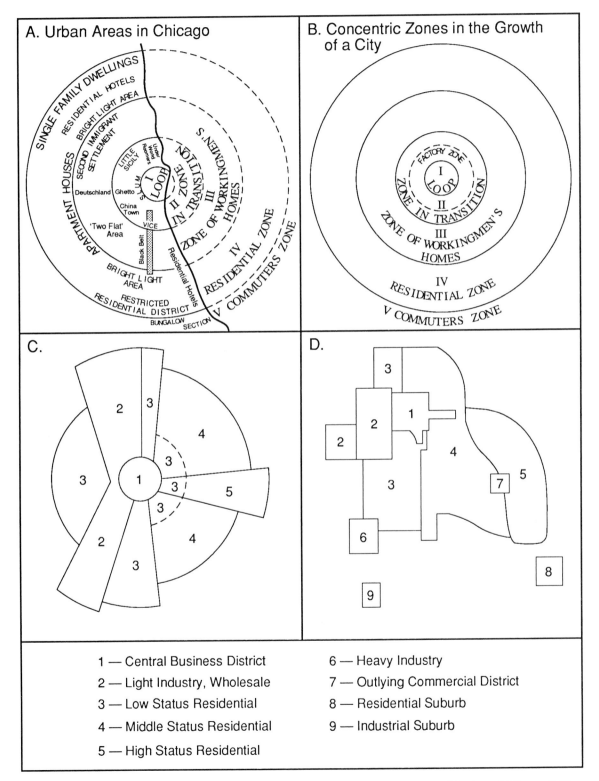

A. Urban Areas in Chicago

B. Concentric Zones in the Growth of a City

C.

D.

1 — Central Business District
2 — Light Industry, Wholesale
3 — Low Status Residential
4 — Middle Status Residential
5 — High Status Residential

6 — Heavy Industry
7 — Outlying Commercial District
8 — Residential Suburb
9 — Industrial Suburb

Figure 3.1 Spatial models of land-use and structure (after Park 1925; Hoyt 1939; Harris and Ullman 1945)

may be useful in one city, it makes absolute comparisons between cities impossible. This unsophisticated technical approach is rather surprising, given the fact that other investigators at the time (Tryon 1955) were demonstrating how multivariate techniques such as cluster analysis could be used to integrate a set of variables and produce clusters of areas of similar social characteristics. Despite these deficiencies, Shevky and Bell's work became the standard for many investigations of the social differentiation of cities, providing a link between theoretical considerations and empirical classifications.

Factorial Ecology

Factorial ecology is the application of factor analysis techniques to urban ecology (Berry 1972). Its growth in popularity was linked to the spread of quantitative techniques in sociology and geography and the increasing use of computers in the 1960s. In methodological terms the value of the approach lay its ability to use a larger number of variables than in the urban ecological and social area phases. In addition, it used precise statistical measures of similarity, such as correlation coefficients, to summarize the degree of association between each variable measured in every community area, or more usually, in census tracts. The heart of the method, the factorial phase, can be considered as a type of statistical induction. Each factor is a new mathematical vector that entails the rewriting of the data set in more concise form; summarizing a common source of variation in the similarity matrix. Each factor, therefore, can be considered as a quantitative measurement of a dimension or component of variation, or constructs lying behind the empirical reality of the individual variables. The factor matrix shown in Figure 3.2 has a series of values, associated with each variable on each factor. These values, or factor loadings, run on a scale from +1.0 to –1.0 and measure the strength of the relationship between each variable and the factor, with 0.8 accounting for ($.8^2$), i.e. 64 per cent of the vari-

ability of the variable on the factor or axis. Also of real importance is that factor scores for each factor, or source of variation, could be derived. These scores measure the importance of each area on a factor. In other words, the factorial approach provided a method for integrating the measurement of the social dimensions — the factors or sources of variation — and the areas — the factor scores on each dimension or construct.

Fascination with this new-found ability to employ multivariate procedures led to an explosion of interest in the techniques and their application to many cities. However, most of the early studies were rather crude in a technical sense, and were of limited scope in terms of data sets used and cities analysed. Gradually, however, the various options available were explored and the utility of procedures adopted was established. This progression to a more systematic body of literature has been described in detail elsewhere (Davies 1983; 1984). Here the stages that need to be considered are summarized in diagrammatic form in Figures 3.2 and 3.3. The first summarizes the key differences between what can be called social indicators, structures, typologies, patterns, regions and models, and provides examples of the different results at each stage. The second summarizes the major technical decisions to be made in the factor analysis itself.

The question of how many dimensions of social variation are needed to characterize the social variability of intra-urban areas is still a fundamental research question in the field. Booth's (1894) single axis of variation was extended to three dimensions by Shevky and Bell (1955), and to four with McElrath's (1968) addition of Migrant Status. Since that time many factorial ecologists have extended the number of axes they consider to be important, perhaps paralleling the changes in psychology, where intelligence was measured by Spearman's (1904) single axis at the turn of the century, and now is considered to be represented by many different dimensions. In the field of personality assessment the number of different personality types continues to grow, and factor analysis has played an important

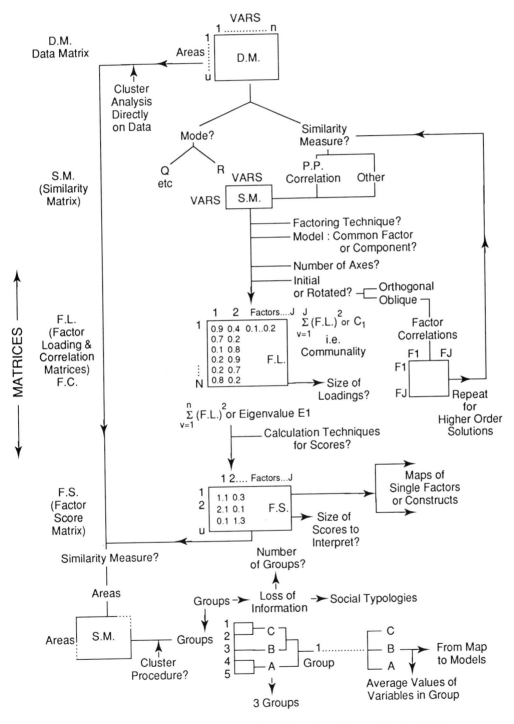

Figure 3.2 Technical decisions and stages in factorial ecology (*Source:* Davies 1991)

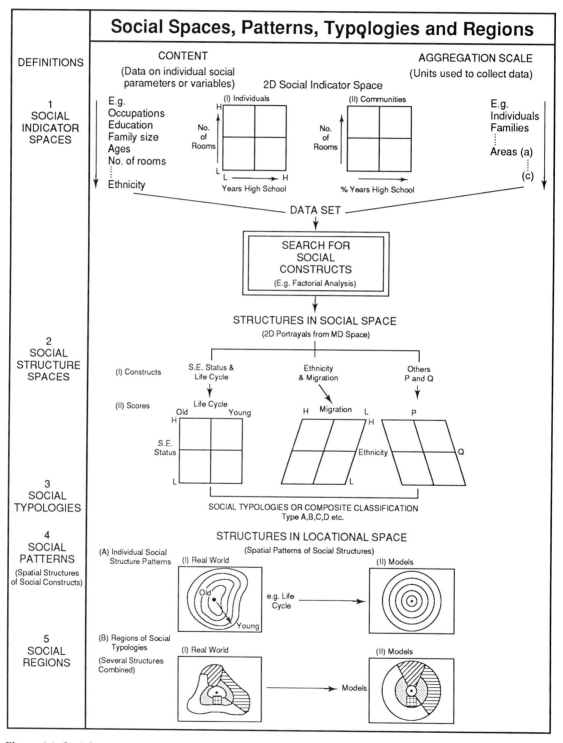

Figure 3.3 Social spaces, patterns, typologies and regions (*Source:* Davies 1983)

part in the derivation of these sources of differentiation. Unlike the psychologists, however, many factorial ecologists have been slow to extend the variety of data included in their data sets, to standardize the indicators used so that results can be replicated, and of really crucial importance, to organize their results into testable dimensions and sets of categories.

Hunter (1974), using community areas defined by the city of Chicago, demonstrated the utility of the three standard Shevky-Bell axes in a factorial framework in describing the social changes in the city between 1931 and 1972. He showed that the level of explanation of the solutions declined through time and Family Status became less important than the other two factors. However, it must be emphasized that Hunter used a limited data set of only nine variables, so the comprehensiveness of these results must be questioned. Moreover, many of the earliest attempts to follow factor procedures did not use rotation to improve the comprehension of the factors, whilst data sets were dominated by ethnic indicators. Hence the results were not always satisfactory. Once wide-ranging data sets were employed to explore the dimensionality of census data sources, many additional axes of differentiation were uncovered. Davies (1984) demonstrated that the results from different cities indicated variations owing to the industrial–post-industrial transition in western society, the influence of cross-cultural differences, or the influence of time. Timms (1971) suggested that the four major axes of McElrath could be combined in a series of ways to derive different social area types. Davies (1984) integrated them into a suite of types, and extended the set by postulating a split in the axes in western cities, especially the fission of Family Status. The evidence seems conclusive that there are more than three axes of differentiation and these vary according to society, region and time.

Part of the problem in this field relates to the fact that so much of the evidence comes from studies of single cities. This means it is difficult to know the extent of place-particular differentiation in the factors, whilst the scores are measurements unique to the data set and are difficult to compare with those from other cities. Davies and Murdie (1991; 1992a) attempted to solve these problems by adopting the *joint analysis* approach (Davies 1975) in their study of all twenty-four Canadian metropolitan areas (CMAs). They used thirty-five variables, representative of fourteen hypothesized dimensions derived from Statistics Canada census tract data. Almost three thousand census tracts, with a mean population of 4,575 people, for the twenty-four metropolitan areas of over 100,000 population were amalgamated in a single study, in total accounting for 13.6 million people or 57 per cent of the Canadian population. Careful scrutiny of a series of alternative results led to the decision to interpret a nine-factor solution accounting for 85.8 per cent of the variance in the similarity matrix.

A later study (Davies and Murdie, 1992b) revealed the loadings and titles shown in Table 3.3. Many of the axes shown are familiar from earlier studies. *Economic Status* is one of the clearest dimensions, although it is worth emphasizing that there is also an *Impoverishment* axis. This is indexed by low-income people and single female parent families; in the main these are a rapidly increasing group of people living in poverty. Ethnicity is also a typical dimension found in most factorial studies. However, it must be stressed that the data set did not explore the variety of specific ethnicity in this increasingly multicultural country, not only to avoid biasing the variable set by this source of variation, but also in the knowledge that many ethnic groups are concentrated in particular areas. Ethnicity, therefore, was measured by the percentage of immigrants: those of French ethnic origin, and those of non-British and French ethnic heritage: namely, those not belonging to the founding nations. The results, therefore, can measure only the extent of ethnic deviation from the largest stock — those of British Isles origin; the specific ethnicity must be measured in other ways, such as by Bourne et al.'s (1986) use of dissimilarity indices.

Unlike the social area analysis approach, Table 3.3 shows that four family and age-

Table 3.3 Canadian metropolitan areas (1986): factors and loadings

Variables	Component Loading for 1986			All Metropolitan Census Tracts		
	2 Economic Status	3 Impoverish-ment	4 Ethnicity	9 Migrants 1 (Distant)	10 Migrants 2 (Local)	6 Occupation (Female Clerical)
Female Income	84					
University Education	91					
Male Managers	85					
Median Income	65					
Low Education	-49			-41		
Blue Collar	-93					
Female Parent Families		86				
Low Income		71				
Renters		55				
Female Unemployment		49				
Male Unemployment		36				
Two Parent Families		-85				
Female Participant Rate		-33				
Immigrants			97			
Other Ethnic			92			
French			-67	-50		
Long Distance Movers				74		
Apartments						
Local Movers					97	
Female Clerical						-95

Source: Davies and Murdie, 1992b

Table 3.3 Canadian metropolitan areas (1986): factors and loadings (Continued)

	Order of Extraction and Titles of Component Rates				
Variables	3 Early-late family	11 Family and Age	8 Non- family	5 Young Adult	7 Housing
Young Children	88				
Adult 25-34 yrs	88				
Movers	56				
Older Children	-78				
Early Middle Age	-82				
Late Middle Age	-53				-47
Apartments		-82	35		
Completed Family		-49	-42		-34
Old Age		-42		-50	
Renters		-43			
Person/Family		50	35		37
Children		40	42		41
Female Unemployment		-39	-30		
Male Unemployment		35	-48		
Non-family Ratio			-94		
Singles			-56	45	
Divorced Ratio			-72		
Childless Family			N.A.		
Young Adult				77	
Female Participant Rate				54	
Old Housing (Poor)					-92
New Housing					86

related dimensions can be recognized. The *Early and Late Family* dimension distinguishes the new suburbs from the older areas full of what are called 'empty-nesters'; *Old Age* identifies the completed family areas; *Pre-Family* separates the areas dominated by those in their early twenties who live apart from their families; and *Non-Family* indexes the areas that have high levels of people who live in non-family units or have been divorced. Two other dimensions were also considered important: *Housing* identifies areas of poorer housing and length of occupancy, whilst a *Migrant* dimension is based on the separation of areas that have high values of people who have migrated between provinces from tracts of high local mobility. Although it could be argued that the presence of so many family-related axes reflects the variable set used in the study, if these differences were not present the analysis would have produced a single axis of family variation. Hence the study illustrates the way in which the social differentiation of large Canadian metropolitan areas are structured on the census tract scale and display much family-related variation. It is also worth noting that the analysis used census tracts, which are defined by the census authorities on a consistent basis. Although these do not necessarily coincide with community areas defined by the cities, the sizes are approximately the same, and results of single city studies using community areas have produced parallel results (Davies 1978a). Studies in other countries using similar extensive data bases have demonstrated that the three-axis model proposed by Shevky and Bell (1955) is too restrictive as a description of the social differentiation of the western city. However, the use of higher-order analyses in cities such as Leicester (Davies and Lewis 1973) and Cardiff (Davies, 1983) have shown that the smaller axes are often correlated, grouping together in higher-order components that parallel McElrath's four-axis model. In addition Davies (1983) has shown that the structures identified will vary on different geographical scales and that city and society-specific variations in the factorial axes can be expected. Unfortunately,

few attempts have been made in recent years to tease out these variations in any systematic manner and there has not been any convincing theoretical demonstration of the reasons why the structures should emerge, although the key issues have been noted by Davies (1984, Chapter 9).

When the factor scores for the various dimensions are plotted, systematic patterns are often found, despite the inevitable place-particular variations. Murdie (1969) demonstrated that the *Family Status*, *Economic*, and *Ethnic* dimensions displayed concentric, sectoral and clustered patterns respectively, demonstrating that the three classical ecological patterns of Burgess (1925), Hoyt (1939) and Harris and Ullman (1945) were not competitive patterns, but were found in all cities and associated with particular factorial dimensions. Davies (1984) extended this idea for medium-sized cities with a single major node. Substandardness or *Impoverishment* as well as the *Pre-Family* dimensions often displayed a cluster pattern, although on different sides of the city centre. *Non-Family* was also concentrated in the inner city, whilst *Late Family* was usually found as a concentric zone in the inner suburbs, one usually broken by the pattern of major roads with their associated commercial and apartment development. *Migration* also displayed concentricity, with high levels of local migrants in the outer suburbs and long-distance migrants concentrated in the inner city. The *Urban Fringe* areas also displayed a.concentricity around the built-up city, whereas council housing estates often formed distinctive clusters. In big multi-centred metropolitan areas these simplistic patterns are rarely found, for the size and presence of many subcentres makes the social mosaic far more complex.

The factor scores need not only be used to describe individual patterns. They can be aggregated, via techniques such as cluster analysis, to provide two summary characterizations of areas. There are a large number of very different cluster routines, each with different decision rules, so care must be taken in the establishment of the most suitable procedure. The most popular procedure consists of the use of a Euclidean Distance measure of dissimilarity to compare the similarity between each pair of places, followed by a grouping procedure that sequentially combines the most similar two cases until one group remains. Normally the pattern of relationships is such that a big break in the distribution of dissimilarity values at a particular grouping stage is found. Each of the groups can then be summarized to provide the average characteristics of the factor scores for the cluster and these can be mapped to provide a summary of the social mosaic of the area of study. Figure 3.4 shows a generalized model of social regions in British cities, using results from a number of published studies.

So far these results have not been explained adequately by any comprehensive theory of social change leading to what has been proposed as the multivariate-structural phase of investigation (Davies 1983). Nevertheless, there has been much success in fulfilling the rationale that inspired Booth's work a century ago: the creation of a quantitatively-based classification for describing the social areas in cities throughout the world.

The social area analysts and factorial ecologists achieved their greatest success in the basic task of **classifying** residential areas. These classifications or typologies rested upon the qualities of the **methods** which they adopted and especially upon the **data** which they were able to use. Whereas the censuses did present wide ranges of social and demographic variables, they also set the limits to what this type of analysis could achieve. In the study of communities within the city there were perhaps two main limitations. First, the residential classification studies could not properly deal with **process** and the dynamics of residential change. Second, the reliance upon census data meant that the typologies or classifications which they produced could not approach a full understanding of the nuances and subtleties of urban life. Census data do not cover quality of life, attitudinal and behavioural variables of the kind that many community analysts would prefer. Ways in which other approaches sought to remedy these deficiencies can be discussed, under the headings of residential area change, generational change, community change and selective loss.

Residential Area Change

Analysts of urban residential structure from the urban ecologists to the factorial ecologists paid too little explicit attention to the details of residential change. These were not static communities or residential areas, they were in a constant state of flux as many studies of migration within the city have shown (see Rossi 1980). The general fact of change was of course always recognized. Burgess (1925) referred to his famous zonal model as one of structure and growth and turned to the ecological processes of invasion and succession as the vehicles of change. Factor ecologists have been able to offer classifications of the same city at different census dates (usually ten-year intervals) and to discuss change in relation to the different patterns which they observe (Murdie 1969). Real interest in residential change had to await the early 1970s after a realization that the concentration on pattern was missing the real forces which underpinned communities in the city. Rees (1970) spoke of the need to study the myriad individual decisions being made on **where to live** as a way of coming to grips with an understanding of residential change. In one sense he was right and a powerful thrust of research into residential mobility became concerned with that question. However, geographers have also long since recognized that for every household which makes a choice there are others which do not have the ability to do so; the constraints upon individual households are often very great. The other parts of the residential change question therefore concern the workings of the housing market and of the structural forces in society which underpin the social geography of the city. These themes are well described in the literature (Knox 1987; Herbert and Thomas 1989) and will not be discussed further in any detail here. The focus will be rather on the implications of these processes for **community change**.

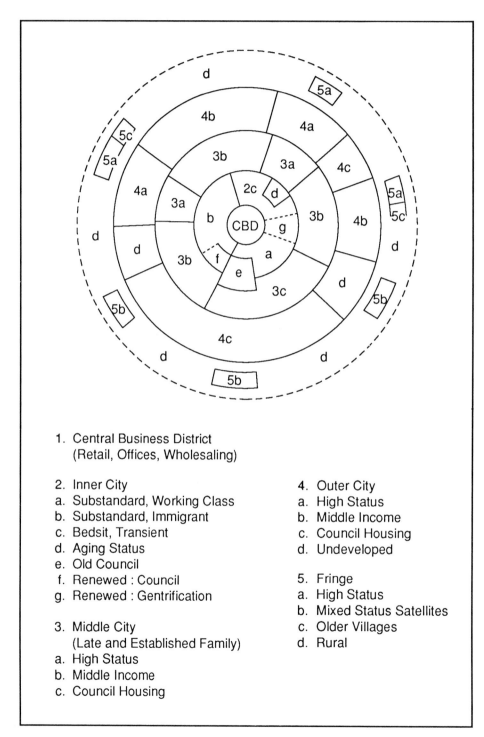

1. Central Business District
   (Retail, Offices, Wholesaling)

2. Inner City
   a. Substandard, Working Class
   b. Substandard, Immigrant
   c. Bedsit, Transient
   d. Aging Status
   e. Old Council
   f. Renewed : Council
   g. Renewed : Gentrification

3. Middle City
   (Late and Established Family)
   a. High Status
   b. Middle Income
   c. Council Housing

4. Outer City
   a. High Status
   b. Middle Income
   c. Council Housing
   d. Undeveloped

5. Fringe
   a. High Status
   b. Mixed Status Satellites
   c. Older Villages
   d. Rural

Figure 3.4 A model of social regions in British cities (*Source:* Davies 1983)

The earlier studies of residential change were strongest in dealing with the idea of **area** change. When Burgess (1925) applied ideas of invasion and succession, the main thrust was the ways in which neighbourhoods could change in status and character over time. Similarly, the Hoyt (1939) sector theory was developed in relation to the growth of neighbourhoods and especially to the movement of high-status residential **areas**. These approaches suggest that communities emerge, although they are vulnerable to change which may lead to their replacement with others of a different character. This is the explicit theme of invasion and succession, and the **filtering** concept suggested by Hoyt — widely used since — envisages changes in neighbourhood status as dwellings filter down the housing market. Although this process of community change is complex, there are two major strands. First, the physical fabric of the area is changing over time. As housing and environment grow older, they may deteriorate unless maintained and given continuing investment. Second, the population of the neighbourhood will itself experience ageing if a relatively stable population moves through its life cycle *in situ*. Interwoven with both processes is the fluidity of residential movers within the city; stability is often less common than a continual shifting of households seeking to adjust dwelling type to their changing family composition and economic or social status.

Communities will clearly vary in their experience of both forms of residential change. Some inner-city neighbourhoods will be unable to halt a downward spiral of physical decay and the poorest sections of the population will be locked into the most substandard conditions. Other parts of the inner city may have qualities of architecture or location which attract investment and an influx of new kinds of people which may transform it to a higher level. Suburban areas perhaps to a lesser extent may have similar experiences, the contrast being sharpest between the most favoured private suburbia and the least favoured problem estates in the public sector of social housing. Simply in demographic terms, residential areas

may progress from being predominantly young families with children at the time of construction to becoming dominated by older age-groups as the **area itself** ages. Some researchers have described a concept of **community careers** as the estate or district itself appears to have a life cycle which buildings and people pass through together. One outcome of factorial ecologies has been the ability to classify areas in demographic terms with labels such as young family, middle age, empty-nesters and old age. There are fabric implications for this 'people' life cycle because the buildings and services created for a new neighbourhood may not match the needs of its population with generational change.

Generational change

Generational change is most easily exemplified in terms of the demographic changes being experienced by the populations of major cities. As a group the elderly are increasing numerically and form higher proportions of the overall population; the over-65-year-olds now form around 12 per cent of the total population in the United States and 11 per cent in Canada, and almost 20 per cent of the population of northern Europe is over 60 years of age. A distinction is now being made between the young-old (65–74 years) and the old-old (over 75 years). Phillips and Vincent (1986) estimated that the former increased 25 per cent between 1951 and 1991 and the latter by 100 per cent. Given the longer survival rates of women, this latter group in particular has a marked gender imbalance. Whereas the term 'geriatric ghetto' has no reality at present, there is evidence that clusters of old people are found within parts of cities. Indices of dissimilarity for the elderly range up to about 40, on a scale of 0–100, showing a level of segregation below that typical of ethnic minorities and of social class groups. Clusters of old people can be found in particular residential districts. A minority of old people have migrated to environmentally attractive retirement areas, such as the sun-belt states in America, Victoria in Canada, and southern parts of Europe. However, Golant (1987) showed that one must not forget the migration streams within metropolitan areas, for he estimated that between 1975 and 1980 American central cities lost some 558,000 elderly, mainly through migration to suburban locations. Local clusters of elderly also occur in cities because developers have provided housing designed for their needs (see Chapter 8). Similar purpose-built accommodation ranging from caravan parks to condominiums to special suburban development are frequently found in the outer urban area. Most of the clustering of old people, however, is occurring in central cities where many remain in the homes and neighbourhoods which they have occupied during the latter part of their working lives. This is the largest group of urban elderly, and it is likely to be the most disadvantaged because it is often part of the residual population marooned in the central city and perhaps occupying substandard housing in an increasingly hostile local environment (see Chapter 5). One expression of generational change therefore is the higher numbers of urban elderly. Communities which include more old people are an increasing feature of western cities. Again, there is more gender separation with the breakdown of traditional forms of family life.

Community change

An ageing population implies demographic change which in turn impacts on those communities where the elderly live. There are also processes of change which can be generalized to the life history of an area or district. **Places** go through a process of change and are different kinds of areas at one point in time than they are at another. The idea of residential community careers has been developed in most detail in the study of crime. Reiss (1986) argued that communities, like individuals, can have careers in crime and that today's safe environment can become tomorrow's dangerous one. Included in the sequence of community 'careers' are demographic processes of births, deaths and migrations, presence or absence of local organization and facilities, and the range of externalities. Reiss (1986) argued for longitudinal research designs to examine ways in which communities change over time. These arguments were specific to community crime careers although they clearly can be generalized.

Community change was also recognized in studies of the life history of areas subject to infiltration and take-over by different kinds of people or land uses. Burgess (1925) used invasion-succession to study such processes which are most common in communities located near the city centre or other points of high accessibility or job opportunity. Such communities are especially prone to this type of change. Burgess's (1925) famous concentric zone model based on Chicago envisaged a constant process of invasion and succession, with each use expanding into its surrounding area, producing a succession of land use. In Chicago, the inner-city 'zone of transition' located outside the manufacturing and wholesale zone that bordered the CBD was a real mixture of land uses and the home of the lowest income and transient groups. Although invasions come in many different forms, they can be generalized into five broad types and these are most evident in the communities in the inner city. Again it must be stressed that although the discussion identifies separate analytical categories, there can be combinations of these types, notably the increase in density and ethnic change.

Historically, the most typical was the spillover of businesses from the downtown area, producing a *conversion to commercial or public use* from businesses or governments seeking a location close to downtown without incurring huge land costs. The decline in many downtown areas in western cities in the past thirty years has led to the dereliction of many of these areas and it has been the public sector which has often rebuilt at least part of the areas with administrative or entertainment complexes.

The second typical type of invasion is an *increase in the density* of some areas, resulting from either the construction of new high-rise apartment blocks or the development of 'bed-sitters' in existing buildings. The former is often part of public housing projects although high-income projects can also be found. The public housing and bed-sit developments lead to a decline in social status and usually a lowering of the average age of the population, with the latter producing the bed-sit land of transients found in so many inner-city areas or areas close to educational establishments.

In the past twenty years these trends have been complemented by a third trend, the process of *gentrification*. Many areas close to downtown have been invaded by middle-income and professional families who seek proximity to the jobs and entertainment of downtown instead of the long commute to suburbs, as well as, perhaps, a capital gain by their improvement of the existing property through either renovation or replacement. The result has been the physical as well as the social upgrading of the community. However, the change has not always been tranquil. It has led to conflict between the way of life and attitudes of wealthier and educated incomers with the older or working-class families. Planning controls over the size of new residences to ensure the back gardens of older properties are not reduced to being constantly in shade or overlooked have often been introduced to minimize the impact of the intrusions.

Another important process has been the *change in ethnic composition* of many areas, frequently complemented by the increasing density described above. Many ethnic areas have their origin in a smaller enclave near downtown, where the low income and status of the original pioneers of the group usually ensure that they are restricted to the most obsolescent area, or to areas that others do not want — such as those prone to flooding. The spatial concentration may also have been reinforced by discrimination through statute or police action. The extent of subsequent growth in surrounding areas is a complex process. It depends on four major variables:

1. the amount of pressure from incoming migration streams into the city from this ethnic group;
2. the extent to which the ethnic group is subject to community opposition to the expansion in the surrounding areas;
3. the desire of the group to continue to concentrate, a product of the extent of their voluntary segregation, perhaps linked to the need to be near their kin, or to a place of worship or cultural facilities (see the discussion in the next section);
4. the extent to which the individual members are economically successful enough to be able to buy houses in other areas and are not subject to discrimination in these areas.

In the United States there are many examples of groups, particularly various east Europeans, who were once concentrated in virtual ghettos and who have now dispersed. In the past thirty years the old hope for the melting-pot of American society has faded. Instead it is clear that ethnic variety remains an important source of variation between intra-urban communities, with blacks, various Hispanic groups and a series of new Asian groups showing increased concentrations. In some cities ethnic groups have succeeded one another in particular areas, the Irish followed by Jews and then blacks is a typical sequence in some of the larger cities of north-eastern America. The changes in social composition as a result of ethnic change can be duplicated by concentrations of people with particular lifestyles, such as the gay or orthodox Jewish groups in many of the bigger American cities.

Ethnic residential segregation is often the most pronounced form of concentration of social groups within urban areas, and historically the ethnic areas — frequently linked with recent immigration — have been regarded as close-knit communities within the city. The persistence of ethnic areas is strongly underpinned by a number of well-known economic and discriminatory constraints (*involuntary* segregation) which maintain the concentration of ethnic groups (Knox 1987). However, there are also *voluntary* choice mechanisms and these provide advantages for the concentration to endure. Boal (1978) identified four such choice-related functions for some ethnic minorities:

1. *Defence*. This is a function which reduces the isolation of an ethnic minority and enables self-protection within a clearly-defined area. The term 'ghetto' (originally the Venetian *geto* for Jews) has this kind of meaning.
2. *Avoidance*. This function emphasizes the need for self-support within the ethnic area, and particularly for recent migrants, allows contact with familiar languages, customs, behaviour and values rather than contact with the unfamiliar.
3. *Preservation*. This is a function which gives the minority group the opportunity to maintain its own cultural mores and to create a subculture within the wide society. Wirth (1928) suggested that for the Jews the geographically separated and socially isolated community provided the best means of preserving the traditional facets of their lifestyle. Asian communities in British cities are driven by similar sentiments in their choice of residential location. Many Chinatowns in Canada have deliberately adopted historic designs — in building or street furniture ornamentation to proclaim their distinctiveness and improve their image and economic success.
4. *Resistance or Attack*. This function uses neighbourhood as a power-base for reaction against discriminatory policies and as a platform for change.

These functions have sometimes been referred to as *choice* mechanisms underpinning ethnic areas, and they could equally be regarded as responses to constraints. Although some element of choice undoubtedly exists, constraint is the overarching force and the persistence of ethnic areas has to be explained largely in those terms.

Boal (1978) also used his concept of choice constraint to form a typology of the spatial outcomes of the ethnic residential segregation which he labelled as *colony, enclave*, and *ghetto*. *Colony* is a temporary form of ethnic area where although the barriers to assimilation are not high, early migrants need a foothold in a new society. They tend to disperse as the passing of time allows the assimilation to have full effect. *Enclaves* are more permanent ethnic areas which, although they may be affected by constraints upon assimilation, they have strong elements of choice. Jewish, Chinese and Asian ethnic areas are sometimes cited as examples of enclaves. *Ghettos* are more forcibly and obviously the product of constraints and black communities in American cities are taken as the exemplars of such places. Cater and Jones (1989) argue that the ghetto results from a one-sided and seemingly perpetual black–white conflict which is essentially racial. They invoke the black nationalist concept of a ghetto as the 'internal colony' occupied by an underclass for whom separation and non-acceptance is accompanied by disadvantage and oppression. Similarly, Darden (1987, 37) concluded that 'black residential segregation is best explained by exclusion and discrimination motivated by racial prejudice'.

Selective Loss

Many of the impacts that account for the change in the character of communities over the long term come from the selective loss of part of the existing population, rather than generational aging or ethnic invasions. Chapter 2 has already described the background changes which have led to the decline in place communities in cities, especially since the Industrial Revolution. It has been the differential or selective loss of different income groups from their original location in the city centre which has had a most profound effect. Although many of these changes are linked to the availability of a new phase of transportation, it must be remembered that they are bound up with a series of related social and economic factors. The result has been to create new communities on the edge of the city with high levels of internal social homogeneity, with the consequent reduction in the degree of social mixture in the areas left behind.

This process of selective out-migration is well established in the history of urbanization. The Romans built villas in the country to escape the noise and congestion of the city: as wealthier groups achieved personal mobility they were able to place distance between work and residence. By the last quarter of the nineteenth century the growth of trams and railways had opened up the possibility of 'suburban' living to greater numbers of people, although it was always a selective process.

With the universal ownership of cars and an increasingly affluent society after World War II, the working class as well as lower middle-income groups were catered for by a new suburban boom. New roads and motorways initially provided rapid links between the employment and residential areas, creating a new and larger flight to the suburbs. However, the loss must be combined with other factors, especially central city congestion, the increasing negative externalities of the car upon the inner city, and the obsolescence of its building structures. Hence it can be argued that the expansion of the suburbs aided the dereliction of many inner cities. Only the poorest, transient and elderly remained in many areas. The addition of low-income disadvantaged minorities — especially, though not exclusively, black — accelerated the trends. At the same time the decline of the city centre in commercial terms due to the addition of commercial strips and large-scale shopping-centres in the suburbs meant that the centres of many North American cities declined in relative importance. Moreover, in financial terms the city's ability to cope was hindered by the fact that many of the suburban areas were incorporated as separate political entities, thus reducing the tax base of the centre at a time when there was a need for renewal. Only in those centres with a strong office sector, such as in the regional and national capitals, was the inner city able to maintain its vibrancy. By the 1960s many inner cities became areas of even greater disadvantage, and in America, frequently of abandonment. Shells of buildings

set in a wasteland of dereliction, violence and crime have been vividly shown in films such as *Fort Bronx*, its title conveying the idea of the depressed inner city as frontier. Although selective out-migration of people and industry has certainly been a major cause, it is the combination of several factors which provides a more complete explanation. Nevertheless, the patterns are not completely gloomy. Planners in European countries have deliberately maintained the primacy of the city centre as a commercial area. Many others have been transformed by deliberate policy. A combination of public and private developments has revitalized many areas, with new shopping malls, markets, entertainment complexes and open spaces, although critics such as Whyte (1988) have commented on the inhuman scale of many of the developments.

The last quarter of the twentieth century has witnessed the continuation of selective out-migration. As a result the concept of **residual** populations of have-nots in inner-city areas has been more real and pointed, and the poverty areas in more generalized form are spreading outwards to include older suburbs. People most affected are those with least ability to move, and many of these become dependent on communities where facilities, opportunities and conditions are all far below any level of acceptability. Other aspects of this 'dependency' are discussed in Chapter 4.

Classifying Communities: The Alternative Perspectives

The second deficiency of social area analysis and factorial ecology was their inability to deal properly with more qualitative aspects of community life. Allied to this was the fact that many social areas as derived statistically from these studies were only crude approximations of 'communities' in the full sense. Their boundaries were determined by census subdivisions and in aggregate they were often far too large to resemble communities. Closer definition of community has had to turn to more detailed approaches, such as those based on mental maps, cognition and actual behaviour which are discussed in Chapter 5. There also have been attempts to form typologies which do take account of 'affective domains' and qualitative indicators not included in census data. For the last part of this chapter some of these attempts can be reviewed.

The revival and growth of neighbourhood organizations and concern about inner-city decay and renewal in the 1960s and 1970s led to an explosion of interest in the topic and many attempts to produce additional types of neighbourhood classification. These went beyond the social structure typologies produced by multivariate analysis (Chapter 3), in the sense that they included behavioural variables and attitudinal variables. Relatively few rigorous quantitative studies have confirmed the differentiation of these distinctions. Burkhardt (1971) was an early exception. He used factor methods on a six-variable data set to confirm his hypothesized difference between what he called 'perceptual' and 'behavioural' sources of variation, although the term 'domain' is a more useful summary. Most of the typologies produced were far less sophisticated. The majority were essentially verbal summaries, at best assigning descriptors, such as 'diverse or homogeneous social character' or 'limited internal interaction', to the various elements of neighbourhood character. Moreover, many of the key elements that have been identified in the discussions on the variety of domains and dimensions were excluded in the construction of community types.

One of the earliest examples of the approach is represented by Hojnacki's (1979) article 'What is a neighbourhood?' Many of the features of neighbourhood character identified in

Table 3.4 Elements used in Hojnacki's typology

Basic Elements of Communities	Hojnacki's Neighbourhood Types		
	2 Emergent	3 (Intermediate)	4 Traditional
1) Area size	Very Large	Smallest	Small
2) Social Character	Diverse	Homogeneous	Homogeneous
3) Area Boundaries	No Common Boundaries		Clearly Defined
4) External Threat		Low Threat	High Threat
5) Future Satisfaction	High Optimism	Low Optimism	Moderate
6) Neighbourhood Organisations	None	None	Many
7) Sub-Group Interaction	Limited	Little	Organised
8) Personal Interaction	–	–	Yes

Source: Revised from Hojnacki (1979)

Table 3.5 Six neighbourhood types (adapted from Warren and Warren, 1977)

Types from three dimensions	Identity	Interaction	Linkage
	Sense of belonging	Active behaviour	Outside contacts
Integral (Integrated: Internally and Externally) This means that the neighbourhood meshes with other institutions in the large community. It is a cosmopolitan as well as a local centre where residents are in close contact with each other and share many concerns, they also participate in activities of the larger community. Although it often has a number of middle class professionals, it may also be an inner city or blue-collar industrial community. This type of neighbourhood is relatively rare. It exerts a good deal of control over directions in which it changes.	Yes	Yes	Yes
Parochial (Localised) This neighbourhood has a strong ethnic identity or homogeneous character. It is self-contained and independent of the larger community. It has ways to screen out what does not conform to its own norms.	Yes	Yes	No
Diffuse (Inactive and Poorly Connected) This is an homogeneous setting, such as a new subdivision or inner-city housing project. The residents have much in common, but there is no active internal life because neighbours are not involved with each other. As a corollary, there is little connection to the life of the larger urban community. This is a neighbourhood vulnerable to decline.	Yes	No	No
Stepping Stone (Short-term stay) The activity of this more uncommon neighbourhood resembles "musical chairs". People participate in neighbourhood community *not* because they identify with the neighbourhood, but because they want to "get ahead" in a career or some other non-local point of destination.	No	Yes	Yes
Transitory (Residual and Mixed) This type of neighbourhood is commonly understood. It is a place where population change has been or is occurring. Residents break into clusters of "old timers" and "new comers" and view each other with suspicion or hostility. As a result, little collective action or organisation takes place. On the other hand, much neighbourhood organising has been successful in such locales.	No	No	Yes
Anomic (Disorganised) This is really a non-neighbourhood. There is a great social distance between people. There are no protective barriers whereby it can resist change from outside influences. It lacks a capacity to mobilise from within for common actions. This is not necessarily a poor neighbourhood. It could be housed in luxury condominiums or exist in a fast-growing suburban area. This neighbourhood is the most vulnerable of all to decline, because it is the most difficult to organise.	No	No	No

Source: Adapted from Warren and Warren 1977, 96–97; descriptions in brackets added by authors

Table 3.2 were recognized as key elements: demographic composition, physical characteristics, the presence of neighbourhood organizations, subgroup and personal interaction. However, Hojnacki accepted the opinion of Suttles that 'externality' and 'residential attitudes' were vital components of community differentiation: they could be measured by the degree of satisfaction about the area and the perception of threat. In the former case this was related to the perceived distinctiveness of an area: the distinctions that people make between their own neighbourhood and others that are perceived as different and, perhaps, less desirable. In the second case it described the degree of optimism about the future. The attitude was that out-migration would increase in areas within which negative change was expected, increasing its problems by leaving only low-income and transient people. Hojnacki combined a residential attitude variable with some of the more traditional components of community character to produce a basic twofold typology of areas: *emergent* and *traditional*, together with an *intermediate* class which was considered to be a 'pocket' within the first two. Unfortunately for those seeking precision in the construction of the typology, the descriptive words used to identify each feature were far from precise. Table 3.4 attempts to clarify the classification by identifying the components or sources of neighbourhood variation used in the description of community character in Table 3.2. Gaps in the cells mean that the element was not linked to the neighbourhood type identified.

Not surprisingly, the characterization of intra-urban areas communities as falling into only two types was not considered to be comprehensive, although at least the study pointed the way to more effective classifications. Warren and Warren (1971; 1978), in an extensive study of neighbourhood change and organizations and change in Detroit, produced a more extensive typology of neighbourhoods — identifying six types and emphasizing the dynamics of these areas (Table 3.5) They summarized the differentiation of neighbourhoods in terms of three sources of variation, called interaction, identity and external linkages. Although the typology proposed by the Warrens has proved useful in identifying differences between areas, it paid relatively little attention to suburban areas and does not explicitly link specific elements of community differentiation to the various area types, or even isolate them in a measurable form. Moreover, it is clear from Table 3.5 that social class and ethnic variations were included although these were not part of the triad of differentiating types. Although this neighbourhood classification certainly provided an advance on Hojnacki's typology, not only in its more complex typology but also in methodological terms, the study is far from analytically clear. It is also important to note that many of the elements or dimensions emphasized by previous workers are ignored or downplayed: the absence of references to 'area facilities', such as schools or shops, provides one example. Moreover, Rivlin (1987, 4) observed that the impression was given that the six types were spatially separate entities, whereas she maintained several types could coexist in one neighbourhood. So despite its initial utility, the classification does not produce an entirely satisfactory summary of the range of elements of neighbourhood differentiation.

The essentially descriptive method of the Warrens can be compared with the recent fourfold typology produced by Weenig, Schmidt and Midden (1990) shown in Table 3.6. This contains a much more explicit attempt to demonstrate the dimensions on which a typology of areas can be based. After reviewing research on neighbouring, social networks and 'sense of community', the authors concluded that there were two basic features of neighbourhood character: 'neighbouring' and 'sense of community'. The former was linked to indicators measuring the degree of interaction: in conversation, visiting, and in the provision of social support to friends and neighbours. The latter was associated with variables of identification or attachment, shared emotional connection, degree of mutual participation, and pressure to conform. All of

Table 3.6 A typology of neighbourhoods

| | | SENSE OF COMMUNITY | |
		Strong	Weak
NEIGHBOURING	+	A-type	B-type
	−	C-type	D-type

Type A: Strong sense of community and many neighbouring activities. In this type of neighbourhood, information diffusion will probably be relatively fast, and social influence will presumably be rather strong.

Type B: Weak sense of community although many neighbouring activities. In this type of neighbourhood, information may be disseminated rather rapidly, although probably without much behavioural influence.

Type C: Strong sense of community and sparse neighbouring activities. Although information may not rapidly diffuse in this type of neighbourhood, social influence on behavior and decisions will probably be high (mostly through commonly shared norms and the existence of a limited number of strong ties).

Type D: Weak sense of community and few neighbouring activities. In this individualistic-oriented type of neighbourhood, information diffusion will presumably be rather slow and almost without any influence on behaviour or opinions.

Source: revised from Weenig et al., 1990

these features had been previously recognized as important elements of community differentiation. Princals Analysis (Gifi 1981), a form of non-linear factor analysis allowing the use of non-interval scale data, was applied to the results of a series of questions administered to 912 respondents in eight Dutch towns. The results confirmed the presence of two major sources of variation, called *neighbouring and sense of community*, which were used to produce the fourfold typology of communities shown in Table 3.6. The authors considered their results an advance on Warren and Warren's (1977) classification, despite the fewer types, emphasizing: 'it is inaccurate and even confusing to treat in one typology the evaluative identification dimension on the same level as the factual interaction dimension' (Weenig et al. 1990, 49). Although this is an important point it must be emphasized that the study cannot be considered comprehensive because of its failure to incorporate many of the other components of the social character of area identified above. So even though the typology proved to be useful in designing neighbourhood information programmes and relating them to an area's social fabric, it is clear that the results can only be a partial representation of neighbourhood character. Obviously there is a need for much more work conclusively identifying and measuring the dimensions of community variation, and combining the characteristics into typologies of intra-urban community variation. Nevertheless one must be careful. It is unlikely there can be one comprehensive typology of communities, suitable for all purposes and as one example of a place-specific classification, Table 3.7 shows an attempt to place residential areas in American cities into a set of identifiable categories.

Table 3.7 A classification of American residential areas

Prosperous Suburbs		
Blue-blood estates	-	wealthiest neighbourhoods
Furs and station wagons	-	new money in suburbs
Pools and patios	-	older upper-middle class suburbs
Young suburbia	-	outlying, child-bearing suburbs
New homesteaders	-	ex urban boomtowns of young families
Grey power	-	upper middle-class retirement communities
Golden ponds	-	rustic cottage communities
Upmarket and gentrified areas		
Money and brains	-	posh urban enclaves
Urban Gold Coast	-	upscale urban high-rise
Young influential	-	yuppie condominiums and apartments
New beginnings	-	suburban singles complexes
Blue-collar areas		
Blue-chip blues	-	wealthiest blue-collar suburbs
Rank and file	-	older blue-collar industrial suburbs
Old Yankee rows	-	working class row houses
Single city blues	-	downscale, urban singles district
Blue-collar nursery	-	middle-class child-bearing areas
Levittown USA	-	aging, post 1940s tract sub-division
Ethnic areas		
Black enterprise	-	black middle and upper class
Emergent minorities	-	black working-class neighbourhoods
Downtown Dixie style	-	Aging Southern black neighbourhoods
Hispanic mix	-	Hispanic barrios
Public assistance	-	inner city ghettos
New melting pot	-	new immigrant areas
Others		
Bohemia mix	-	inner city bohemian enclaves
Two more rungs	-	comfortable multi-ethnic suburbs

(adapted from Weiss 1988)

Conclusions

This chapter has summarized some of the elements which need to be considered in the study of local communities in cities. First, it has demonstrated the contributions made by geographers towards the classification of residential areas in a tradition that began with the Chicago School and its concern with natural areas and has assumed modern form in factorial ecologies. Second, it has recognized the fact of residential change and the dynamic nature of the urban environment. Communities change over time and the processes which underpin that change are vital components of our understanding. Third, it has been acknowledged that definitions of community need alternative forms of measurement. In order to introduce the essential qualitative perspective, there is a need to adopt very different methodologies to collect the data and different measurement scales to identify the importance of each feature. Some — such as demographic character — can be obtained from census sources; others, such as neighbouring, need interviews to obtain the data; cognitive approaches require attitudinal surveys, producing data very different from the typical interval scale or rank order and ordinal scales of many of the first two data sets. A real problem in the field is that of integrating so many different elements, although this has been eased by the adoption of multivariate techniques.

References

Banerjee, T. and Baer, W. C., 1984, *Beyond the neighbourhood unit: residential environments and public policy*, Plenum Press, New York, 1984.

Berry, B. J. L., 1971, The logic and limitations of comp. fact. ecology, *Econ. Geog.*, 47, 209–19.

Boal, F. W., 1978, Ethnic residential segregation, in D. T. Herbert and R. J. Johnston (eds), *Social areas in cities*, John Wiley, Chichester, England, 502–10.

Booth, C., 1894, Life and labour of the people of London, Presidential Address, *Journal of the Royal Statistical Society*, 55, 557–91.

Booth, C., 1902, *Life and labour of the people of London*, reprinted 1969, A. Kelley, New York.

Bourne, L. S., Baker, A. M., Kalbach, W., Cressman, R. and Green, D., 1986, *Canada's ethnic mosaic*, Major Report No. 24, University of Toronto, Centre for Urban and Community Studies.

Burgess, E. W., 1925, The growth of the city, in Park, R. E. et al. (eds), *The city*, University of Chicago Press.

Burkhardt, J. E., 1971, The impact of highways on urban neighbourhoods, *Highway Research Record*, 356, 85–95.

Cater, J. and Jones, T., 1989, *Social geography: an introduction to contemporary issues*, Edward Arnold, London.

Darden, J. T., 1987, Choosing neighbours and neighbourhoods; the role of race in housing preferences, in G. A. Tobin (ed.), *Divided neighbourhoods: changing patterns of racial segregations*, Urban Affairs Annual Review, 32, Sage, London, 15–42.

Davies, W. K. D. and Lewis, G. J., 1973, The urban dimensions of Leicester, England, in Social patterns in cities, *Institute of British Geographers Special Publications*, 5 (March), 71–86.

Davies, W. K. D., 1975, Variance allocation and the dimensions of British towns, *Tijdschrift voor Economische en Sociale Geografie*, 66 (6), 358–271.

Davies, W. K. D., 1978a, Alternative factorial solutions and urban social structure. *The Canadian Geographer*, 22, 273–297.

Davies, W. K. D., 1978b, Charles Booth and the measurement of urban social structure, *Area*, 10, 290–6.

Davies, W. K. D., 1983, *Urban social structure: a multivariate structural study of Cardiff and its region*, University of Wales Press, Social Science Monograph 8, Cardiff.

Davies, W. K. D., 1984, *Factorial ecology*, Gower, Aldershot.

Davies, W. K. D., 1992, *Affective dimensions of community character*, unpublished paper read to IGU Commission on Urban Systems and Development, Detroit.

Davies, W. K. D. and Murdie, R. A., 1991a, Consistency and differential impact in urban social dimensionality: intra-urban variations in the 24 metropolitan areas of Canada, *Urban Geography*, 12 (1), 55–79.

Davies, W. K. D. and Murdie, R. A., 1992a, Measuring the social ecology of Canadian cities, in Bourne, L. and Ley, D. (eds), *The social geography of Canadian cities*, McGill-Queens Press (forthcoming).

Davies, W. K. D. and Murdie, R. A., 1992b, Changes in the social complexity of Canadian metropolitan areas: 1981–86, *Canadian Journal of Regional Science* (forthcoming).

Doxiadis, C. A., 1968, *Ekistics: an introduction to the science of human settlements*, Hutchinson University Library, London.

Engels, F., 1844, *The condition of the working class in England*, Panther, London (reprint 1969).

Firey, W., 1945, Sentiment and symbolism as ecological variables, *American Sociological Review*, 10, 140–8.

Firey, W., 1947, *Land-use in central Boston*, Harvard University Press, Cambridge, Mass.

Galster, 1986, What is neighbourhood? An externality–space approach, *International Journal of Urban and Regional Research*, 10, 242–63.

Gifi, A., 1981, *Non-linear multivariate analysis*, University of Leiden, Netherlands.

Glass, R., 1948, *The social background to a plan: the study of Middlesbrough*, Routledge and Kegan Paul, London.

Golant, S. M., 1987, Residential moves by elderly persons to U.S. central cities, suburbs and rural areas, *Journal of Gerontology*, 42, 534–39.

Haggett, P., 1967, *Locational analysis in geography*, Edward Arnold, London.

Harris, C. D. and Ullman, E. L., 1945, The nature of cities, *Annals, American Academy of Political Science*, 242, 7–17.

Herbert, D. T. and Thomas, C. J., 1989, *Cities in space: city as place*, David Fulton, London.

Hillery, G. A., 1955, Definitions of community, *Rural Sociology*, 20, 779–91.

HMSO, 1969, *Communities attitudes survey*, Royal Commission on Local Government, Research Study 9.

Hojnacki, W., 1979, What is a neighbourhood? *Social Policy*, September/October, 47–52.

Hoyt, H., 1939, *The structure and growth of residential neighbourhoods*, US Federal Housing Administration, Washington, DC.

Hunter, A., 1974, *Symbolic communities*, University of Chicago Press, Chicago.

Johnston, R. J., 1971, *Urban residential patterns*, Bell, London.

Jones, K. and Simmons, J., 1987, *Location, location, location: analysing the retail environment*, Methuen, Toronto.

Kitawaga, E. and Taeuber, K., 1963, *The Chicago local community fact book*, Chicago.

Knox, P. J., 1987, *Urban social geography*, Longman, London.

Lynch, K., 1960, *The image of the city*, MIT Press, Cambridge, Mass.

McElrath, D. C., 1968, Societal scale and social differentiation in Accra, Ghana, in S. Greer et al. (eds), *The new urbanization*, St Martin's Press, New York, 33–52.

Mumford, L., 1961, *The city in history*, Martin, Secker and Warburg, London.

Murdie, R. A., 1969, *The factorial ecology of Toronto*, Department of Geography, University of Chicago Research Paper No. 116.

Park, R. E. (ed.), 1925, *The city*, University of Chicago Press, Chicago.

Phillips, D. R. and Vincent, J. A., 1986, Private residential accommodation for the elderly: geographical aspects of development in Devon, *Transactions, Institute of British Geographers*, 11, 155–73.

Rees, P. H., 1970, Concepts of social space, in B. J. L. Berry and F. E. Horton (eds), *Geographic Perspectives on Urban Systems*, Prentice Hall, New York, 306–94.

Reiss, A. J., 1986, Why are communities important in understanding crime? in A. J. Reiss and M. Tonry (eds), *Communities and crime*, University of Chicago Press, Chicago, 1–33.

Reps, J., 1965, *The making of urban America*, Princeton University Press, New Jersey.

Rivlin, L., 1987, Neighbourhood, personal identity and group affiliations, in I. Altman and A. Wandersman (eds), *Neighbourhood and community environments*, Plenum Press, New York.

Rossi, P. H., 1980, *Why families move*, Sage, London.

Shevky, E. and Bell, W., 1955, *Social area analysis*, Stanford University Press.

Spearman, C., 1904, General intelligence, objectively determined and measured, *American Journal of Psychology*, 15, 201–93.

Suttles, G., 1972, *The social construction of communities*, University of Chicago Press, Chicago.

Timms, D., 1971, *The urban mosaic*, Cambridge University Press, England.

Tryon, R. C., 1955, *Identification of social areas by cluster analysis*, University of California Press, Berkeley.

Warren, R. B. and Warren, Donald I., 1977, *The neighbourhood organizer's handbook*, University of Notre Dame Press, Indiana.

Weenig, M., Schmidt, T. and Midden, C., 1990, Social dimensions of neighbourhoods and the effectiveness of information programs, *Environment and Behaviour*, 22, 27–54.

Weiss, M. S., 1988, *The clustering of America*, Harper and Row, New York.

Whyte, W., 1988, *Rediscovering the city centre*, Doubleday, New York.

Williams, M. R., 1985, *Neighbourhood organizations*, Greenwood, Westport, Connecticut.

Wilkenson, K. P., 1989, The future for community development, in J. A. Christenson and J. W. Robinson (eds), *Community development in perspective*, Iowa State Press, Ames, 337.

Wirth, L., 1928, *The ghetto*, University of Chicago Press, Chicago.

4

Interactions, Social Networks and Communities

Introduction

The second major domain of community differentiation is that which is associated with the behaviour or interaction of people — with the way they engage in social and economic contacts with others, in and around their area of residence. This chapter deals with this general issue in three ways. First, it identifies the various components or separate dimensions that can be isolated. Second, it examines the continuing roles or functions of neighbourhood as a place-defined, locality-based community, set within the more general context of the study of social networks. Third, it will examine the significance of the local community to some groups — such as the elderly, women and ethnic minorities — who will be more dependent on their local environment and for whom a general notion of widely dispersed, non-place networks may be inappropriate.

Domains and Dimensions of Behaviour

Most definitions of community refer to the important integrative role played by the variety and frequency of interaction between people living in a local community and those outside. Unfortunately, an early tradition in urban ecology was to stress the intra-community issues at the expense of a wider perspective. Many of the early ecologists regarded the communities, the 'natural areas' of the Chicago School, and eventually the city, as an aggregate of neighbourhoods. Another was to see the neighbourhood as the microcosm of the

city, a social world within the larger urban structure. Moreover, the community or even the neighbourhood was viewed as a convenient spatial unit for administrative purposes for academics and city officials. Wellman and Leighton (1979, 366) pointed to the resultant problem in their discussion on the 'community lost, saved and liberated' alternatives (see Chapter 2). 'The identification of a neighbourhood as a container for communal ties assumes the a priori organizing power of space. This is spatial determinism.'

Nevertheless, the idea that proximity has a profound effect on the formation of social relationships has had a long history in the field. A much quoted study by Festinger, Schacter and Back (1950) showed how students located in rooms close together had higher levels of friendships than those in more distant rooms, a product of higher levels of chance encounters leading to more intimate relationships. Similarly, Cooper (1975) reported that families living in cul-de-sacs in a housing project in Easter Hill Village of San Francisco visited 40 per cent more families in the project than did the residents in traditional row houses. This type of finding buttressed the long-standing intuitive belief in the power of cul-de-sacs and clusters of houses around a green to increase local interaction, and accounts in part for the widespread adoption of these design principles in new town and neighbourhood unit schemes (see Chapter 8). Another example of behavioural variations was provided by a study of two contrasting patterns of children's playgroups in Toronto (Bordessa and Bunge 1975). The play partner groups of 8-year-old males in the inner city are restricted, for the roads are often dangerous and represent barriers because of increasing through-traffic. By contrast, the suburban groups display larger and more curved ellipses, a function of the more diffuse nature of contact patterns in the suburbs in general, as well as the fact that the streets are less dangerous because of limited access to through-traffic.

This type of concentration upon space alone as a basis for friendship formation is inappropriate in an age of high mobility. A variety of other factors, such as age and family status, perceived social distance and personal preference are as influential. Thus, members of the same ethnic group often interact more, as do those in the early stages of child-rearing, because both have shared interests. Hence Wellman and Leighton (1979) maintained that we should be cautious about exaggerating the effect of proximity upon interest communities, without denying that it is one of the variables that is at work. They argued that even the presence of local relationships does not necessarily create discrete neighbourhoods and that an exclusive focus on the common locality base can omit other major spheres of interaction. Hence the big question in local community study is the extent to which the interactions between people are restricted to, or concentrated on, the area around the residence. If they are — thereby overlapping and reinforcing one another — they provide the daily contact and integration between people which is assumed to represent the heart of the historic place community. However, it is as important to investigate the flows and contacts outside the area of interest.

Before the extent to which local interaction is organized on a locality base can be assessed, an inventory of the range of alternative behaviours that are included must be provided. Unfortunately, there is little consistency in the range of behavioural characteristics identified by various workers in the field, although Chapin's (1965) schedule of alternative activity types and his concept of action spaces are among the most used. The review of the elements of community character previously discussed in Chapter 3 (Table 3.2) also identified seven major types of interactional behaviour.

Activity or Facility Use. The first of these behaviours refers to the way residents obtain their various needs from that area. The functions performed by these various interactions consist of the *satisfaction of various needs and requirements*, such as food, shelter, work and recreation. Today few of the needed goods and services may be available locally. Instead there is a complex spatial pattern of commercial and recreational activities in western cities (see Chapter 7).

Informal Interaction. Social interaction can be classified into two broad types. The first of these covers the informal interaction between people in which four basic types can be recognized: interaction with neighbours, workmates, friends and kin. Obviously these can be expanded and need not be exclusive: kin can be friends, neighbours and workmates. Although there are different ways in which these relationships can be measured, all provide the basic function of *sociability*. In addition they can provide an increasing scale of intimacy, from simple *companionship* to various degrees of *emotional support*.

Mutual Co-operation. Once the contacts between people reach the stage of providing *mutual aid*, such as helping a neighbour or friend start a car, or look after children, a different category of behaviour should be recognized: one that is best described as mutual co-operation. It may be worth following Unger and Wandersman's lead (1985) in differentiating between *instrumental* and *informational mutual aid*. The former entails some exchange of goods or services, the latter relates only to information, such as advice on how to find a bargain in the purchase of a good or the quickest way of reaching another place. It is still, however, informal. An important question is: Why should people extend this type of aid? Bulmer (1986, 10) summarized the views of the late Philip Abrams in identifying four reasons why people extend informal help:

1. *altruism*, or a belief in the need to help others or to be engaged in 'good works';

2. *tradition*, or accepted rules for behaviour which became guiding principles;
3. *status*, or the prestige attached to the act of helping others; and
4. *reciprocity*, or the doing of favours in the expectations of some return gesture.

As more and more relationships in society become specialized, and two income-earners in the family allow adults less time to cultivate informal linkages during the day, many of the informal activities that provided mutual aid or emotional support in the past are replaced with provision by paid workers. Although such services may be more sophisticated, the inevitable professional detachment that goes with them often means that they are provided without the emotional support of the traditional care-giver.

Organizations (formal). The next category refers to the creation of an organization to fulfil some need of the group or some ordering. An organization occurs only when there is some **formal** mechanism for the creation of the association, such as a membership fee, constitution or a hierarchy of officials. A multitude of very different organizations can be found in areas of the city. Some, such as churches or ethnic groups, may have their own meeting-places and test of membership. Others may relate to a common interest, such as bird-watching. The category of greatest concern here is the community organization, the formal association dedicated to the mobilization of the people in the residential area to protect their rights or supply services. Keyes (1987) has described the multiple roles played by these organizations: the *area or turf-based defence* of areas under threat; increasing *local control* over area-impacting decisions; the provision of a form of *resident participation*; recognition of the need to increase *resource access*, from city or national funds; increasing the amount of *communication* between local needs and the city; to which could be added the development of *liaisons*, linkages with the broader needs of the city and other groups and regions. Keyes showed that in the 1980s the first three of these roles had

become less important compared with the resources and communication functions.

Political Participation. The variety and influence of political associations in an area could be considered as a subset of the previous category. However, it is considered to be a separate category because the linkages are externally related since they connect the residents of a local area to city, regional — whether district, state or province — and national political power. In democratic countries individuals in a local area in the city vote in elections to send representatives to the higher levels of government and can lobby or demonstrate against or for these individuals in order to have their problems resolved. Except for 'at-large' voting structures, these representatives are selected on the basis of voting in specific areas. Normally a local area is only part of the areal unit represented by a politician, and aldermanic or local city council jurisdictions do not coincide with regional or national political districts. All these factors make it difficult for a layman to know which elected official is responsible to which bureaucracy for what services, and they make it a real possibility that individual problems will be shifted between the different politicians or officials, each with their rules and regulations. This confusion and complexity of regulation has created a virtual bureaucratic jungle of alternative and overlapping agencies in the most impoverished parts of the cities, often strangling initiative. This is why many community-based programmes have, as a first priority, a reduction in the byzantine labyrinth of regulations. Nevertheless, they cannot ignore the outside power sources that provide the necessary money and resources.

Supportive Milieu. The importance of interaction outside the area must also be stressed in relation to community character. This is not the informal or kinship linkages, or the affective assignments of meaning; it is the tangible relationships that people have with external organizations, whether city, corporations, or national government, which can help improve the area. Political scientists such as Williams (1985) have re-emphasized Park's (1925) point that communities need to have links to a *supportive environment*, one that has the resources and desire to implement change if improvements are to be made.

Economic or Capital Flows. This is a very different type of interaction, and is one which is too easily overlooked in the more usual concern with interactions between people. It has been referred to already in Chapter 3. The key question is whether money is being invested in the area or taken away. If the capital flow in the local community is one of persistent loss, then the area is likely to be on the road to obsolescence and dependency.

Place-communities in cities will vary in the patterns of these seven broad categories or domains of behaviour, and the extent to which the interactions are directed upon the local area. The next section demonstrates how a new approach to the study of informal interaction and informal mutual co-operation, called social network analysis, has helped investigators understand the emerging pattern of behaviour in cities. Further related issues will be discussed in Chapters 6 and 8.

Perspectives from Social Network Analysis

Identification of the various sections of the behavioural system is obviously only part of the issue. It is necessary to investigate these interactions in a local place or community context. A series of different methodologies and techniques can be recognized in the first three of these interactions, from surveys of individual indicators, whether movements to shop or to visit friends, to analyses of so-called activity spaces, to the particularistic study of all behaviours of a small group. Despite the theoretical views that space no longer plays an important part in structuring patterns of behaviour, many studies, such as those quoted above, have shown that distance still plays a role, although not the determining one of the

past. Far more shopping visits today are made to more distant places because of the decline in the number of local commercial outlets (see a longer discussion in Chapter 8). In terms of personal contacts, Stutz (1973) identified three types of social visiting in San Diego: with friends, relatives and neighbours accounting for 40 per cent, 35 per cent and 25 per cent respectively. However, the relationships of these contacts with distance were very different. There was no distance-decay in the spatial pattern found in the group of relatives, the number of contacts were similar for residences within one mile, as for those twenty miles apart. By contrast there was a rapid decline in the number of friendship contacts after six miles, and there were virtually none after fifteen miles. Not surprisingly, all the neighbours were within a mile of the residence.

A common problem of all these behavioural studies has been that of coping with the volume of data required, and the teasing out of the important relationships from the kaleidoscope of potential interactions and movement over a series of different spaces. All too frequently data has been aggregated to a set of spatial areas that cannot be subdivided, so the nuances of spatial relationships are easily lost. Fortunately, the social network approach, originally developed by Bott (1957) and Mitchell (1969), has proved to be particularly useful in interpreting the relationships between people in a number of different ways. By organizing each connection between individuals as a matrix, it provides a method for summarizing complex interpersonal relationships and can also be applied to flows between places. An example of the approach in a community organization is shown in Figure 4.1a, which indicates the connections between the seventeen key members in the Monroe Community Association in Philadelphia. Ley (1974) used the participant observation technique to isolate a basic pattern of contact, coding the matrix with 1 for friendship patterns and 0 for antagonisms, based on his knowledge of the relationships between people over several months. From this he constructed a graph isolating each person and the two persons with whom each

a)

	CS	SS	AG	RM	LB	A	EL	DD	AL	BL	FW	DM	JP	TK	JT	CV	NV
CS		1	0	1	0	0	1	0	0	1	0	0	0	1	1		1
SS	1		1	1	0	0	1	1	1	1	0		0	1	1	1	1
AG	1	1			0		1				0		0	1	1		1
RM	1	1			0	0	1	1	1	1			0	1	1	1	1
LB	0	0	0	0		1	0	0	1	1	0	0			0	1	0
A	0	0		0	1		0	0			0			0			0
EL	1	1	1	1	0	0		1	0	1	0	0	0	0	0	0	0
DD	0	1		1	0	0	1		0	0	0	0	0	0		0	0
AL	0	1		1	1		0	0		1	1			1	1	1	
BL	1	1		0	1		1	0	1					1	1	1	
FW	0	0			0	0	0	0	1				1		1		1	0
DM	0						0				1						
JP	0	0		0			0	0									1
TK	1	1	1	1			0	0		1		0			1		1
JT	1	1	1	1	0	0	0	0	1	1			0				1
CV		1		1	1		0	0	1	1	1			1	1		
NV	1	1	1	1	0	0	0	0	1	1	0		1	1	1		

b)

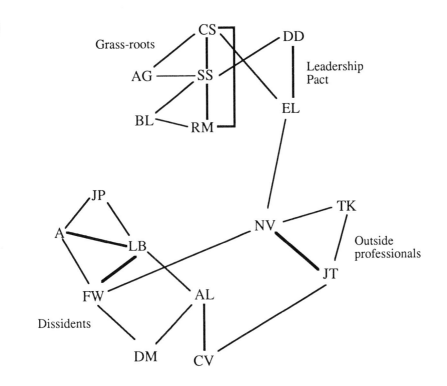

Figure 4.1 A social network for a Philadelphia voluntary association (Ley 1983) (a) matrix of network; (b) graph of first and second neighbours

person shared the most similar pattern of friends and enemies (Figure 4.1b). This revealed four basic clusters called Leadership Pact; Grass-roots; Dissidents; and Outside Professionals. The Dissidents were unable to act together to form a united front against the Leaders and their Grass-roots allies, yet these two groups could not eliminate their opposition. The result was that the organization atrophied. Under pressure from outside funding sources who wanted the community programmes to continue, a steering group of outside professionals was formed to provide them. Figure 4.1b shows that these professionals had links to all the groups. Although in a behavioural sense it was understandable, since they provided co-ordination between the cliques, from a citizen's participation perspective it was not satisfactory because it led to control by outsiders. Unfortunately this type of dissension and the formation of rigid cliques is typical of many voluntary organizations without a hierarchical and authority structure linked to outsiders, and it is one of the reasons why grass-roots organizations at a community level fail to maintain themselves (see also the discussion in Chapter 7).

The conversion of interpersonal linkages to a matrix and graph form lies at the heart of the social network approach. In the example shown in Figure 4.1a the matrix entries are in their simplest binary form and represent a judgement by the investigator about the nature of the relationships. Today the social network idea is often used to plot all contacts between people. Obviously the simple presence of such a connection tells one nothing about the type, strength or significance of the linkage. However, there is nothing to prevent the matrices being adjusted to contain such data. As a data-gathering exercise, the network approach has the potential for being unmanageable if all components and their linkages are checked all the time. This is rarely possible except in small samples or closed networks, so analysts have treated a network as 'significant, informal "community ties" defined from the standpoint of a "focal person". Their research has relied on large-scale surveys, with investi-

gators relying on respondents' accounts of their networks for reasons of economy' (Wellman 1987, 8). A number of very different measures have been used to define the structure of informal interaction in networks. Four of the major measures used are:

1. *size*, or the number of potential and actual contacts;
2. *composition*, or the membership, such as what percentage is kin;
3. *structure*, the character of the network, such as the density of interconnections; and
4. *contents*, such as measures of levels of supportiveness in the network.

In addition, a variety of mathematical techniques derived from graph theory have been applied to these matrices to summarize or identify various parts of the structures of the pattern of interaction. Many networks are very complex and may need complicated mathematical procedures to isolate relationships.

During the last decade the analysis of personal interactions between individuals by the social network approach has established an important niche in the research literature (Wellman 1987; Wellman and Berkovitz 1988). The 'community lost, saved and liberated' argument of Wellman and Leighton (1979) discussed in Chapter 2 showed the utility of the approach in developing the idea of personal communities as networks of significant, informal ties, in which the extent to which such communities are localized in place is relatively incidental. Although Wellman is anxious to free these 'interpersonal communities' from the 'shackles' of local place, he is never dismissive of neighbourhood as a *separate* concept, and some of his empirical evidence recognizes the roles of neighbourhoods and neighbours, namely the place and the people living in close proximity. He further argued that even the presence of local relationships does not necessarily create discrete neighbourhoods and that focus on the common locality base can omit major spheres of interaction. In their empirical work on a sample of people from East York in

Toronto, Wellman and his associates found that the respondents spread themselves over a range of spatially-diffuse networks which were strands of the large metropolitan area rather than localized social worlds. Hence Wellman (1987, 8) argued that the definition of 'community' has been expanded to account for 'far-flung sparsely knit ties stretching beyond the boundaries of neighbourhood or kinship solidarities'. Local associations certainly continued, although they were maintained over larger areas. Rather than being members of *one* local solidarity group, modern city-dwellers maintain limited memberships in multiple, specialized, interest-based communities. Wellman (1987, 5), in assessing the progress of the 1980s, stated that the 'rediscovery of community has been one of sociology's greatest post World War II triumphs', although we must stress again that he is referring to 'community' in the context of informal associations, rather than place-communities.

The network analytic approach and the main findings of Wellman and his co-workers in Toronto have led to considerable replication and support elsewhere. For example, Connerly's (1985) work in the Detroit metropolitan area both supported and elaborated the thesis that the interactive community has been substantially, if not completely, liberated from the physical confines of neighbourhood. These sentiments were echoed by Fischer (1982) who argued that although living in cities affects personal networks, it does not disintegrate them; instead it engenders a variety of distinct and intense social worlds (see Deng and Bonacich 1991). As people were freed from spatial constraints, they became embedded in social support systems that extended across the metropolitan area (Fischer et al. 1977). Again: 'Different kinds of people, with different kinds of social preferences, tend to prefer different kinds of places. People with opportunity and resources to do so will sort themselves out according to those preferences' (Fischer 1982, 8). However one must be cautious and note that most of the empirical work has been restricted to white middle-aged people in inner suburban areas. Inner-city and ethnic areas may have quite different patterns.

Many attempts have been made to summarize the basic character of personal networks. Wellman (1987) provided a typology for the composition of informal communities (Table 4.1). From his and other work it is possible to summarize some of the essential features of contemporary personal networks, emphasizing that they provide support which is efficient, low-cost and flexible.

In terms of the *size* of networks, there is a big difference between the availability of people for interaction and the actual interaction. Wellman estimated that 2,700 adults (estimated number of people *known* to a typical East Yorker) were potentially available for interaction in his sample from East York, whereas *actual ties* were on average 400. These results were derived from a modal group which he defined as white, employed, once-married, North American, 40 years old with a child in primary school. Killworth et al. (1990) suggested that the United States average in research findings was 1,526, a figure very similar to Wellman's original estimate of 1,500 in Toronto. Killworth and his associates produced figures for Jacksonville, Florida (1,700, + or – 400), Orange County, California (2,025) and Mexico City (600). These are clearly estimates only, although they give some indication of size and also of cross-cultural differences with a less mobile society.

The networks are moderately *knit* with fewer than half the members of a person's network being linked with one another. This confirms the change in contemporary society, contrasting with the older societal patterns formed by inclusive, overlapping relationships.

Four basic *types of tie* were recognized by Wellman (1987), and these provide a scale of increasing degrees of interpersonal support and companionship: namely *active, interactive, intimate* and *confidant ties*, with those in the last category having the closest bonds. Wellman fitted average sizes, or number of people, to each of these categories, namely: active (20), interactive (10), intimate (5) and confidant (2). The category of actual ties includes the whole range from weak acquaintances to strongly-bonded confidants. Although interactors are more frequently seen, for they are likely to be neighbours and workmates, intimates are more socially close and they are much more likely to be kin. Most personal networks contain only one or two intimate neighbouring or co-worker relationships, and half a dozen weaker community ties with neighbours and co-workers. Friends clearly figure in the networks, often not only as neighbours or co-workers, but also as individuals with shared interests of one kind or another. Wellman's categories of intimates, interactors and confidants apply to both kin and friends, as did the scheme developed by Boissevain (1974) who offered a typology of informal relationships (Figure 4.2).

The rapid reduction in the number of meaningful relationships, from over 1,500 potential contacts to under half a dozen active associations, and a couple of really close ties at the level of strongest emotional support, seems to confirm that for many humans the real pattern of relationships has hardly progressed beyond the numbers found in the historic hunting and gathering bonds — despite the availability of so many people to whom one could turn. However, it is important to note that these figures are averages: some people are more gregarious and others are content with virtual social isolation. Nevertheless, the finding that networks have so few significant ties may be compared with the persistent finding from recent censuses that people are living in smaller residential groups and increasingly alone.

The significance of *kin* in personal networks can also be also measured in networks. Only 9 per cent of actual ties were with kin, although kin accounted for 40–50 per cent of network members in the interactors, intimates and confidants categories. Wellman concluded that the new communities are apt to be mixed in composition and structures, kin form a key core cluster for communicating needs and co-ordinating support. So even though the general role of kin has been reduced, their significance remains. In the words of Fischer (1982, 132):

'we typically have a good time with friends but turn to relatives in a crisis.' This is gender specific, for Philip Abrams (quoted in Bulmer 1986) found that 90 per cent of informal community care was provided by kin, almost all by women. The importance of kinship bonds has been recognized by others: 'you lose a neighbour by moving away, you lose a friend by failing him, you never lose a relative except through death' (Keller 1968, 27).

Given the limited number of intimates and confidants, it is just as well that kin are still available, although the progression to smaller and one-parent families provides obvious danger signs for the future of our relationships. Yet there remains the question of why kin is still so important. Allan's (1979) work on informal relationships provides some clues. He defined a sociable relationship as one which was entered into by an individual for primarily *non-instrumental* reasons and concentrated upon systems of exchange and emotional and affective ties. In his discussion of the difference between family and friends, Allan distinguishes between those bonds which can be made or unmade at will (friends) and those which cannot (family). Whereas the cultural norms of amity encourage the provision of support to kin without an expectation of strict reciprocity, friendship is but the exploitation of an implicit right to reciprocity. There are individuals who indulge in very high levels of social interaction and those who participate in very little; Irving (1978) referred to those as 'social lions' and 'social recluses' respectively. Within any personal network the strength of the friendship tie will vary and attempts to classify these (see Table 4.2) invoke criteria such as frequency and nature of contact.

Another point of relevance to this discussion concerns the *spatial relationships* of the networks. Two related issues need to be noted. The logic of the social network approach is that spatial relationships need not be confined to locality, place or neighbourhood. In spatial terms Wellman's (1989) Toronto sample showed that about three-quarters of the active ties extended beyond neighbourhood and one-

Table 4.1 Types of ties in networks

Type of ties	No. of ties	% of above	No. of kin ties	% of above	% kin of all ties
Directly available*	2,700	17	55	100	2
Actual	400	15	35 (30-45)	64	9
Active	20 (14-23)	5	6 (6-10)	17	30
Intimate	5 (5-7)	25	3 (2-3)	50	50
Interacting	10 (3-15)	50	4 (5-7)	67	40
Confidant	2	40	1-2	50	50

* estimated number of people who should be known to a typical East Yorker (after Wellman, 1989); i.e. column 3 is initially based on 16,000 potential ties; column 5 is % of column 3; column 6 is % of column 4

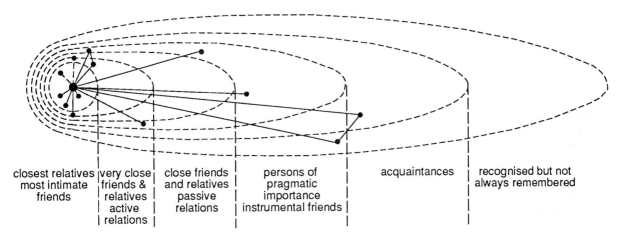

closest relatives | very close | close friends | persons of | acquaintances | recognised but not
most intimate | friends & | and relatives | pragmatic | | always remembered
friends | relatives | passive | importance |
| active | relations | instrumental friends |
| relations |

Figure 4.2 A typology of informal relationships (after Boissevain, 1974)

Table 4.2 Classifications of social interaction

A. Irving (1978)

Interaction types	Duration features	Frequency features
1. Low intensity	Half-day or less	Less often than once a week
2. Long frequent	Whole day or more	Less often than once a week
3. Middle range	One hour or more	Once or twice a week
4. Short frequent	Half-day or less	More often than twice a week

B. Raine (see Herbert and Raine, 1976)

Type of relationship	Form of social interaction
1. Acquaintance	Pass time of day if we meet, but never been in house
2. Quite friendly	Chat in street if we meet, but rarely, if ever, go in house
3. Friendly	Always chat when we meet, only occasionally go in house (1/month)
4. Very friendly	Chat regularly in street, frequently visit home (1 or 2/week)
5. Very close friend	Chat daily, regularly visit home (4/week)

C. Abrams (see Bulmer, 1986)

Type of relationship	Form of social interaction
1. Acquaintance	Awareness of neighbours, casual greeting
2. Sociable	Chatting, visiting, shopping together
3. Communication	Exchange of information, gossip
4. Participation	Invite to family occasions
5. Collective involvement	Local neighbourhood events

third beyond the metropolitan region. Intimate ties were even less likely to be local, with seven-eighths in the Toronto sample extending outside neighbourhood. He also cites evidence from a study of black residents in Los Angeles (Oliver 1986) which showed that half of the intimate ties were with non-neighbours. This evidence supports the generalization that local social interactions in the form of ties and interactions among the members of personal social networks are not necessarily, or usually, confined to the immediate neighbourhood in the modern western city. However, one must be cautious about generalizing these findings, for Wellman's sample consisted only of white, middle-aged people in the inner suburbs. Although Wellman (1987) acknowledged that even though most ties are non-local, it did not imply the disappearance of neighbourly ties; most people engage in selective neighbouring, and by maintaining friendly relations they achieve a sense of security and belonging.

Again in his 1989 paper, Wellman argued that whereas most people have an important minority of active and immediate kin living nearby, most *local* contacts are with neighbours and friends who provide support and companionship. Connerly's (1985) work in Detroit found that sizeable percentages of residents participated in the life of their neighbourhood. His four highest-ranking indicators were the 76.9 per cent who perceived neighbourhood as home, the 59.3 per cent who knew half or more of their neighbours, the 56.4 per cent who got together with neighbours at least once a month, and the 56.1 per cent who used stores within one mile of their homes.

A final summary comment about the cross-cultural differences in the use of linkages is also worth making. Wellman (1989) observed that in the western world, networks are primarily used for personal, friendship relationships, since nepotism or favouritism is usually frowned upon or outlawed, although scientists often depend upon them to disseminate their results and ideas. In traditional Latin American and even communist countries, the bureaucratic dominance of so many aspects of life mean that people use their connections to bypass these ever-pervasive structures in their search for documents and permits. In many Third World countries, the problems posed by the incessant search for the essentials of life means that personal networks are often used to find jobs for friends and family.

There is little doubt that the social network approach has improved our understanding of the nature of informal interactions in contemporary cities, although it has not been without its critics. Four points can be made. One relates to the increasingly technical nature of the inquiry. The constant fascination with the techniques of analysis deals not with content, but with procedures that are often difficult for outsiders to read. A second line of criticism relates to the abstraction of the informal interaction from the larger set of relationships — again a problem that faces most scientific endeavour. Connerly (1985)'s view of the idea of neighbourhood as a locality community of limited liability is important. Although it can be accepted that the neighbourhood makes only partial claims on each resident's social ties, it still contributes to a symbolic sense of community. This means that we should note that analyses of interpersonal ties do not define fully the dimensions that characterize the content of *local* community life, issues described in Chapters 3 and 5 as the areal content and cognitive-affective dimensions. The roles of neighbourhood in service provision, locational identities, as 'havens', and as bases for the evolution of 'localized' concerns are additional to the interactions of actors in a social network. To be fair, it is a point that has been recognized in Wellman and Leighton's (1979, 385) original hypothesis: 'we must be concerned with neighbourhood *and* community rather than neighbourhood *or* community ... the two are separate concepts which may or may not be closely associated'. In etching out the essential qualities of networks, they have proved that although they overlap with neighbourhoods,

they are different. The proof of the existence of the former with its particular form does not negate the continuing value of the latter. Another recent recommendation can be linked to this general problem, the need to relate social network analysis with theoretical frameworks, such as the structuration theory of Giddens (1984). As Haines (1988, 178) observed: 'social network analyses continued to operate with a deficient account of human agency'. In this context, of course, the whole range of cognitive and affective dimensions described earlier will have to be applied, for much of the strength of the local neighbourhood derives from the human agency values which attach to it.

Another critique of the social network approach to the study of community and of neighbourhood arises from its reliance on *strong* ties within the networks, perhaps a large number of daily meetings, as among workmates. Wellman (1987) acknowledged this as one of the 'debits' of social networks analysis. Greenbaum (1982) had argued that 'weak ties' or acquaintanceships among neighbours which are rarely used can lead to a false impression of their potential. Their existence can provide the basis of a local social cohesion. Although strong ties, particularly those with close kin, have continuing central roles, a locality-based ambience resting on a 'mutuality' of well-disposed individuals, can go some way towards fostering a neighbourhood sense of place. Freudenburg (1986) discussed the 'density of acquaintanceship', defined as the average proportion of people resident in a local community who are known by the inhabitants of that community: 'knowing' is a general awareness of, rather than a close tie with, other residents. This kind of argument has also been advanced in discussions about private space, parochial realm and public realm. Lofland (1989) defined the public realm as spaces in a city occupied by people who are strangers to one another or who know one another only in terms of roles. In the 'ideal community' there may be no public realm, private and public merge into one, although the scale of urban life makes the public realm inevitable and creates a world of strangers. Hunter (1975) defined the parochial realm as characterized by a sense of commonality among acquaintances and neighbours who are involved in interpersonal networks that are created within communities. *Weak ties* are sufficient to allow such parochial realms to exist and to have purpose in urban life.

A fourth criticism is the limited scope of the studies available to date. Although new studies are widening the range of types of people used in network analysis, the original 'modal group,' described above is basically white, middle-aged North Americans of British-Canadian ancestry. Indeed Wellman's latest research is based only upon a sample of thirty-three from this group, in which ten hours of interview were needed to establish the whole interactional patterns of individuals. This forms a big contrast with the limited set of relationships that are normally studied in the type of large-sample surveys normally used, such as Wellman's initial study based on the responses of 845 people to a request for information on six intimates. This restriction to a small sample may have improved our knowledge of the real relationships of people, not just a selected few, even if the type of people analysed must condition many of the generalizations. It is clear that the form of both personal network communities and neighbourhoods will vary with the types of people studied, and this is particularly true in cities with a large ethnic population. Society falls into groups with internally common characteristics and these groups will differ in their interactions and their attitudes towards neighbourhood. Fischer's (1982) definition of subcultures within cities, of people who share a common defining trait and lifestyle, bears similarity to this idea. Some of the defining qualities of these groups or subcultures are well understood and easily recognized. In the context of his Detroit study, Connerly (1985) judged that family status, length of residence, location and Catholicity were the best predictors of type and degree of neighbourhood participation. Location appeared to be a good indicator of a range of economic and social differences, although he also drew out the contrast between propin-

quity-based neighbouring, typical of newer suburbs, and the kinship, ethnicity and religious bases to neighbouring in the central city and older suburbs. Freudenburg (1986) also showed length of residence as a key explanatory variable, providing the strongest single influence upon his 'density of acquaintanceship' index.

Neighbourhood-Dependent Groups

There is some evidence that specific groups of people are more dependent upon local place than others. This dependence will vary over time, impacts differently on different stages of the life cycle and will vary from place to place. One could expect dependence upon local place to be stronger for groups which share some constraint upon their physical mobility. Such constraints may arise from a diversity of causes. Poverty imposes constraints in that movement normally has a **cost** attached to it, and discrimination or prejudice may reinforce such constraints. Banerjee and Baer (1984) found that residential area tended to shrink with declining income and minority status.

Old age imposes constraints in that it is often accompanied by increasing infirmity, lack of physical mobility and a loss of confidence. Such constraints are exaggerated by the greater vulnerability often felt by the elderly in complex urban environments. Gender imposes constraints in that women are often placed in roles that inhibit their freedom of movement. The routine rhythms of household chores and responsibilities, the needs of young children and the caring role all act as limits on mobility. Women also share some of the felt vulnerability of old people and tend to limit the number of places which they can safely and acceptably visit. Whereas everyone has a personal community network, for groups such as these the extent to which these networks correspond with local neighbourhood is high.

There are clearly some general conditioning factors which strengthen the significance of place and locality. Age, stage-in-life cycle and length of residence warrant this description. If a neighbourhood is composed of many people who have lived there for a long time, progressing through the same life stages in a stable community, these are conditions which would generally enhance the significance of locality. There is empirical evidence that specific groups of people are more dependent on local place than others. Banerjee and Baer (1984) revealed that nearly 90 per cent of their Los Angeles sample thought neighbourhood-living to be at least of **some** importance and 60 per cent **very** important; however, among low-income blacks the **very** important score reached 91 per cent of the sample, 70 per cent for the elderly and 65 per cent for children. Some of these subgroups are used to explore this idea of **neighbourhood dependency**.

Ethnic minorities

Ethnic residential segregation is often the most pronounced form of residential separation within cities, and historically **ethnic areas**, frequently linked with recent immigration, have been regarded as close-knit communities. The question of classifying ethnic areas and of understanding the balance of choice and constraint processes which underpin their persistence has already been discussed (see Chapter 3). The changing nature of ethnic areas communities, however, and their roles as dependent neighbourhoods can be exemplified.

Wilson (1987) argued that there have been fundamental changes in the American ghetto in the last quarter of the twentieth century. The key changes result from the movement of black middle-class professionals out of the ghetto neighbourhoods; this movement has begun to affect **stable** working-class black families. Inner-city ghettos become places for the **truly disadvantaged**, the poor blacks typified by unemployment, low-income, single-parent (female-headed) families who constitute the modern **underclass**. The ghettos become residual, deprived of the more stable social infrastructure which the out-migrants had provided. Whereas prior to 1960, inner city communities 'exhibited the features of social

organization, including a sense of community, positive neighbourhood identification and explicit norms and sanctions against aberrant behaviour' (Wilson 1987, 3), the underclass ghettos of the 1990s have lost much of this local sense of community. As Aponte (1991) argued, a substantial inner-city minority in American urban areas is 'hopelessly mired in poverty'. These are not only black minorities but also include Hispanic and Chinese populations. Against this picture of change, there is a range of evidence with which to evaluate the nature of ethnic areas as local communities.

Increasingly in the United States there is a tendency to talk about the **historic ghetto** and the nature of its community life. Wilson (1987) views the indicators of this change as unmistakable, and for him life in the inner city is now less pleasant and more dangerous than it was prior to 1960. Anderson (1978) and Breton (1964) recognize the institutional completeness of ethnic communities where the organizations set up by social entrepreneurs gave the means to integrate and internalize local community life.

Evidence from other kinds of ethnic areas suggests that personal network communities have corresponded with local place. Gans (1962) in his classic study of Italians in Boston, Suttles (1968) in Chicago and Phillips (1981) in an analysis of Asians in Leicester all demonstrate this fact.

> Now nearing a position of institutional completeness, the community is able to offer many religious facilities, shops and services which provide employment, reinforce ethnic values and constitute a framework for the traditional way of life. They also allow the community relative autonomy and free many members from unwanted interaction with the host society. (Phillips 1981, 1)

In its **historic form** therefore, the ethnic community acts as local neighbourhood and fills roles associated with choice despite the fact that in reality the constraints are dominant. This kind of ethnic area in American cities has undergone significant change. Clark (1987) described the process of black suburbanisation which increased the black population in suburbs by almost 50 per cent between 1970 and 1980. This phenomenon was not restricted to blacks for rates of Hispanic migration to suburbs from the city centre were greater than those of blacks. The destinations have been the ring of inner suburbs, and although the rate of change is high the absolute numbers are relatively small. The larger problems of inner-city poverty remain and are not likely to be diminished by out-migration (Clark 1987).

It is the loss of middle-class blacks that Wilson (1987) and others regard as highly significant. In their analyses the community-bonding features of neighbourhood institutions and the role models provided by stable black families are removed in ways which undermine the meanings of place and local social interaction. The traditional ethnic areas become different kinds of places in which the old notions of locality no longer apply. New ethnographic studies (Marks 1991) emphasize the extreme problems which beset the traditional ghettos. Unemployment is very high, job prospects are few, traditional family life has collapsed, crime and drugs become the hallmarks of the communities. Anderson (1978) showed that with a dearth of well-paid jobs, the reliance on welfare and drug-trafficking become behavioural norms: the dramatic increases in black and Hispanic female-headed lone-parent families is one indicator of this change.

Inner-city ethnic areas become dangerous places and residents have to adjust and find suitable lifestyles. Anderson (1978) talks of new rules of conduct based on residual values: people negotiate and settle for what they can have in terms of deference and self-regard. Residents acquire very localized codes of street etiquette, mental notations which guide them on what is to be avoided and what is left as a liveable community. These are almost strategies for survival which leave little room for the positive development of local community. This portrayal of the black inner city poses one extreme view of the ethnic area as community. Although there is of course variety and change,

ethnic communities continue to provide internalized worlds with many features of neighbourhood dependency.

The elderly

There is growing evidence that the elderly are increasing numerically, forming higher proportions of the overall population and emerging as a group with distinctive social and spatial characteristics (see Chapter 3). As a group the elderly are distinctive socially as a component of the **dependent** population, most have retired from paid work and spend far more time in their homes and neighbourhoods. Many studies emphasize the diversity of the elderly as a group with chronological age in itself as only an approximate indicator of health, morale and the ability to cope with urban environments. Although diversity also applies to the material wealth and life quality of the elderly, by all indices of poverty and deprivation, many old people are amongst the most disadvantaged in society. Some indication of the way in which poverty is distributed among the elderly is revealed by Duncan and Smith (1989), who show the percentage of old people living beneath the official poverty level in the United States. This was 6.9 per cent for white males, 13.3 per cent for white females, 24.2 per cent for black males, 35.5 per cent for black females, 18.8 per cent for Hispanic males and 25.5 per cent for Hispanic females. There is a clear indication here of the disadvantages of both ethnic minorities and also of women, many of whom are in the over-75s or **old-old category**. The study also revealed a concentration of old people just above the official poverty level.

As already discussed, there is evidence of clustering among the elderly, even if this does not amount to anything approaching the **geriatric ghetto**. Most of the clustering is located in city centres, where many old people remain in the same homes and neighbourhoods that they have occupied for the latter parts of their working lives. This largest group of urban elderly are those likely to be the most disadvantaged and constrained to a local environment, which may enhance their feelings of vulnerability. As Warnes (1989) shows, however, some British inner-city residential areas are not uniformly hostile environments for the elderly. Although housing is often poor, services and welfare systems are easily accessible and the elderly live in accustomed places among friends and relatives.

This empirical evidence on the social and demographic changes affecting the elderly can be related to theories of ageing. The more pessimistic **disengagement theory** has the old withdrawing from activities, especially in the wake of catastrophic events such as loss of spouse, whereas the more optimistic **activity theory** envisages the substitution of new roles to sustain activity and participation. A theory particularly relevant to the containment of old people in neighbourhoods is that termed **environmental docility**. For old people the environment and its hazards, from steep slopes to unsafe areas, assumes more significance and their movements in space become more restricted. Herbert and Peace (1978) found distance to be a major constraint on the elderly and few respondents were able to walk more than a quarter of a mile. Mental maps of the elderly confirmed this dependence on local space. In terms of local social interaction, Chappell and Badger (1989) argued that **counts** of contacts were less relevant to the well-being of the elderly than were the **qualitative assessments** of companionships and confidants.

Old people have network links, especially with family, which extend outside neighbourhood, although with the onset of old age they tend to live their lives within local neighbourhood. Hunt and Ross (1990) contended that immediate neighbourhood may be more important to the well-being of old people than the residence itself. Johnson and Barber (1990) concentrated on the black elderly and showed that although about 20 per cent could be classed as isolates, most had extensive friendship and associational networks. There were important cultural differences which distinguished the black elderly. Immediate family members were often less important, because of the preoccupation with their own economic survival, than those who were less close kin. The local church was important to older blacks, and they used their ability to **redefine** who was regarded as kin to establish a close set of supports.

Rowles (1978) captured many of the realities of life for the elderly in his study of the **prisoners of space**. Rowles showed how old people tend to retreat to into more limited spaces in which home, surveillance areas and neighbourhood assume greater importance in their lives. As the elderly become less able to cope with social interaction entailing journeys, they rely on visitors to their homes and begin to substitute **fantasy** or memories and images of other places for actual activities. These remembered places, although no longer visited or seen, have great significance for the elderly and allow them in Rowles's words to be prisoners of space but occupants of a prison without walls. As with ethnic minorities, it is important to stress the diversity within the elderly group, mainly in wealth, health and morale. Many old people remain active and are not necessarily distinct from the rest of the population. Ageing, however, is a progressive process which takes its toll on energy, confidence and mobility. Local neighbourhood increasingly dominates their lives: for much of the **third age**, home and neighbourhood **contain** activities.

Women and children

The place of women in society still varies dramatically from one part of the world to another and even within given societies, despite so-called liberalization. Women are most closely aligned to locality and neighbourhood in their traditional roles of child-rearers and home-carers. It can be argued that this traditional role has been seriously challenged. If, for example, one takes the narrow definition of a traditional family in which the husband works, the wife stays at home, there are two children, and the couple have always been married to each other, only 4 per cent of British households, fall within this category. There are in fact a greater number of single-parent households, though a broader definition of married couples with one or more dependent children does capture 29 per cent of households. There is change in the organization and form of family life which affects women in particular: 'most women's lives no longer conform to the pattern of unpaid married women living at home, caring for children, and doing housework while the man goes out to earn the money' (Lewis and Bowlby 1989, 220).

However, there are other facts which demonstrate the persistence of traditional roles. The average woman still spends three-quarters of her adult life in marriage; during much of that time she still carries much of the burden of domestic and child-care roles. Even women in paid work undertake 300 per cent more hours of housework than do men, and long and fixed hours of paid work discriminate against women by creating norms of employment they find difficulty in meeting. Some changes in the norms of family life work against women. The percentage of black families which are female single-parent increased from 17.9 per cent in 1940 to 41.9 per cent in 1985; for Hispanic families the recorded increase was from 16.7 per cent in 1973 to 22.8 per cent in 1983. Women in this position have no spouse support in family-raising and rely upon kin, friends and welfare.

Women also face access problems. About one-third have cars and only half of the women in car-owning households have regular access to the family car. There may be a reliance upon public transport, although as Figure 4.3 shows, the multiple roles of worker, mother and housewife may make considerable demands on daily travel. The women's role as carer may extend beyond the immediate nuclear family and often does not cease when a child leaves home. On the one hand there are the demands of looking after grand-children, on the other the responsibility for the care of older dependent family. Daughters especially tend to carry the main burden in the support of elderly parents, and this is a role which can extend over long periods of time. Again for older women

in particular their perceived vulnerability becomes a major constraint in itself on movement within the city.

The roles of women as mothers and child-minders underpin their close ties with local neighbourhood for large parts of their lives. Although children clearly progress through a spatial learning process which progressively enlarges their images and uses of urban space, through most of their primary school years they live a large part of their lives in the neighbourhood. At this time school itself is a very significant anchoring-point around which children orientate their awareness of space. In their detailed studies of the child in the city, Michelson, Levine and Spina (1979) emphasized the need not to neglect the importance of home and school environments which occupy a major portion of a child's daily life. This dependence on neighbourhood does change over time and 'with increasing age, children are considered to have the capacity and motivation to cover larger and larger territories when they are not required to be at home or school' (Michelson, Levine and Spina 1979, 415). Lynch (1977) in his studies of several contrasted societies found that there were cross-cultural differences, although for many children the neighbourhood was a compact, well-identified reality.

The thrust of this argument is that most women for large parts of their lives have constraints upon their movements and activities which serve to make neighbourhoods more central. The dependants, both children and elderly relatives, for whom they typically care, are neighbourhood-bound and this in turn affects many women. Many of the 'norms' of society, forms of work and feelings of risk, further serve to localize women's activities. As Wellman (1987) acknowledges, women may sacrifice parts of their personal network communities if the competition for time and energy becomes too great. He also argues (Wellman and Wortley, 1990) that only full-time home-makers tend to be in densely knit networks of neighbours. Proximity often makes active neighbours a principal source of companionship for women with common concerns.

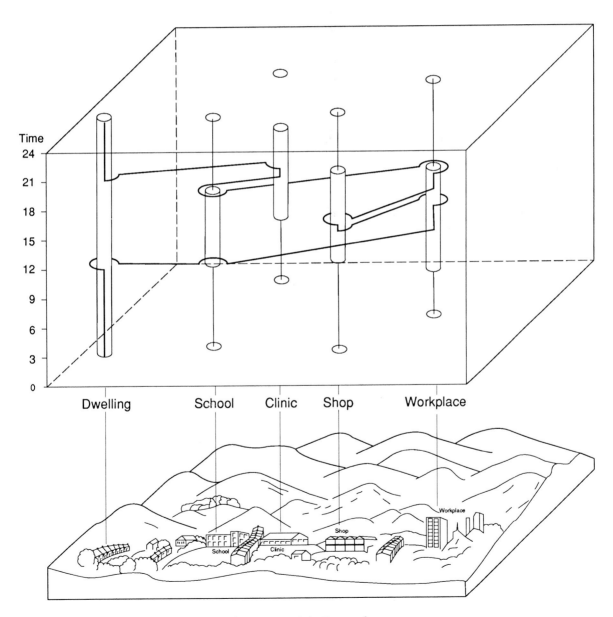

Figure 4.3 Gender constraints; a woman's movements in time and space

For these three groups the correspondence between their network and the local neighbourhood is often high. There are clearly some general 'conditioning' or factors which strengthen the significance of place and locality. Nevertheless, we must be careful. So far there have been few attempts to apply techniques such as network analysis to disadvantaged groups in order to test their local self-sufficiency in social interaction.

Neighbourhood Effects on Behaviour

The influence of residential area upon the people who occupy it has been referred to as the 'neighbourhood', 'milieu' (Sprout and Sprout, 1965), or the 'context' effect. In simple terms this hypothesis suggests that individual behaviour or attitudes will be influenced by the local environment, especially the typical values and role models present within any neighbourhood. In relation to the groups described in the previous section, age, stage in life cycle, and length of residence usually enlarge the significance of locality. This is increased if a neighbourhood comprises many people who have lived there for a long time, and who have progressed through the same life cycle stages in a stable community. In a more behavioural context many researchers have argued that the prevailing norms affect behaviour. Robson (1969), for example, showed how parental attitudes towards the education of their children were affected by the neighbourhoods within which they lived. He maintained it was not class, but aspirations, in family attitude to schooling, which was of crucial importance in understanding transfer rates to senior schools. Johnston (1974) has described how the consensus view within a residential area will influence individual voting behaviour. Herbert (1976) found evidence that youths resident in specific neighbourhoods were more likely to become delinquent, and this, in part at least, could be attributed to the prevailing behavioral norms

within the area. In wider contexts, Wynne-Edwards (1965) demonstrated the impact of territorial control by animal species upon population densities and conservation of resources, whilst the journal *Environment and Behaviour* has published many detailed studies of topics such as crowding and territory/behaviour interactions. Isolating the context or neighbourhood effect has always been a very difficult task, and Jencks and Mayer's (1990) extensive review of the literature found a fair measure of conflicting evidence. They showed that in general the presence of advantaged neighbours led to several effects: it discouraged crime among some youths and discouraged teenagers from having children out of wedlock; also it encouraged teenagers to finish high school, and increased teenagers' future earnings. The epidemic theory of social problems (Crane 1991) suggests that social problems are 'contagious' and spread through peer influence. As neighbourhood 'quality' declines, there will be a sharp increase in problems and individuals resident in such areas become vulnerable to a neighbourhood effect. In all, although a general neighbourhood effect is not inevitable, there is sufficient evidence to suggest that it can exist and will influence the life chances of young people in particular.

As the 'social structures' focus (Wellman and Berkovitz 1988) has grown out of network analysis, it has assumed familiar forms. Statements about the need to understand processes, structures of relations, and how large-scale social transformations affect community, are common. Wellman (1987) is explicit in his intent to accommodate network analysis with political economy perspectives. Network analysts begin with a set of relations and draw inferences from the whole to the part, structure to categories, behaviours to attitudes. In the attempt to accommodate the political economy perspective, it is necessary to recognize that all relationships are potentially uneven in the resources to which each party has access and in the power which they have over one another. These arguments are far removed from the detailed analysis of the networks of East Yorkers and modal groups defined to remove a great deal of the uneven- ness studied by political economists. There is some danger of convoluting a reasonably clear method of studying human relationships.

In some senses the neighbourhood concept is reductionist, and it is certainly as much con- cerned with human agency as it is with the broad structures within which people and places are contained. However, concern with the one is not to be unaware of the significance of the other. Hunter (1979) maintained the cen- tral thesis of neighbourhood is that of a uniquely linked unit of socio-spatial organiza- tion between the forces and institutions of the large society and the localized routines in their daily lives. Indeed he quotes E.W. Burgess's observation that to think of neighbourhood in isolation from the rest of the city is to disregard the biggest fact about it. The relevance of the many structural postures is clear: many things do filter downwards from societal structures; decisions made and values prevailing at societal levels do impact upon neighbourhoods. Nevertheless, people are not merely passive recipients of structural conditions, they are cre- ators of meaning which is a well-spring of human action and historic change. 'Structural forces do not create monuments for social change, people do' (Fisher and Kling 1989). The need to recognize structural forces, processes, and various forms of structure, is a truism. There is also a need to achieve 'openings' between the concentration on structure on the one hand and that on human agency on the other; structuration theory and the holism– individualism debate is one means of achieving progress in those directions (see Haines 1988; Giddens 1984). Meanwhile for those scholars who choose to investigate human diversity and values, the neighbourhood as a local place- community remains a fertile field of study.

Conclusions

This chapter has reviewed the various strands that exist in the behaviour of people in local communities in cities. It then concentrated upon the utility of social network analysis in uncovering the structure of informal relation- ships between people, discussing the problems of particular groups who are the most affected by local neighbourhood, although leaving the organizational and service delivery parts of the community interaction question to subsequent chapters (6 and 7). The typologies discussed in Chapter 3 based on interactional data have underestimated the variety of potential rela- tionships and need revision. A major theme has been the tension between the concept of community as developed by social network analysts, where it is really used to describe the structure and patterning of informal associa- tions, and neighbourhood as a place concept. By defining community without the place com- ponent and with the attention on ties, network analysis has changed its meaning. It has not so much freed the community question from its concentration on solidarity and neighbour- hood, as given the question a new interpreta- tion. There are now two questions: one is concerned with personal network communi- ties; the other with local community or neigh- bourhood. Although they overlap, they are different in conception. If community is inter- preted as a personal social network, then clearly it has no necessary coincidence with neighbourhood as local place. Patterns of social interaction are not contained within neigh- bourhoods and many links in the network lead to at least a metropolitan scale. The weight of this evidence for middle-income families is to prove that social interaction occurs in networks which are not local: there are diffuse 'commu- nities' of contact as defined by network analysis. It does not follow that neighbour- hoods have no significance. First, some con- tacts are neighbourhood-based, as virtually all empirical studies show. Second, weak ties are important, and the fact that acquaintanceship is a real though not close tie, is significant. It can be used as a way into a person's confi- dence, perhaps to solicit information, espe- cially in business. Perhaps it is worth noting the historic habit of writing letters of introduc- tion for friends or even casual contacts, pro- viding the traveller or job-seeker with some of the benefits of the writer's connections. More specifically in a neighbourhood sense, Downs (1981) showed that neighbours have an 'inescapable interdependency', emanating from common local concerns such as house values, safety and status consciousness. It will be shown how these have been built upon in different ways, from the selling of new communities (Chapter 4) to the protection of areas by block watch (neighbourhood watch) programmes (Chapter 7). Weak ties can become strong bonds if these are threatened. Another important argument is that by concentrating on interactive ties, the social network analysts take only a partial interpretation of neighbourhood. When O'Brien and Ayidiya (1991) concluded that a sense of community has measurable consequences for the larger life experiences of neighbourhood residents, they are not talking about networks but about the affective, generalized feelings which relate to a sense of place. That the locality remains as one of the bases for interaction is inescapable. As will be shown in the next chapter on the community as a 'sense of place' (Chapter 5) and that on community organizations (Chapter 6) it remains important to *all* of the people for *some* of the time, and to *some* of the people for *most* of the time.

References

Allan, G. A., 1979, *A sociology of friendship and kinship*, George Allen and Unwin, London.

Anderson, E., 1978, *A place on the corner*, University of Chicago Press, Chicago.

Aponte, R., 1991, Urban Hispanic poverty, disaggregations and explanations, *Social Problems*, 38, 516–28.

Banerjee, T. and Baer, W. C., 1984, *Beyond the neighbourhood unit: residential environments and public policy*, Plenum Press, New York.

Boissevain, J. H., 1974, *Friends of friends: networks, manipulations and coalitions*, Basil Blackwell, London.

Bordessa, R. and Bunge, W., 1975, *The Canadian alternative: survival, expeditions and urban change*, Monograph No. 2, Geography Department, York University, Toronto.

Bott, E., 1957, *Family and social network*, Tavistock Publications, London.

Breton, R., 1964, Institutional completeness of ethnic communities and the personal relations of immigrants, *American Journal of Sociology*, 70, 193–205.

Bulmer, M., 1986, *Neighbours: the work of Philip Abrams*, Cambridge University Press, Cambridge.

Chapin, F. S., 1965, *Urban land use planning*, University of Illinois Press.

Chappell, N. L. and Badger, M., 1989, Social isolation and well-being, *Journal of Gerontology*, 44, 169–76.

Clark, T. A., 1987, The suburbanisation process and residential segregation, in G. A. Tobin (ed.), *Divided Neighbourhoods*, Urban Affairs Review, 32, Sage, London, 15–42.

Connerly, C. E., 1985, The community question: an extension of Wellman and Leighton, *Urban Affairs Quarterly*, 20, 537–56.

Cooper, C., 1975, *Easter Hill village*, Free Press, New York.

Crane, J., 1991, The epidemic theory of ghettos and neighbourhood effects on dropping-out and teenage childbearing, *American Journal of Sociology*, 96, 1226–59.

Deng, Z. and Bonacich, P., 1991, Some effects of urbanism on black social networks, *Social Networks*, 13, 35–50.

Downs, A., 1981, *Neighbourhoods and urban development*, Brookings Institute, Washington.

Duncan, G. J. and Smith, K. R., 1989, The rising influence of the elderly, how far, how fair, how frail? *American Sociological Review*, 15, 261–89.

Festinger, L., Schacter, S. and Back, K., 1950, *Social pressure in informal groups*, Stanford University Press, California.

Fischer, C. S., 1982, *To dwell among friends*, University of Chicago Press, Chicago.

Fischer, C. S., Jackson, R. M., Steuve, C. A., Gerson, K., Jones, L., McAllister and Baldassare, M., 1977, *Networks and places*, Free Press, New York.

Fisher, R. and Kling, J., 1989, Community mobilization: prospects for the future, *Urban Affairs Quarterly*, 25, 200–11.

Freudenburg, W. R., 1986, The density of acquaintanceship: an overlooked variable in community research, *American Journal of Sociology*, 92, 27–63.

Gans, H., 1962, *The urban villagers*, Free Press, New York.

Giddens, A., 1984, *The constitution of society: outlines of the theory of structuration*, Polity Press, Cambridge.

Greenbaum, S. D., 1982, Bridging ties at the neighbourhood level, *Social Networks*, 4, 367–84.

Haines, V. A., 1988, Social network analysis, structuration theory and the holism–individualism debate, *Social Networks*, 10, 157–82.

Herbert, D. T., 1976, The study of delinquency areas: a geographical approach, *Transactions, Institute of British Geographers*, 472–92.

Herbert, D. T. and Peace, S. M., 1980, The elderly in an urban environment: a study of Swansea, in D. T. Herbert and R. J. Johnston (eds), *Geography and the urban environment*, 3, John Wiley, Chichester, England, 223–55.

Hunt, M. E. and Ross, L. E., 1990, NORC, a multivariate examination of desirability factors, *The Gerontologist*, 30, 667–74.

Hunter, A., 1975, The loss of community: an empirical test through replication, *American Sociological Review*, 40, 537–52.

Hunter, A., 1979, The urban neighbourhood: its analytical and social contexts, *Urban Affairs Quarterly*, 14, 267–88.

Irving, H. W., 1978, Space and environment in interpersonal relations, in D. T. Herbert and R. J. Johnston (eds), *Geography and the urban environment*, 1, John Wiley, Chichester, England, 249–84.

Jencks, C. and Mayer, S. E., 1990, The social consequences of growing up in a poor neighbourhood, in L. E. Lynn and M. G. H. McGeary (eds), *Inner city poverty in the United States*, National Academy Press, Washington, 68–186.

Johnson, C. L. and Barber, B. M., 1990, Families and networks among older inner-city blacks, *The Gerontologist*, 30, 726–33.

Johnston, R. J., 1974, Local effects on voting at a local election, *Annals, Association of American Geographers*, 64, 418–29.

Keyes, L., 1987, The shifting focus of neighbourhood groups, *Policy Studies Journal*, 16 (2), Winter, 300, 306.

Keller, S., 1968, *The urban neighbourhood: a sociological perspective*, Random House, New York.

Killworth, P. D., Johnsen, E. C., Barnard, H. R., Shelley, G. A. and McCarty, C., 1990, Estimating the size of personal networks, *Social Networks*, 12, 289–312.

Lewis, J. and Bowlby, S., 1989, Women's inequality in urban Britain, in D. T. Herbert and D. M. Smith (eds), *Social problems and the city: new perspectives*, Oxford University Press, Oxford, 213–31.

Ley, D., 1974, The Black inner city as frontier outpost: images and behaviour of a Philadelphia neighbourhood, *Association of American Geographers Monograph*, 7, Washington, DC.

Lofland, L. H., 1989, Social life in the public realm, *Journal of Contemporary Ethnography*, 17, 453–82.

Lynch, K. (ed.), 1977, *Growing up in the city*, MIT Press, Cambridge, Massachusetts.

Marks, C., 1991, The urban underclass, *Annual Review of Sociology*, 17, 445–66.

Michelson, W., Levine, S. V. and Spina, A. R., 1979, *The child in the city: changes and challenges*, University of Toronto Press.

Mitchell, J. Clyde, 1969, *Social networks in urban situations*, Manchester University Press.

O'Brien, D. J. O. and Ayidiya, S., 1991, Neighbourhood community and life satisfaction, *Journal of Community Development*, 22, 21–37.

Oliver, M., 1986, Beyond the neighbourhood: the spatial distribution of social ties in three urban black communities, Paper presented to: Minorities in the post-Industrial City, UCLA, Los Angeles.

Park, R. E. et al., 1925, *The city*, University of Chicago Press, Chicago.

Phillips, D., 1981, Social and spatial segregation of Asians in Leicester, in P. Jackson and S. J. Smith (eds), *Social interaction and ethnic segregation*, Institute of British Geographers, Special Publication 12, 101–21.

Robson, B. T., 1969, *Urban analysis*, Cambridge University Press, Cambridge.

Rowles, G. D., 1978, *Prisoners of space: exploring the geographical experience of older people*, West View, Boulder, Colorado.

Sprout, H. and Sprout, M., 1965, *The ecological perspective on human affairs*, Princeton University Press, New Jersey.

Stutz, F., 1973, Distance and network effects on urban travel fields, *Economic Geography*, 49, 134–44.

Suttles, A., 1968, *The social order of the slum: ethnicity and territory in the inner city*, University of Chicago Press, Chicago.

Unger, D. G. and Wandersman, A., 1985, The importance of neighbours: the social, cognitive and affective components of neighbouring, *American Journal of Community Psychology*, 13 (2), 139–69.

Warnes, A. M., 1989, Social problems of elderly people in cities, in D. T. Herbert and D. M. Smith (eds), *Social problems and the city: new perspectives*, Oxford University Press, Oxford, 197–212.

Wellman, B., 1987, *The community question re-evaluated*, University of Toronto, Centre for Urban and Community Studies, Research Paper No. 165.

Wellman, B., 1989, *The place of kinfolk in personal community networks*, University of Toronto, Centre for Urban and Community Studies, Research Paper No. 176.

Wellman, B. and Leighton, B., 1979, Network, neighbourhoods, and communities: approaches to the study of the community question, *Urban Affairs Quarterly*, *14*, 363–390.

Wellman, B. and Berkovitz, S. D. (eds), 1988, *Social structures: a network approach*, Cambridge University Press, Cambridge.

Wellman, B. and Wortley, S., 1990, Different strokes from different folks: community ties and social support, *American Journal of Sociology*, *96*, 558–88.

Williams, M. R., 1985, *Neighbourhood organizations*, Greenwood, Westport, Connecticut.

Wilson, W. J., 1987, *The truly disadvantaged: the inner city, the underclass and public policy*, University of Chicago Press, Chicago.

Wynne-Edwards, J., 1965, Self-regulating systems in populations of animals, *Science*, *147*, 1543–1558.

5

The Social Construction of Communities: Creating and Identifying Senses of Place

Literature as a Source of Sense of Place

During the last twenty years it has been recognized that areas of distinctive character within cities cannot be understood only by objective empirical studies of their content, as areas of bricks and mortar containing people of different ages, economic status or ethnic backgrounds, or as patterns of interactions. Rather than viewing neighbourhoods and communities in an ecological context, primarily as *bundles of activities* located in areas, or as being defined as sets of *common behaviours*, the new approaches pioneered by Lee (1968), Lynch (1960), and Suttles (1972) emphasized that the areas were viewed differently by people. Individuals and groups have feelings about these areas and attribute meanings to places. This means that urban places, or rather our knowledge of them, are not given, concrete entities; instead in Suttles's (1972) phrase, they should be considered as *social constructions*, in which there may be very different experiences. This means that our understanding of the differentiation of places is really a product of the way individuals or social groups interpret or construct their character, a result of our perception of these places and the meanings that we assign to them.

These breakthroughs by social scientists must not be thought to be entirely original. Novelists have been particularly skilled in providing perceptive descriptions of the places in which their works unfold, defining their distinctive, idiosyncratic character. Imaginative literature is a particularly rich source of the 'meanings' of local areas or neighbourhoods.

Qualitatively and subjectively they offer a window through which to study the whole idea of local communities in cities and provide a rich source of ideas. Novelists consciously endow their settings with this distinctiveness: for example, D. H. Lawrence (1969, 12) claimed that the 'spirit of place is a great reality', whilst Lawrence Durrell (1969, 163) stated that the great books 'are tuned into the sense of place'. In an interpretative context Barrell's study of the 'geographies' of Hardy's Wessex identified these distinctive features in the various ecological zones. The distinctiveness was not only a simple matter of the physical differences, but also the highly localized sense of place of the heath folk, a sense derived not only by sight and sound, but also 'by smell, by tread — the feel of the earth underfoot' (Barrell 1982, 349). Writers certainly vary in their depiction of place; Barrell (1972) argued that whereas John Clare's 'sense of place' was very specific, Wordsworth tended to look *through* places, so the exact place was not always significant to him.

Writers of prose fiction variously evoke a sense of place, often as an essential and integral part of the story of human relationships which represents the core of the novel. Literary critics have gone further, as in Williams's (1977) idea of the 'structure of feeling'. Although in many ways it is an amplification of the 'sense of place' concept, it goes beyond it, providing a bridge between local and societal or cultural scales as well as time. Williams (1981, 207–9) defined culture as 'a realized signifying system: a set of signs and symbols that are embedded in a whole range of activities, relations and institutions, only some of which are manifestly cultural, others being overtly economic, political or generational'. Williams did not describe sense of place in purely humanistic terms, but tried to define the *qualities* that structure that experience. This concept comprises particular qualities of social experience and relationships, feelings which constitute a structure in the sense that they are a 'living and interrelating continuity'. To a sense of place is therefore added a sense of time and the 'generational investment in place' which gives its meaning. However, many of these attitudes in terms of literature are quite new. For example, it is worth noting Lodge's (1991) argument that the creation of a sense of place was a fairly late development in prose fiction. He claimed that it was the romantic movement which 'pondered the effect of *milieu* on man, opened people's eyes to the beauty of landscapes and then to the grim symbolism of industrial cityscapes' (Lodge 1991, 20).

There are certainly considerable caveats in using a source such as imaginative literature to throw light upon a real-world concept such as local community or neighbourhood. The aspects of reality that have been chosen and passed through the filter of the novelist may be different to those of others. Also descriptions can vary according to the kind of literary genre which is being used. Romantic literature, for example, will portray aspects of the world in a particular light; realist literature in something closer to 'objective' reality. In addition the views of an 'insider' may be very different from those of an 'outsider'. Thomas Hardy, perhaps the best-known of the English regional novelists, spoke of his use of the term 'Wessex' as a partly real, partly dream country (Birch 1981, 349). However, beyond the filter of the novelist there are also the filters of the readers, and what they make of the images which are portrayed. Barrell (1982, 347) suggested that the places in Hardy's novels are constructed 'by the characters in the novels ... by Hardy in his narrative, and by us as we read.' This emphasis upon the *construction of the text* in a novel has led to a major debate in English literature faculties. It has led many to the view that the novelist and readers may have several dif-

ferent interpretations of the 'text' and there can be no primacy for any one of these views. Readers may obtain very different interpretations from the text, whilst the novelist or essayist may not be successful in communicating particular intentions. The so-called deconstructionist approach takes one back to the uniqueness and individualism of the humanistic experience and can be rather unsettling to those who search for generalizations, for consistent meanings in novels, which we all share. The same problem can be seen in the interpretation of all landscapes, which some post-modernist geographers (Soja 1989) have claimed can be read in different ways like a 'text'.

Most geographers who have used literature to interpret landscape or places have drawn upon rural and historical settings, although urban landscapes have not been completely forgotten. The novels of Dickens contain graphic descriptions of life in parts of Victorian London, whilst the writings of Arnold Bennett vividly portray the character of the Potteries in England. Regional novelists have a particular skill in capturing the essence of inner-city communities. Alexander Cordell (1984) illuminated the sharp contrasts among the inner-city districts — clearly place-communities in the sense described here — of the boom town of Cardiff in the earlier part of the twentieth century when its volume of coal exports made it the biggest port in the world. Moreover, he shows both a *process of change* and the often ignored *diurnal rhythm* in these areas.

> Tiger Bay was a bit removed from Newtown; they could be called sisters because both were poor, but there the similarity ended. There was about Newtown an impoverished respectability; an Irish oasis within a community of sometimes hostile Welsh or English. Newtown built by the immigrant Irish, stayed Irish; its wakes, its lore, were essentially of the Green fields of Erin, which was one of its pubs ... But slowly, inexorably, the surrounding Welsh influence crept into Newtown; like tide gaining inch by inch ... But Tiger Bay, formed between the canal and Bute Street ... was an enclave that was neither Welsh or Irish, but of its own; a melting pot of every

nationality from Greece to China and Arabia to Spain. Here the administrators ... worked from nine until six and then travelled north for home and respectability, leaving their offices deserted ... after dark ... another world of seamen gambled and ate opium and made love until dawn cleansed their revelry — a multi-nation race. ... Here came the lovesick libertines in search of ale and love. (Cordell 1984, 142–3)

Similar vivid descriptions can be found in many novels and successfully capture the stark contrasts in intra-urban character. Nevertheless, it is always too easy to romanticize life in these colourful areas. J. Wreford Watson, an award-winning Canadian poet as well as distinguished geographer, used Crane's novel (1892) of life in inner New York in his Presidential Address to the Institute of British Geographers to illuminate the desperation of life in such areas:

> the whole atmosphere of the district bred conflict. The tenement was in a lane popularly known as Rum Alley. A tall, ungainly, begrimed 'careening building' it stood in a 'dark region' from which the sun was shut out by the big apartment blocks and by factories and warehouses near the river. The tenement 'creaked' from the weight of humanity stamping about its bowels. It was made up of 'dark staircases and ... gloomy halls' from which two-roomed flats were reached. (Cited in Watson 1979, 109–10)

It was not only the poor neighbourhoods which found expression in American literature. Watson drew the contrast between the *lower* world of Crane's *Maggie* and the *upper* world of Fitzgerald's *Gatsby* (1925, 120): the upper world occupied 'what Henry James called that "chain of villas" thrusting themselves out from their suburban woods and lawns ... loud, and assertive' (Watson 1979, 110). The Canadian novelist Mordecai Richler also offers insights into upper-income areas, the 'room at the top' syndrome so characteristic of many cities.

> Westmount was where the truly rich lived in stone mansions driven like stakes into the

shoulder of the mountain. The higher you climbed up the splendid, tree-lined streets the thicker the ivy, the more massive the mansion, and the more important the men inside. (Richler 1964, 170)

In his use of literature to portray the contrasts within urban America, Wreford Watson goes beyond the descriptions of areas, by also looking for the *values and meanings* which are portrayed. However, he never loses sight of the social, economic and political *contexts* within which these values and meanings are placed. The strivings of the Lonigan family to survive in a hostile city were contained within the Irish-Catholic world; Gatsby's reaching for a class position was always constrained by his deficiencies of tradition and lineage. Watson (1979) used a 1930s novel by Farrell (1932) on Chicago to show how it is possible to go beyond areal description to derive the *elements of change*:

> the family would have to be moving soon. When he had bought their current building Wabash Avenue had been a nice decent respectable street for a self-respecting man to live with his family. But now, well, the niggers and the kikes were getting in, and they were dirty. (Farrell 1932; see Watson 1979, 89)

This passage was used by Watson to describe the process of change and the creation of what he called an inner-city *shatter-belt*, similar to the urban ecologists' transition zone,

> where the changing geography of the city had led to the rapid deterioration of a formerly stable working-class area. Here family homes lost out to the invasion of shops, offices and tenements; those that were not abandoned to them were squeezed out by them. More significantly, Irish Catholic homes became threatened by the influx of Jews and Negroes. (Watson 1979, 85)

All these uses of imaginative fiction portray a subjective insight into the 'worlds' about which they write. Nevertheless, as Barrell (1982) reminds us, it is important to understand literary conventions and methods of narrative. Farrell (1932) for example, must have had some awareness of his contemporaries in the Chicago School of human ecology — indeed the key to his story is the place of the Irish-Catholic in the changing ethnic mix of Chicago in the 1930s.

Many other literary and artistic sources can offer insights into the character of urban communities. Lowry's paintings offer a still-life snapshot of Lancashire towns in the first half of the twentieth century. The tradition continues into modern literature, though the theme is often one of portraying the integrated close-knit neighbourhoods of childhood. For example, Mordecai Richler has set several of his novels against what can be called a *remembered background*, a childhood in a poor Jewish area in Montreal. Richler writes about St Urbain in ways which reflect his class and ethnicity. It emerges through the 'filters' of his characters in ways which enrich our understanding of the subtle differences in city neighbourhoods at that time, and the crucial difference in understanding between what must be seen as the *insider's* view and that of the *outsider*:

> To a middle-class stranger, it's true, one street would have seemed as squalid as the next. On each corner a cigar store, a grocery, and a fruit man. Outside staircases everywhere. Winding ones, wooden ones, rusty and risky ones. Here a prized plot of grass splendidly barbered, there a spitefully woody patch. An endless repetition of precious peeling balconies and waste lots, making the occasional gap here and there. But as the boys knew, each street between St. Dominique and Park Avenue represented subtle differences in income. No two cold-water flats were alike. (M. Richler 1964, 13)

Thus St Urbain was a neighbourhood built on internal cohesion and with lines of conflict drawn up between other ethnically different inhabitants of the inner city. At times of conflict with the French-Canadians, the normal 'order' of St Urbain and the official sanctioning of its activities were disturbed:

> Police cars cruised slowly up and down St. Urbain. Store-owners and pool-room proprietors were fined for infraction of city by-laws that had not been enforced for years ... On St. Urbain, stores shut down early and hardly anybody went out after dark. (M. Richler 1972, 126)

Richler's characters look back on St Urbain with nostalgia not so much for the character of the place but for the values it held, the cherished people with whom it was shared. It is described variously as:

> suffocating St. Urbain ... urban backyards, wherein you dumped punctured tires and watermelon husks and cracked sinks and rotting mattresses, boys grew up dirty and sad, spiky also, like grass beside the railroad tracks ... this is nowhere, St. Urbain. We're nothing here. We have to leave. (M. Richler 1972, 130)

Nevertheless, the bond with the place and its valued memories was there: 'Again and again he was driven back to St. Urbain to linger before the dilapidated flat that had once held Hanna, Arty, Jenny' (M. Richler 1972, 373).

However, these places were not frozen in time. Virtually all the characters and their close contemporaries had achieved upward and outward movement and had reached Toronto or London and even upper-income areas of Montreal, for 'students graduated from cold-water flats to buy their own duplexes in the tree-lined upper income streets of Outremont' (M. Richler 1964, 7).

Although these types of descriptions can be duplicated from the work of many other novelists, a feature of the modern urban novel is that it increasingly depicts a world of placelessness, in which the local community is undermined: 'Places are altered daily, disrupting bonds and perceptions that people develop over years of residence. In urbanised portions of North America, many residents may be condemned to become "strangers" in their own place in a lifetime' (Hay 1987, 285). Porteous (1985) has gone further, developing the *no-place* idea with a matrix designed to classify novels according to the strength with which they portray the concept of place. He cites Lowry (1947) who sees cities as 'symbols of fear ... merciless predators on human life'. Richard Ford (1986; 1988) is another contemporary American writer who portrays the transient nature of life for those on the margins of society, occupying the motel-strips of 'no-place'. 'Families and friendships fall apart; this is a world where nothing can be relied upon, where betrayal is commonplace. Everyone is moving on in search of something better' (Ford 1986, frontispiece). The kinds of urban worlds which Ford (1986) describes in *Rock Springs*, his collections of short stories about people trying to make sense of their lives, are far removed from a utopian concept of community, or remembered familiar safe havens of childhood. His qualities are those of transience, disorder and placelessness: to him suburban New Jersey is the 'wasteland.' This approach is not entirely new. Jack Kerouac's breathless novels of the 1960s expressed the new mobility and standards of his time. Earlier and more devastating was Gertrude Stein's cutting reference to Oakland, California in the 1930s: 'When you get there, there's no there, there,' (quoted in Pocock and Hudson 1978, 81). Although this undoubtedly reflects the smart, cynical put-down of a New York-based critic, there is an uncanny ring of truth about the description of the Bay Area's less legible settlement. Perhaps one of the problems of this century has been the growing homogeneity of places, a major theme in the urban landscape of the mid-twentieth century that novelists and popular artists have managed to highlight. 'No-place' is the antithesis of place and may typify many contemporary urban landscapes from suburbs to inner-city areas. It was succinctly satirized by the contemptuous comment in the popular 1960s song: 'Little boxes, little boxes ... and they are all made out of ticky tacky and they all look just the same.'

It could be argued that some of the reason why placelessness seems so widespread is the lack of intimate contact that people have with particular places: they spend little time in areas outside the workplace and home and are driven to and from places — producing a separation of humans and localities. Yet as

important may be the fact that so many buildings, and also the materials from which they are constructed, are repetitions of those in other areas: standard designs of streets, malls and homes are found throughout the western world and beyond. More generally it is produced from the 'suppression of local context and culture, and the imposition of uniformity as a means to universality' (Ley 1989, 60). Perhaps it is fortunate that the homogeneity of the contemporary period is being challenged by post-modernists who have argued for uniqueness; for the need to design on a human scale and to use deliberately the artistic device of a 'collage' to create distinctive mixtures of different styles. Individual places need to be created, and with time they may lead to distinctive human feelings about these areas.

It must be stressed that the worlds which the novels describe through the eyes of their characters or those of the folk singers of the present are not necessarily real worlds. Nevertheless, they often crystallize the character of neighbourhoods, or cities and their process of change. Certainly the ways in which neighbourhoods are depicted often reflect the lives and experiences of the authors. As Richler dwells upon his memories of a childhood in Montreal to recreate the experience of life in different neighbourhoods, so Ford draws out the more modern experience of loss of community. Although the imaginative literature of the novel provides us with vivid descriptions of local place-communities, the processes of change and sources of the 'meanings' of neighbourhood, the approach does create problems. It does not provide a systematic body of replicable knowledge, one that is amenable to the cumulative identification and refinement of the various components of community character. To achieve such ends one has to turn to very different academic tradition, mainly to the work of social scientists, where the differentiation of place can be summarized in terms of two different sets of concepts: those of the *cognitive and affective domains*. The former deals with the recognition and identification of places, particularly their spatial patterning; the latter with attitudes to the place-communities, to the values and emotional associations which are linked to these areas.

Cognitive Variations

During the late 1960s and 1970s, the growth of behavioural approaches in geography and related fields led to a new interest in the topic of cognitive images and mental maps, namely our perception and definition of the places, one of the by-products of which was a series of useful techniques with which to identify and define neighbourhoods. An important catalyst in the development of this interest was a book by the eminent economist Kenneth Boulding, whose primary proposition was that all behaviour was dependent on an image (Boulding 1956, 6).

> For any individual organism or organization there are no such things as 'facts'. There are only messages filtered through a changeable value system ... . This does not mean that the image of the world possessed by an individual is a purely private matter or that all knowledge is simply subjective knowledge ... . Part of our image of the world is the belief that this image is shared by other people who are also part of our image of the world ... and if a group of people are exposed to much the same set of messages in building up an image of the world, the value systems of all individuals must be approximately the same. (Boulding 1956, 14)

This initial point on the 'generality' of the image is of importance to our understanding of place-communities and neighbourhoods: if an image were wholly individual and idiosyncratic it would be unmanageable as a concept. Lowenthal's (1961) brilliant summary essay on the role of imagination in geography also recognized that there could be as many images as individuals, a set of 'personally apprehended' milieux, although he maintained the sharing of needs, ideals and loyalties induces group images (see also Tuan, 1977). Canter has summarized the objectives of the cognitive ap-

proach: 'We must identify the units of which the cognitive system is composed ... show how they relate to each other spatially ... [and obtain] a full description of the places and of the reactions which people have to them' (Canter 1977, 31).

The analysis of people's attitudes to places must be left to a subsequent section. The next sections summarize our understanding of cognitive variations in four parts: naming; cognitive mapping; territorial marking; and people identity (see Figure 3.2).

Naming

Perhaps the most primitive part of these cognitive images is the *naming of places*. This can be regarded as the identification of an object, its denotation by the allocation of a distinctive name to some territory. Although the discussion in the previous section has indicated that there is an increasing problem of anonymity, of 'no-place', it is apparent that most cities are full of different areas with distinctive territorial names. Although they can be a label, an identification, they also contain meanings to others. Some may be the informal labels attached by residents, or even outsiders fearful or envious of their character: for example, the general term Skid Row generally applied to rundown areas of cities, or the specific Tiger Bay in Cardiff described by Cordell (1984) come into the former situation; whereas Knob Hill, derived from the Indian word nabob or ruler, is an example of the latter. Increasingly names for local areas in cities are not generated by residents: they are allocated to areas by municipal authorities either attempting to differentiate the area for a range of services or to establish community areas or are named by developers. Increasingly the name is not based on their family or old home, but is chosen as part of a selling process, commodifying them like any product in the market. On a more detailed scale we are accustomed to the marking of territory by street and house addresses in the western world, although this is a relatively recent phenomenon, part of our ordering of life. Travellers to Japanese cities find it confusing that individual and unique house addresses are not common. In the west one of the most widespread current trends in community planning is the practice of allocating separate names to what are supposed to be neighbourhood units within larger community developments (Figure 8.6). This is done deliberately to create a sense of identification (see also Davis (1990) on the naming of Los Angeles suburbs such as Sunburst, New Horizons and Bravo). However, Gill's (1989) study in the planned town of Tumbler Ridge showed that over a third of local residents could not supply a neighbourhood name to their immediate areas, although this might be a function of the fact that the town was only three years old at the time of her survey.

Cognitive Mapping

A more general attack on understanding the cognitive images of place in an urban context can be seen in an influential work of Lynch (1960). He maintained that people simplified the complexity of urban areas with their multitude of roads, buildings and people. People possessed images of the spatial relationships of urban areas and these images were structured around a set of basic features that he described as the *elements of urban images*. These elements could be viewed as the cognition of the spatial patterning of areas. Lynch derived a set of 'collective images' from the correspondences in a set of sketch maps from American downtown areas provided by individuals, thereby identifying the common as opposed to the unique images. Lynch's major concern was to interpret the 'cityscape' as a set of messages which could be read by individuals. The term *legibility* was used to identify the strength of the messages, namely, 'the ease with which its parts [the city's] can be recognized and can be organized into a coherent pattern' (Lynch 1960, 2–3).

The qualities of legibility and imageability were considered to be important facets of the urban landscape and conditioned people's atti-

tudes about the places, illustrating that this analytical approach to the separation of the various components of images is artificial, although perhaps necessary if we are to uncover the various parts of the multidimensional character of places. Lynch studied three American cities, Boston, Jersey City and Los Angeles, interviewing thirty citizens in Boston and fifteen in each of the other two, and combining this with the observations of trained observers.

> The basic office interview consisted in its essentials of a request for a sketch map of the city, for the detailed description of a number of trips through the city and for a listing and brief description of the parts felt to be most distinctive or vivid in the subject's mind. (Canter 1977, 23)

Lynch's main innovation was the use and summary of these sketch maps which were seen as the metaphor for what was in the person's mind. The 'mental map' was 'that image, derived from knowledge of the real world and from cartographic and other communications that we carry as a guide to our spatial activities' (Goodey 1974, 24). These individual 'maps' were considered to be simplifications of reality and contained five separate parts or *elements*:

1. *paths* are the channels along which people move;
2. *nodes* are points of convergence;
3. *edges* are boundaries or barriers;
4. *landmarks* are physically distinctive objects;
5. *districts* are recognizable territories — essentially areas that can be entered.

Lynch's approach has been widely replicated in studies in various parts of the world and has been used to compare places in terms of legibility and imageability. By identifying the degree of correspondence that people showed in their sketches, the relative legibility of each element could be shown in map form. An important part of Lynch's original study was his finding that Jersey City and Los Angeles had much less legibility than Boston, where there was a high degree of common identification about the individual parts of downtown.

Applications of urban imagery techniques to the particular case of the definition of neighbourhoods, considered to be the smallest place-community in cities, have adopted various methodologies, though generally with the objective of teasing out the mental map of local residents. One of the earliest methods of identifying the spatial bounds of neighbourhoods was developed by Lee (1954), who referred to the units identified as 'socio-spatial schema'. Respondents were asked: 'Please draw a line around the part which you consider acts as your neighbourhood or district'. This technique was based on the stimulus provided by the name, and attempted to define the precise area and boundaries of the named area — the districts and boundaries in Lynch's terminology. Although Lee found that about 80 per cent of the people could delineate a neighbourhood, these were personal and idiosyncratic. It is clear that there are various ways in which respondents can be asked to represent their images of neighbourhood. For example, Lee experimented with a method in which respondents were presented with a list of places around their home and were asked to say which were in their 'neighbourhood' and which were outside.

Other studies have explored the variations in the images of different groups of people. Ladd (1970) studied black youths whom she asked to draw maps of their Boston neighbourhood and obtained a variety of responses which ranged from pictorial drawings to maps with specific landmarks. Herbert and Raine (1976) experimented with a number of techniques to define local communities in Cardiff. The first method (Figure 5.1a) entailed presenting respondents with a set of nominated locations and asking them to score them as definitely in, possibly in or definitely not in their neighbourhood. These mental maps provide a composite approximation of the territorial extent of the local community. For example, Area A, a low-income area of terraced houses in the inner city, is compactly defined and is strongly influenced by

boundaries, with the railway on one side and Newport Road on the other. Area B is more extensive as a mental map and has a lower-level intensity of recognition; this was a high-income suburb. The example shows boundaries at levels of recognition and highlights contrasts between neighbourhoods of different socio-economic status and length of residence. This analysis of spatial neighbourhood did contain elements of environmental quality and local social interaction which gave the study some clues about appraisive or affective attitudes. Residents of Area A showed high levels of informal social interaction and awareness of local environmental problems. Residents of Area B also had high levels of social interaction, although these were expressed in more formal forms of visiting, based on invitations, whilst the district contained few environmental problems.

Figure 5.1b shows the same two areas where the mental map of neighbourhood is obtained by asking respondents to identify the point at which their neighbourhood ends, using various directions from their homes. Lynch's terminology of edges and nodes is used, though node could be read as landmark in some cases. For Area A, the dominant edges are the railway and Newport Road, and the hospital is an important node. For Area B, there is a well-defined edge which forms a compact central part to the neighbourhood, though some respondents recognized boundaries outside this area. By contrast, Area A has a well-defined outer boundary with inner partitions, for some residents looked to the smaller collection of streets within which they lived. A final method in the Cardiff study, though with two different areas, was to use a technique called the standard deviational ellipse. The question was standard because respondents were asked to identify on a map the district they considered to be their home area. Using this method (see Herbert and Raine 1976, 330) the locations of the edge of the neighbourhood at ten-degree intervals could be translated into co-ordinates, from which the 'ellipse', really a summarizing spatial form, could be calculated. In the two examples used, the size of the perceived home

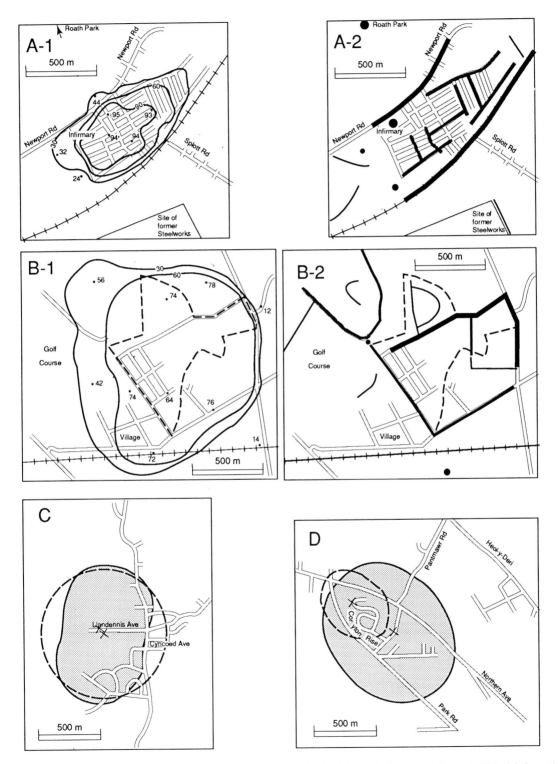

Figure 5.1 Defining neighbourhoods by different methods (after Herbert and Raine 1976); (a) Location counts, (b) Boundaries and (c) and (d) Standard deviational ellipses

area ellipse varied from 79 hectares for Area C to 23 hectares for Area D, even though these are similar middle-income suburbs.

Also shown in Figure 5.1c are the ellipses derived from information on where neighbourhood friends lived, and where they travelled for local services, though such interactional issues are more thoroughly dealt with in Chapter 4. For Area C the two ellipses have a high level of concordance, whereas for Area D, the perceived home area ellipse is much smaller than the friendship– services ellipse. It is in the area where congruence between perceived friendship and services ellipse is lowest that the former is smallest in extent.

A number of studies has examined the neighbourhood mental maps of particular groups, and not surprisingly have shown that there are *variations by type of people*. Lee's pioneering (1954) study was restricted to housewives in Cambridge, whilst Herbert and Raine (1976) similarly studied women's mental maps in Cardiff suburbs. By contrast Ladd (1970) studied the images of black youths in Boston. Matthews's (1984) study of primary school-children showed that his subjects were able to describe the area around their home in the richest terms, noting more than twice the amount of detail that they could record for their journey to school. In the context of neighbourhoods this supports the contention that children have a sense of their surroundings by the time they arrive at school and suggests that their spatial maps are stronger than their sequential maps. He also showed that children's environmental cognition shows a complex relationship with age: 'With age children increasingly achieve more information about places. The six year old's view of space is much narrower in conception than that of the eleven year old' (Matthews 1984, 95). Bowden (1972, 227) went so far as to claim that neighbourhoods were best defined as 'the territorial and perceptual range of advanced pre-adolescent males regardless of society or geographic location'. He justified this claim by observing that smaller children and females were not allowed the liberty to stray far from home,

whereas adolescents go beyond the bounds because they are given greater range and responsibility. Bowden went on to argue that the home–meal–bed dependency created limits to the territorial range, for older children break out of the pattern by overnight stays. Barriers such as main roads and rivers defined areas and schools, whereas shops and play areas were boundary markers, not the centre of neighbourhoods, because the core was the sleeping-quarters of the young males. Environmental cognition among children will be affected by the freedom they have to explore their neighbourhood and mental maps may have declined substantially since the earlier decades of the twentieth century. This can be attributed to both the changing physical fabric and social environment of the neighbourhood. Gaster (1991), in a study of Manhattan, showed that the extent to which neighbourhoods were supportive of children's play declined between 1915 and 1976.

Many studies of the cognitive maps of older people have been carried out and have found rather different patterns. Herbert and Peace's (1980) study of elderly people in several contrasted neighbourhoods in Swansea found that their mental maps were highly localized and specific, reflecting a lack of mobility and a greater reliance on home and neighbourhood with increasing age (Figure 5.2). Despite the criticisms of the approach, mental maps have provided one method of identifying and communicating subjective images of areas, such as neighbourhood, although the weight which can be attached to them and the roles they play have been questioned. Walmsley (1988) placed importance on the 'schemata' idea developed by Lee (1976), maintaining it is a 'framework which enables an individual to *remember* a city' (Walmsley 1988, 49). In this sense they represent useful generalizations, and as such are not that dissimilar from attempts to develop a typology of neighbourhoods or local social interaction (Irving 1978).

Although Lynch's work was applied in many empirical studies in the 1970s, serious debate soon emerged on ways of interpreting mental maps. The approach was criticized as

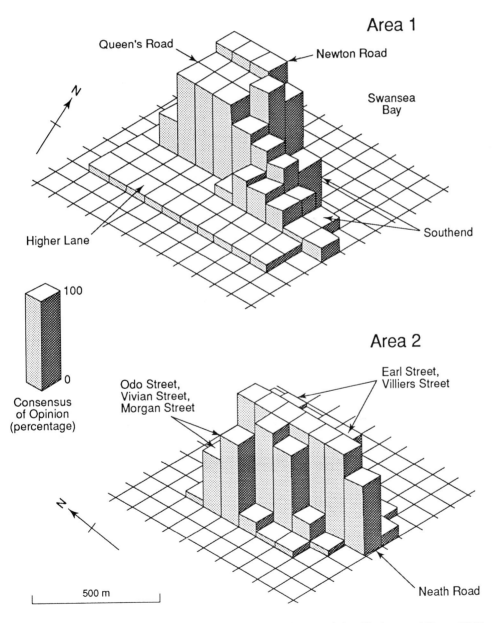

Figure 5.2 Mental maps of old people in two Swansea districts (after Herbert and Peace 1978)

often representing the extent to which people were unfamiliar with, or simply wrong about their city's patterns, suggesting that the term 'ignorance maps' may be as appropriate. In addition it could be argued that Lynch imposed the five elements, rather than conclusively determining that the elements are essential parts of the relational part of the image. Pocock and Hudson (1978) summarized many of the other criticisms, identifying four limitations of the urban image approach as a mental representation of the real environment. They maintained it is:

1. partial — for it does not include all parts of the environment;
2. simplified — because it excludes information about the parts it does include;
3. distorted — owing to inaccurate statements of distance and direction;
4. idiosyncratic — since it relates specifically to the individual.

Downs and Stea (1973) also identified a number of important questions about the composition, arrangement, extent, stability and variability of the image. In addition, Walmsley (1988) noted that some of the elements, particularly landmarks and nodes, are not always easily separated, and there is a concentration on the visual to the exclusion of all other sensory reactions to the city. Further, *the image will vary among individuals* for a variety of reasons which include not only perceptual and cognitive skills of the individuals but also more general parameters such as *social class, educational level, age, ethnicity, gender and length of residence*. This latter set of attributes is of particular importance, for it is from this factor that the bases of common images are likely to emerge. The structures can, however, be learned. A study by Kirasic and Mathes (1990) showed that map study was one of the most effective ways of conveying environmental information to elderly adults.

It was appreciated at an early stage that there were different types of image which fulfilled different purposes, even apart from the distinctiveness of *appraisive images* (Pocock and Hudson, 1978) which will be dealt with in the next section. Another distinction was between *spatial* maps and *sequential* maps. Whereas sequential maps were concerned with the linkages between locations or places, spatial maps looked at the elements within an area. People may hold both spatial and sequential images for different purposes, perhaps the former when imagining their neighbourhood or local community, the latter for a trip to the local stores or to the city centre.

Walmsley (1988) pointed out that most researchers have preferred to concentrate on the *cognitive map* rather than the process of *cognitive mapping*. However, Beck and Wood's work (1976) had shown how this could be conceptualized, identifying eight steps in a process model of cognitive mapping (see Table 5.1).

This model shows a set of logical steps in a process which leads to an image. However, given the fact that seven of the eight steps are internal processes, the issue of testing them is problematic though they can be theorized (see Canter 1977). In general this scarcity of research on cognitive mapping processes is symptomatic of the stronger interest in empirical description of the real world by geographers and urbanists, rather than in theory or the use of laboratory testing under controlled conditions — the approach favoured by psychologists.

Although the term 'mental map' is attractive and may be useful in identifying the strength of areal cognition, it has always remained a blurred 'image' in practice. Downs and Stea (1973) argued that cognitive maps contained little more than sets of shorthand symbols to describe the environment. Walmsley (1988) makes the point that the term 'map' is merely a metaphor, because it is not known whether the stored 'mental' information is in fact in a form of spatial co-ordinates. So by the early 1980s the value of mental maps was being questioned. There were doubts raised on the measurability of images and their links with actual behaviour; Boyle and Robinson (1979) argued that mental maps would be drawn upon selectively and that for most spatial or place decisions, people would purposefully improve their image by consulting real maps. Walmsley

Table 5.1 A model for the cognitive mapping process

SYNCHRONIZATION	(draws bits together)
ROTATION	(convert to two dimensions)
SCALING	(reduce to manageable size)
GENERALIZATION	(simplify)
SYMBOLIZATIONS	(select symbols)
VERBALIZATIONS	(name places)
REPRESENTATION	(image held in mind)
EXTERNALIZATION	(image presented to others)

Source: Beck and Wood 1976

(1988) suggests that the research emphasis has shifted from the attempt to persuade people to draw their mental maps to one which examines how people handle environmental information. The idea of schemata, which originates in *Gestalt* psychology, can be thought of as 'frameworks in the mind on which information is hung'. Most of the criticism has been of those methods which require respondents to draw maps or to look at and interpret real maps, 'media' with which they may not be familiar. Thus level of familiarity may be a more significant discriminator than others which are used in the analysis of mental maps. Boyle and Robinson (1979) expressed this concern and also doubted whether 'mental maps' had much importance as influences upon activity: they are in their view internalized, mainly visual and have no affective qualities. They experimented with completion tests 'designed to examine specific elements in the image' rather than to produce a whole mental map. For example, the cloze procedure requires respondents to fill gaps in a presented map where certain sections, usually grid cells are left blank. Although it retains difficulties, it overcomes some of the methodological problems of sketch-mapping and has proved a reliable and useful tool.

Territorial Marking

More specific evidence of another type of cognitive understanding can be derived from studies of teenage gangs occupying particular territories or 'turfs' in inner Philadelphia (Ley and Cybriwsky 1974). Graffiti have not normally been regarded as a measurable indicator, rather as a 'folk-symbol in their own right'. Ley and Cybriwsky argued that graffiti allowed teenage gangs to claim some control over neighbourhood space and it becomes an accurate indicator of 'turf ownership', the 'edge of a socially claimed space. As such the marking parallels animal behaviour for many animals mark their territory, although usually by urination, creating a marking by smell, not visual stimuli: 'The walls are more than an attitudinal tabloid; they are a behavioural manifesto ... . Graffiti are a visible manifestation of a group's social space. Moreover, assertive or aggressive graffiti represent more than attitudes. They are disposition to behaviour' (Ley and Cybriwsky 1974, 505). The use of graffiti in this way is one way of ascribing a proprietary meaning to space on the neighbourhood scale, though in fact this particular study was specifically concerned with the attitudes of teenage gangs. Indeed, Cybriwsky (1978) characterized the Fairmount district of Philadelphia as a typical urban village, and it is this largely qualitative concept which has most general meaning. As such it can be related to Gans's (1962) original development of the urban village idea, which attempted to characterize close inward-looking urban neighbourhoods where qualitative senses of local place were high, although these attitudes were usually identified and communicated by descriptive word pictures or ideas. The evidence from this study of graffiti isolates another dimension of the cognition of place, what Unger and Wandersman (1985) usefully described as *symbolic communication*, one that conveys information to strangers as well as neighbours. However, this dimension is best regarded as having subdivisions. One is certainly best seen in the examples provided above; those relate to the marking of space, especially boundaries, which can be real or symbolic. This dimension can be called *territorial marking*, a cognitive alert that indicates ownership, dominance of a group, or even a means of privacy regulation. The other is a personalization of space, the addition of self-expressive qualities to homes and their immediate surroundings which provide an indication of personal identity, as well as status or cultural values (Appleyard 1970). This may be seen in the use of particular colours, door decorations, naming, or even yard ornaments. The term *symbolic decoration* may be appropriate for this dimension. Again one must be careful to note that most decorations may apply more to individual houses than to areas. However, the latter can be found, even though such areal cohesion is usually a product of a developer's plan, rather than an individually derived harmony. Also our understanding of the sense of place provided by these features must go beyond the cognition of these features; they can have various meanings that apply in the affective domain.

People Identity

The fourth set of cognitive features comes from the perception of the people found in particular areas. Much of our identification of the differentiation of areas in cities comes from our awareness of the different people who inhabit an area, especially the various types of ethnic groups. Primitive measurements of the concept we now know as 'social distance' were anticipated in the earliest work of human ecologists and represented attempts to measure the degree of comfort that people feel towards associating with or entering relationships with groups of different ethnic origin (Bogardus 1925). A crude though still useful and readily recognizable set of thresholds that provide for greater levels of intimacy: (6) Exclusion; (5) Admit to Citizenship; (4) Admit to Employment; (3) Admit to Social Club; (2) Admit to Friendship; (1) Admit to Family by Marriage.

However, ethnicity is not the only criterion by which we perceive the differentiation of people in an area and the creation of feelings of compatibility about these individuals. A number of other visual clues are used in the identification that lies behind any feelings of compatibility. For example, many of our clothes and personal possessions communicate what we like and perhaps even our values. The long skirts and bonnets of Amish and Hutterite women and the long hair and hats of the Hasidic Jew or the dreadlocks of the Rastaman communicate membership of various religious communities. Few attempts have been made by geographers to integrate the range of criteria by which we differentiate people in area. Ley (1983, 177–9) identified four basic criteria (age, clothing style, cosmetic management and race) which summarized the range of very different appearances of people entering a Vancouver Park. Each of these criteria were subdivided into a number of detailed features, and ten groups of males were identified as occupying various parts of the park from a graph linking neighbours on the basis of the seating dissimilarity indices. These groups were combinations of the individual criteria:

1. Young Adults (Young Mod, Young Casually Dressed, Native Indian, Young Hippy);

2. Middle-Aged Tramp;
3. Middle Aged-Elderly (Elderly Tramp, Elderly Well-Dressed, Middle-Aged Casually Dressed, Elderly Casually Dressed);
4. Oriental.

The Middle-Aged Tramps supplied the link between the generational clusters for they were the scavenger group that were more appropriately scattered than concentrated. To use the age-old phrase, 'birds of a feather' certainly did flock together to form distinctive groups of people found in different parts of the park, with the elderly near the Cenotaph!

As yet the number of different criteria by which we perceive differences in people is not completely determined, although it will be culture specific in terms of dress and management. Also it does seem appropriate to add other criteria to the set shown above, such as gender, and perhaps even gestures or behaviour which may alert others to a particular lifestyle or preference. There seems little doubt that most of us would feel uncomfortable entering an area containing young male adults wearing bikers' costumes, even in the absence of any unwelcome advances. This means that recognition alone is not the only factor: the types of people act as cues to our feelings in which empathy with the group or fear are particularly important, although these are only two of a range of affective dimensions that apply to places which will be discussed below.

Perspectives from Socio-Semiotics

During the last decade Lynch's work on the relevance of images and the structuring of our understanding of place-communities has been attacked on another set of grounds by those who have applied some of the ideas of semiotics to urban areas. Semiotics was developed originally by Ferdinand de Saussure as the study of signs, the search for the underlying structures behind languages. It has subsequently been applied to many fields, such as literary criticism by Roland Barthes and others, where it is used to identify the social ideology behind literary texts, or in socio-semiotics where the meanings behind material objects are related to the underlying social ideology. More recently its principles have been applied to urban areas (Gottdiener and Lagopoulos 1986). At its simplest level semiotics can be described as a system of signification, where a distinction is drawn between a material object (called the *signifier*), things that can be observed empirically, and the meaning the object portrays (that which is *signified*). The distinction can be expressed in the idea of a word having a denotative and connotative function. The first of these is the name by which it is known, the second is the meaning which the word seeks to convey.

An example may demonstrate the point. Two communities in Calgary are called University Heights and The Hamptons. These names can be viewed simply as terms that distinguish the area from others, perhaps designated by their locational associations. University Heights is adjacent to the university and its southern edge is bounded by a scarp that separates it from the former flood plain of the Bow. However, it is very likely that the name was deliberately chosen to convey other characteristics — a prestige associated with an institution of higher learning and the designation 'heights' to convey some social elevation, for the pejorative term 'flats' would be a more accurate topographical description. The new community of 'The Hamptons' cannot claim any such local association. It has a denotation that is linked to ancient settlements in England and more recent ones in upper-class America, whilst the word 'Estates' implies spacious lots. The obvious question is whether the denotative or connotative functions came first. If the former applies, the prestige associations are those which we have applied to the signifier — they derive from our general knowledge, from other signs or our culture in general. If the latter is the main explanation, then the individuals responsible for choosing the names thought of the need for upper-income associations first, and chose names that reflected the connotative meanings. The order of priority in

description is not a simple academic exercise, but is one fundamental to explanation.

The cognitive approach of Lynch which has been discussed above is based on the belief that the images are derived from our experience, thus implying that the meanings we have of places is derivative. Adherents of the semiotic approach would claim that the connotative function comes first. In our previous discussion on the naming of communities it was observed that planned communities in North America are packaged and advertised like other commodities. The name given to the object is deliberately chosen to convey some message — at least in the mind of the developer or advertiser. So the semiotic view does seem to be the more appropriate explanation.

Five important characteristics of signification must be stressed. First, these meanings cannot be observed directly: they are concepts that are embedded in the particular social or cultural system. Second, the meanings are not given, as in the denotative case — they are socially constructed and linked to the values of the assigning group and are part of a social discourse whereby the group knows or understands the underlying meaning through discourse or from knowledge obtained from previous situations. Third, these meanings may be shared by different groups or classes or they may be specific to individual groups. Fourth, the development industry deliberately searches for names that may be helpful in projecting the desired image. Given the recent riots in Los Angeles it is unlikely that Watts or Brentwood would be chosen for new developments, whereas Monterey or Carmel are acceptable because of their 'historic or upper-income' aura. Indeed, Monterey Park, a new community in the lower-income east side of Calgary, has recently advertised itself as 'come and experience a taste of California living'— although there is nothing in the area that could be claimed as relating to that state! Fifth, it must be remembered that urban landscapes are only what Ledrut (1986) calls pseudo-texts, for they have functions other than their signification. The most obvious example may be a house. Certainly its size and style may have

symbolic meanings to residents and outsiders — nevertheless, its primary function may still be as shelter and refuge. Davis (1990) in his study of Los Angeles provides a range of detailed insights into the naming of parts of the urban area and its symbolism.

Extending the Sense of Place: Affective Dimensions

Cognition, however, is not enough to capture the sense of place that is associated with neighbourhoods and place-communities in cities. Part of the mystique of urban neighbourhoods is that its residents feel some sense of belonging, perhaps an affinity with one another and the 'territory' within which they spend much of their lives. Although it has been shown how novelists create this sense of place in their books as a backcloth for their story, geographers, sociologists and social anthropologists have also sought different ways of expressing this sense of belonging to place. It is worth remembering that Park and his co-workers who developed the Chicago School of human ecology proposed *sentimental attachment* as one of the essential qualities of communities (see Table 3.1 in Chapter 3). However, it was Walter Firey's (1947) study of land-use change which began the systematic description of what has subsequently become known as the *social valuation* of place in which an important quality of the distinctiveness of area comes from the assignment of feelings and meanings to individual locales.

Firey believed it was impossible to explain the persistence of very different areas within central Boston by reference to the economic or ecological explanations of the Chicago School. Beacon Hill had persisted as a high status, exclusive inner-city district despite the pressures of urban growth because of the collective attitudes and actions of its inhabitants. Instead of selling houses to the highest bidder, the upper-class residents stayed because they were motivated by cultural and non-rational sets of values. The district was a symbol of the cultural heritage of the country, the site where many of the leading pre-revolutionary families of New England lived. As such, residents acquired status by living in the area: status in the minds of the élite as much as of the rest of the city. A residence in the area was seen by Firey as bestowing symbolic significance, so *symbolism* was placed alongside *sentiment* as what are now called the basic affective dimensions of place-communities in cities.

Humanistic geographers have been active in showing how shared values and common experiences transform a segment of space into a particular place. For example, Tuan (1977) described places as centres of 'felt value' and argued that what begins as undifferentiated space becomes distinctive 'place' as we come to know it better and endow it with value. Thus urban neighbourhoods are places which initially present a confusion of images to the new resident and which acquire viability through an effort of mind. It is perhaps Relph (1976) in his study *Place and Placelessness* who has provided the most incisive form of words to express 'place' in the humanistic perspective:

> Places are fusions of human and natural order and are significant centres of our immediate experiences of the world. They are defined less by unique locations, landscape, and communities than by the focusing of experiences and intentions onto particular settings. Places are not abstractions of concepts, but are directly experienced phenomena of the lived world and hence are full of meanings, with real objects, and with ongoing activities. They are important sources of individual and communal identity, and are often profound centres of human existence to which people have deep emotional and psychological ties. (Relph 1976, 141)

More recently the humanistic geographer, Anne Buttimer, wrote of the need for *anchoring-points* to which residents of a complex and confusing urban world could reach out in times of need. Also Seamon developed the idea of *place-ballet*: it is a 'community in place grounded in a bodily scale and interpersonal continuity' (see Buttimer and Seamon 1980). For Seamon, such a place must be founded in familiarity, part of which may arise from regularity of movements, although the fact of novelty and the unexpected may add something:

> the spontaneity of childplay, neighbours 'bumping into' one another, a community group quickly organizing to oppose a proposed street widening .... . Place, in other words, requires both regularity and variety, order and change. Place-ballet is one means by which a place comes to hold these qualities. (Buttimer and Seamon 1980, 163)

In addition one must take cognizance of studies more firmly founded on empirical work. Fried's (1963) evidence of 'Grieving for a lost home' is a collection of studies on the impact of urban renewal upon inner-city communities. Studies of this kind evoke a sense of place and attribute it to urban neighbourhoods. There is still a debate on whether such senses of place persist in the modern city or whether they are parts of the sentimentalities, or even the myths, of modern living.

Unfortunately, for those seeking some order or overview, some comprehensive summary of the different components in the affective domain, the humanistic approach has not been entirely successful. Although descriptive comments such as 'place-ballet' may be useful in creating an impression of the character of places, they are difficult to translate into defined concepts that are subject to verifiable study. However, it must be noted that those of an existential persuasion may deny that it is possible to agree on ways of creating common images. By contrast, the work of social psychologists and behavioural geographers is based on the premise that it is possible to identify common ideas and agree on ways in which investigators accept one another's findings. By using a battery of questions carefully designed to elicit particular attitudes, and quantitative techniques that allow the measurement of the distinctiveness of these attitudes and their respective strength, they have been able to isolate very different affective dimensions found in place-communities in cities. Obviously, this does not deny a role for humanistic approaches: their emphasis on individual, everyday experiences provides insights into the 'life-world' of individuals, not the abstracted elements of individual communities; their perception isolates the nuances of place, providing vivid descriptions of actual areas similar to the created world of novelists; and they may identify or provide clues to the isolation of additional affective dimensions. What their methodology makes difficult is the identification of these affective dimensions in more than an individual case or their refinement and measurement of strength. Added to this is the need for conformation from the work of different researchers, for not only have Unger and Wandersman (1985, 144) observed that there is little work on the affective qualities of neighbouring, but also there is a remarkable lack of consistency in the field. A variety of different dimensions have been proposed by many reviewers, for it is clear that the affective bonds that exist between people and place or neighbours are multidimensional. Unfortunately it is quite rare to find a clear separation of affective from other domains: divergent labels have been given to apparently similar dimensions and there seem to be quite substantial disciplinary differences in the content reviewed (see Wolpert et al. 1972; Unger and Wandersman 1985).

Definitions and Functions of Affective Dimensions

Eleven different affective dimensions associated with place-communities in cities can be identified. The list is still tentative, there being a pressing need to refine and probably to extend the dimensions (see Figure 3.2). In the discussion of these dimensions the distinctive function of each is highlighted in bold letters.

Sentiment as Attachment. Early work by Firey (1947) stressed the significance of positive, satisfied attitudes to their area of residence as 'sentiment'. Suttles (1972, 129) showed that sen-

timent was not a single, distinguishing feature: 'sentiments of *evaluation* of the local community and *attachment* to it are separate expressive orientations'. Additional quantitative questionnaire work (Unger and Wandersman 1985) has shown that the original concept needs to be split into two separate dimensions, and perhaps one should be called 'attachment' and the other 'evaluation'. *Attachment* is associated with the original meaning of the term sentiment and is distinguished as a hyphenated word to reflect this origin. It is linked to the function of what can be called the **degree of rootedness or stability** of a population. Suttles showed that positive or negative feelings about the place they live in seem to be related to social class and race, whereas their attachment, their rootedness, is more closely linked to an individual's social integration — the area and their interaction within it. The difference can be summarized in the oft-repeated expression: 'It may be a slum, but I like it because it's home'. Hence although an area may be evaluated as physically deteriorated, it is viewed positively in an attachment context. Nostalgia, even Fried's (1963) 'grieving for the lost home' described above, is often bound up with the attachment dimension, although it may be a separate component in historic communities.

Evaluation now seems to be clearly established as a separate dimension in the affective domain. Its function is to identify the **degree of satisfaction** that people have about their residential areas, in other words, its desirability as a place to live. The idea can be extended to consider *external appraisals*, characteristics that have been measured by many surveys of preferences for living in various areas of a city or region.

Nuisances and Annoyances. Attitudes towards the degree of satisfaction about a community are almost certainly complemented by specific feelings about the number and variety of annoyances felt by the residents, whether lack of privacy, intrusion by outsiders — especially parking — as well as unacceptable noise levels from neighbours or an external source such as aeroplanes or traffic, although Carp et al. (1976) identified noise as a separate source of variation from neighbours. These are often described as negative externalities providing the function of **community dissatisfaction** rather than satisfaction. Elsewhere (Herbert 1992) these have been described as neighbourhood **incivilities**.

Security and Safety. Several students of community variations (Sennett 1973, Tuan 1977) have stressed the need to consider the security or safety of areas, particularly in the often unfamiliar, even hostile, perhaps crime-ridden areas of contemporary inner cities. Much attention is currently being paid to designs and plans that inhibit crime and create defensible space (see the longer discussion in Chapter 8). Unfortunately, the precise character of the dimension has not been systematically measured in conjunction with other dimensions, although it is worth noting that Carp et al. (1976) separate *traffic danger* from safety of *persons and property*. This dimension has the function of identifying the relative degree of **fear or threat** present in different place-communities.

Empowerment. The affective domain should be extended to include a dimension that has the function of identifying the degree to which individuals feel they have **control over their area**, in the sense of being able to influence the future of their community. It has already been shown that the terms 'local control' or 'discretion' (Wolpert 1972) have been used by previous workers to describe this concept. By calling for individuals to become 'helpgivers' instead of 'helpseekers', the desire is to provide a great degree of participation. Empower-ment is really a single dimension, which can be described by a sense of civic duty, political efficacy, perceived personal confidence and the willingness to lead, and is negatively related to alienation. Empowerment may be observed as a continuum by which individuals joining an organization may move through several stages which include observation, various forms of participation and eventually, for some at least,

leadership. Really active organizations may allow this type of progression for each member, although it is far from clear that all individuals would wish to take the group or leadership roles, whilst senior-level opportunities are certainly not available to all who would wish to serve. Empowerment is not simply a matter of the internal issues; it relates to the milieu in which the community is set and in this context there is an important difference between *actual* power and *perceived* power: it is the latter that is in the affective domain in community settings, the feeling that members *really are able* to do something about their concerns.

Symbolism of Place. This was first recognized in Firey's work in Boston (1947) and has been discussed above as the way areas have the function of producing **enhanced or decreased status** for its residents. It must be stressed that the concept is different from that of symbolic communication, which is best recognized as a characteristic of the cognitive domain.

Property Appearance. There seems little doubt that attitudes towards a community are very much influenced by its appearance, especially by its tidiness, its level of maintenance, etc. In part this represents what Williams (1985) described as Internal Reciprocity, which was the link between physical conditions and a resident's perception. Appearance has the function of identifying the extent of **potential social malaise or contentment**. As yet there is little consistency in the scale of criteria used to measure the appearance of areas, in part because the indicators used will vary according to the morphology of different areas. Coleman (1985, 22–30) used the presence of litter, graffiti, property damage, the presence of urine and deposits of faeces as increasingly severe indicators of the degree of social malaise in public housing projects in London, although Coleman's objective was to show there were strong associations with building design and a lack of control by residents over their space — the defensible space argument discussed in Chapter 6). Again, the neighbourhood incivilities label (Herbert 1992) is appropriate.

Latent Participation (Neighbours). This dimension can be related to Carp et al.'s (1976) element called 'neighbours' and Unger and Wandersman's (1985) 'sense of latent mutual aid', the feeling or belief that people in an area really would help if the need arose — such as a family crisis that entailed neighbours looking after children. Intuitively, it seems possible to identify various scales of assumed aid. This concept is very much an attitudinal one, and should be distinguished from the actual provision of aid, the manifest mutual aid and instrumental support that is part of the interactional component of community variation. Its function is simply related to the **level of expected mutual aid**.

Aesthetics should also be considered to be a separate affective dimension, although it must be stressed that the aesthetic sense will be culture-specific. Harrison and Sarre (1975) identified a 'liked and beautiful' versus 'disliked and ugly' dimension among the three dimensions identified in their study of the classic Georgian resort of Bath, England, contrasting the Georgian areas of the city from the working-class, industrialized areas. Aesthetics may prove to be a very complicated dimension to deal with, given very different values and preferences, since its function is linked to features such as **beauty or order**.

Common Values. Many descriptive accounts of place-communities emphasize the way in which areas can be distinguished because the inhabitants share similar beliefs and mores, the whole contributing to the extent to which there can be **interpersonal influence or common behaviour**. Williams' (1985) 'critical consciousness' domain and 'sense of community' come closest to the concept being expressed here. However, it must be emphasized that it is most unlikely that a single set of values apply in any area in the modern world, given the typical diversity of the populace: it may be better seen as a tendency, rather than a rigid characteristic, except in communities founded on adherence to a set of rules which are rigidly enforced. Variations will occur between areas. In the case of the black American ghetto, Anderson (1978, 210) observed: 'when

jobs are not available, living up to rules of conduct based on the values of "decency" become difficult.' Strategies for survival which are weighted down by the negative qualities of areas leave little room for development of the positive sides of local community. There is also evidence that against these odds, the option of withdrawing from neighbourhood is real. Williams and Kornblum (1985) record that teenage mothers in the ghetto spend 'hours and hours' watching television, thus acquiring more ideas from the media than from one another, and increasing their already severe isolation.

Empathy or Sense of Belonging. Less clear is the need to define a separate source of variation linked to *community belonging*. This would be an emotional connection relating to some psychological sense of belonging to an area and its people, one that relates to others and is additional to the degree of rootedness in the attachment construct. As such, the dimension can be considered to have the function of **social cohesion or integration**. Although Unger and Wandersman (1985) identify this feature as a persistent characteristic of communities, the use of different questionnaire data, and varied dimensional titles make it difficult to be conclusive about the presence of the dimension. This dimension is proposed as a separate affective construct, although it is possible that 'belonging' may be that 'sense of community' best regarded as a composite of all these separate dimensions (Weenig et al. 1990).

The distinctiveness of communities, therefore, can be seen as derived from the incidence, strength and combination of these various affective dimensions, together with the various elements from the areal content and behavioural domains. It is possible that empirical research will show additional dimensions or that some of these hypothesized dimensions may be generalized into a number of more limited types. Thus, Unger and Wandersman's summary (1985) identified three basic affective groups containing a series of subdimensions, namely: sense of mutual aid (manifest and latent); sense of community (associated with membership, influence, value-sharing and emotional linkages);

and attachment to place (attachment and satisfaction). It is clear that the subdivisions shown in brackets correspond to some of the dimensions described above.

This summary catalogue of the various components of the affective domain would not be complete without additional reference to the relevance of two of the other basic domains identified in Chapter 3 — those relating to the externality (the various geographical spaces) and to the dynamic changes that occasionally occur in neighbourhoods.

Externality

Place-communities in cities, of whatever size, create attitudes that may be very different in the eyes of *insiders*, those who live in an area, compared with the *outsiders* — whether these be people who work in the area and live outside, residents in the surrounding areas, or city planners, private developers, etc. There is no necessary reason for their attitudes to coincide.

Dynamic change

Two different issues need to be distinguished in the context of time. First there is a time-dependency in a daily, weekly or even seasonal context: this can be summarized as *episodic transformations*. Cordell's description of the day and night changes in Tiger Bay quoted earlier provides one example. In more familiar situations there are probably few parks in which women feel comfortable, or safe, at night, whereas the same group will use them intensively in the day. Similarly, most neighbourhoods can be transformed when an issue acts as a catalyst, transforming the normal relationships. Bell and Newby (1978) and Tuan (1977) described this as the difference between 'latent and active senses of place', the former describing neighbourhoods that 'come to life' on particular occasions, such as at times of celebration or threat. The process of change has been summarized as follows:

Emotion begins to tinge the whole neighbourhood drawing on and extrapolating from, the direct experience of its particular parts — when the neighbourhood is perceived to have rivals and to be threatened in some way, real or imagined. Then the warm sentiment one has for a street corner broadens to include the larger area. (Tuan 1977, 88)

Affected people often band together to prevent change, perhaps heightening their sense of fellow-feeling. So it is at times of crisis, not in normal everyday experience, that the deepest community identifications may be formed. Chapter 6 describes how community activists deliberately seek this type of confrontation in their mobilization of communities. Second, it is clear that *long-term changes* can occur in the affective dimensions through time, just as in the cognitive context. Common experiences that apply to many people will often enhance the degree of cohesion. However, several publicized violent acts may destroy a neighbourhood's safe image.

Finally, neighbourhood, as a local place-community, acquires fullest meaning when it is invested with an individual's experiences and values, a set of remembered contemporaries, and with a generational history which gives continuity over time. St Urban was not only the stage on which Richler's Jewish boys played out their childhood, it was the ethnic hearth in an alien city, the place carved out as haven in the New World by their parents, grandparents and the whole social network of family and friends. The nature of their lifestyle within St Urban was structured by their class, ethnicity and their distance from resources and power. Within St Urban they created a culture, and that culture reflected their position within society as well as their own customs, traditions and values. To paraphrase Jackson (1989), the neighbourhood was imbued with symbolic significance, although it was conditioned also by the material world of which it was part. Social contexts gave neighbourhood its material standards; its inhabitants added the gloss of character which is summarized in these cognitive and affective dimensions.

Applications

This discussion of place community character, a place identity, needs to be complemented by the interactional issues described in Chapters 3 and 4 — issues that relate to the formation of actual contacts and interactions among people. However, the cognitive and affective domains summarized as conceptual identity need not only be considered in an academic or dispassionate sense. Many of the ideas can be used in an *applied context*. The methods that have been used to isolate mental maps of neighbourhood make them available to external reference. Hence the definitions and dimensions produced have been variously used as bases for discussion about new units of local government (Herbert and Raine 1976), as a means of testing the efficiency of political and service area boundaries (Pacione 1984), or helping to evaluate the functioning and maintenance of neighbourhood organizations (Unger and Wandersman 1985). Following his detailed study of a Glasgow study area, Pacione concluded:

> It is possible to extract individuals' cognitive representations of their home areas by employing a carefully designed mapping procedure ... the present investigation permitted the identification of a set of popularly acknowledged urban neighbourhoods with well demarcated boundaries. Political and service-area boundaries generally reflect administrative convenience rather than neighbourhood or local community feeling. (Pacione 1984, 387)

Obviously it would make more sense to base the local delivery of certain services upon the active area recognized by residents; however, most of the units within cities are too small and usually too diffuse to provide the threshold population for commercial or municipal services. On other levels, such as those described in the section on community-of-interest areas between settlements, definitions of new government units have often taken the cognitive and interactive community areas into account in the revisions. In the same way the affective dimensions may be deliberately manipulated to enhance the 'sense of place' of community residents.

More recently attempts have been made to use the principles obtained from these cognitive and affective domains to counteract the trend to increasingly anonymous or 'no-place' areas. Modern planners and developers charged with the renewal of communities seemed, at times, to have accelerated these trends. Johnson (quoted in Ley 1989, 52) described his feelings of modern Texan cities, although it may not be shared by residents: 'There is no sense of place. These skyscrapers are like individual tombstones in a cemetery.'

All too frequently, urban neighbourhoods are often idealized as close-knit, integrated places — *historic remembered places* — on which people look back with nostalgia. This is a harking-back to times before ease of transport, when communities shared a common space and common adversities which drew them together. The 'village in the city' idea, as portrayed in London's East End or New York's Greenwich Village perhaps half a century ago, is one example of this nostalgia. However, criticisms of the present are more than yearnings for the past. When Jacobs (1961) reacted against the onslaught of post-war urban renewal and rational planning, her plea was for the retention of 'people-places', the preservation of communities and the personalizing of space, for neighbourhood on a human scale. More specifically Goodey (1974) proposed a still useful tripartite division of how a place can be 'socially-engineered' by urban design.

1. Sense of place with *the accent on sense* pointed up the responsibilities of designers or planners to anticipate ways in which users will react to their local environments.
2. Sense of place as *feeling of occasion* evoked the time-occasion sense of place and could be linked to the heritage place idea. Events linked to a specific place gave it a special meaning, a sense of place which should be preserved.

3. Sense of place *as an essential ingredient for future environments* reminded planners of the need to incorporate it in new communities, to help form place on a human scale. This is not the place to discuss such issues further. The evolution of attempts to plan areas to create community feelings is discussed in Chapter 8 and demonstrates how at least some of the cognitive and affective dimensions examined here are being incorporated in new communities.

Conclusions

The chapter has reviewed ways in which literary, humanistic and behavioural ideas can be used to understand the elements or components of a 'sense of place' in local urban communities or neighbourhoods. These ideas are now known as the cognitive and affective domains that form the images of places, our social constructions, and have been identified by very different methods to the qualitative and subjective criteria exemplified by the use of imaginative literature. Unfortunately the study of the identification and measurement of these dimensions in intra-urban communities is still in its infancy, and the examples of community typologies that incorporate these features have been shown to be very limited. This is why literature still has an important part to play as a source of the content of area, of ideas, as well as the conveyance of meanings. Although descriptive writing will include accounts of buildings, streets and local point of conflux such as bar, store or school, it is inevitably the people, memories and experiences of particular localities which give them real meaning. As Richler's characters return to look at a street and a building, it is not the fabric of the place which touches their emotions, but rather the recall of events, people and contacts which they associate with it. This is the essence of the humanistic view of place. The test of the continuity of neighbourhood is whether these meanings can still be found or created in our cities. When writers such as Ford convey an image of 'no-

place' they throw doubts on this continuity. The reasons may be many. More self-containment within the home, less reliance on neighbours and life in the street, a diminution in shared values and problems. Although literature reflects these changes, the social science research community needs to develop various ways of testing its reality by measuring the specific types of cognitive and affective dimensions.

The credentials of a humanistic approach to the study of local community or neighbourhood relate to wider issues on the humanistic perspective and the way in which local 'cultures' can be studied. The debate over ways in which the subjective view of neighbourhood can be advanced relates directly to the debate on the tension between the 'local' and the 'structural'. Duncan and Savage (1991) state that culture is not the product of an economic base or social structure; it is the means by which people gain identities and create their social world. Cox and Mair (1991) argue that a conceptual framework is needed which does not lose sight of the reciprocal relationship between localized and wider-scale social processes. Humanistic perspectives developed partly in response to the neglect of people as active agents: now there is some recognition that the urgency to bring back subjectivity, meanings and values may have provoked too radical a reaction:

> In retrieving men from virtual oblivion in positivist science, humanists have tended to celebrate the restoration perhaps too much. As a result values, meanings, consciousness, creativity, and reflection may well have been overstated, while context, constraint, and social stratification have been under-developed. (Ley 1981, 252)

These types of relationships need to be explored in more detail. They will both modify and add to the sense of place idea and provide it with more tangible links to social context. Social contexts gave neighbourhood its material standards; its inhabitants added the gloss of character which is summarized in the cognitive and affective dimensions.

References

Anderson, E., 1978, *A place on the corner*, University of Chicago Press, Chicago.

Appleyard, D., 1970, Styles and methods of structuring a city, *Environment and Behaviour*, 2, 100–17.

Barrell, J., 1972, *The idea of landscape and the sense of place: 1730–1840*, Cambridge University Press, England.

Barrell, J., 1982, The geographies of Hardy's Wessex, *Journal of Historical Geography*, 8, 347–61.

Beck, R. and Wood, D., 1976, Cognitive transformation of information from urban geographic fields to mental maps, *Environment and Behaviour*, 8, 199–238.

Bell, C. and Newby, H., 1978, Community, communion, class and community action, in D. T. Herbert and R. J. Johnston (eds), *Social Areas in Cities*, John Wiley, Chichester, 189–207.

Birch, B. P., 1981, Wessex, Hardy and the nature novelists, *Transactions, Institute of British Geographers*, 8, 347–61.

Boulding, K., 1956, *The image: knowledge in life and society*, University of Michigan Press, Ann Arbor.

Borgadus, E., 1925, Measuring social distance, *Journal of Applied Sociology*, 9, 299–308.

Bowden, L. W., 1972, How to define neighbourhood, *Professional Geographer*, 24, 227–8.

Boyle, M. J. and Robinson, M. E., 1979, Cognitive mapping and understanding, in D. T. Herbert and R. J. Johnston (eds), *Geography and the urban environment*, V, 2, John Wiley, Chichester, England, 418–29.

Buttimer, A. and Seamon, D. (eds), 1980, *The human experience of space and place*, Croom Helm, London.

Canter, D., 1977, *The psychology of place*, Architectural Press, London.

Carp, F., Zawadski, R. T. and Shotrkon, H., 1976, Dimensions of urban environmental quality, *Environment and Behaviour*, 8, 239–64.

Coleman, A., 1985, *Utopia on trial*, Hilary Shipman, London.

Cordell, A., 1984, *Peerless Jim*, Hodder and Stoughton, London.

Cox, K. R. and Mair, A., 1991, From localised social structures to localities as agents, *Environment and Planning*, A, 23, 197–213.

Crane, S., 1892, *An omnibus*, R. W. Stallman (ed.), Knopf, New York, 1950.

Cybriwsky, R., 1978, Social aspects of neighbourhood change, *Annals, Association of American Geographers*, 68, 17–33.

Davis, M., 1990, *City of quartz: excavating a future for Los Angeles*, Verso, London.

Downs, R. M. and Stea, D., 1973, *Image and environment*, Aldine, Chicago.

Duncan, S. and Savage, M., 1991, New perspectives on the locality debate, *Environment and Planning*, A, 23, 156.

Durrell, L., 1969, *Spirit of place: letters and essays on travel*, E. P. Dutton, New York.

Farrell, J. T., 1932, *The young manhood of Studs Lonigan*, Forum Books, New York, 1948.

Firey, W., 1947, *Land use in central Boston*, Harvard University Press, Cambridge, Mass.

Fitzgerald, F. S., 1925, *The great Gatsby*, Schriber, New York, new edition 1953.

Ford, R., 1986, *The Sportswriter*, Collins-Harvill, London.

Ford, R., 1988, *Rock Springs*, Collins-Harvill, London.

Fried, M., 1963, Grieving for a lost home, in L. H. Duhl (ed.), *The urban condition*, Basic Books, New York, 151–71.

Gans, H., 1962, *The urban villagers*, Free Press, New York.

Gaster, S., 1991, Urban children's access to neighbourhood, *Environment and Behaviour*, 23, 70–85.

Gifi, A., 1981, *Non-linear multivariate analysis*, Department of Data Theory, University of Leiden, Netherlands.

Gill, A., 1989, Experimenting with environmental design research in Canada's newest mining town, *Applied Geography*, 9, 171–95.

Goodey, B., 1974, *Images of place*, Centre for Urban and Regional Studies, Birmingham.

Gottdiener, M. and Lagopoulos, A. P. (eds), 1986, *The city and the sign*, Columbia University Press, New York.

Harrison, J. A. and Sarre, P., 1975, Personal construct theory in the measurement of environmental image, *Environment and Behaviour*, 7, 3–58.

Hay, R. B., 1987, Senses of place: experiences from the Cowichan Valley, British Columbia, in R. Letteron, M. Roche and M. Sheperd (eds), *Geography and society in global context*, Proceedings of the Conference of New Zealand Geographers, 278–88.

Herbert, D. T., 1992, Neighbourhood incivilities and crime, *Area*, (forthcoming).

Herbert, D. T. and Peace, S. M., 1980, The elderly in an urban environment: a study of Swansea, in D. T. Herbert and R. J. Johnston (eds), *Geography and the urban environment*, 3, John Wiley, Chichester, England, 223–55.

Herbert, D. T. and Raine, J. W., 1976, Defining communities within urban areas, *Town Planning Review*, 47, 325–38.

Hojacki, W., 1979, What is a neighborhood? *Social Policy*, September–October, 47–52.

Irving, H., 1978, Space and environment in interpersonal relations in D. T. Herbert and R. J. Johnston (eds), *Geography and the urban environment, 1*, John Wiley, Chichester, England, 249–84.

Jackson, P., 1989, *Maps of meaning*, Unwin-Hyman, London.

Jacobs, J., 1961, *Death and life of great American cities*, Random House, New York.

Kirasic, K. C. and Mathes, E. A., 1990, Effects of different means for conveying environmental information on elderly adults' spatial cognition and behaviour, *Environment and Behaviour, 22*, 591–607.

Ladd, F. C., 1970, Black youths view their environment: neighbourhood maps, *Environment and Behaviour, 2*, 74–99.

Lawrence, D. H., 1969, *Studies in classic American literature*, Viking Press, New York.

Ledrut, R., 1986, The images of the city, in M. Gottdiener and A. P. Lagopoulos (eds), *The city and the sign*, Columbia University Press, New York.

Lee, T. R., 1954, A study of urban neighbourhood. Unpublished PhD, Cambridge.

Lee, T. R., 1968, Urban neighbourhood as a socio-spatial schema, *Human Relations, 21*, 241–67.

Lee, T. R., 1976, Cities in the mind, in D. T. Herbert and R. J. Johnston (eds), *Social areas in cities*, John Wiley, Chichester, England, 253–81.

Ley, D., 1981, Cultural and humanistic geography, *Progress in Human Geography, 5*, 249–57.

Ley, D., 1983, *A social geography of the city*, Harper and Row, New York.

Ley, D., 1989, Modernism, post-modernism and the struggle for space, in J. A. Agnew and J. S. Duncan (eds), *The power of place*, Unwin-Hyman, Boston, 44–65.

Ley, D. and Cybriwsky, R., 1974, Urban graffiti as territorial markers, *Annals, Association of American Geographers, 64*, 491–505.

Lodge, D., 1991, The sense of place, *Independent on Sunday*, 20.

Lowenthal, D., 1961, Geography, experience and imagination: towards a geographical epistemology, *Annals, Association of American Geographers, 51*, 241–60.

Lowry, M., 1947, *Under the volcano*, Jonathan Cape, London.

Lynch, K., 1960, *The image of the city*, MIT Press, Cambridge, Massachusetts.

Matthews, M. H., 1984, Environmental cognition of young children: images of journeys to school and home area, *Transactions, Institute of British Geographers, 9*, 89–105.

Pacione, M., 1984, Local areas in the city, in D. T. Herbert and R. J. Johnston (eds), *Geography and the urban environment, 6*, John Wiley, Chichester, England, 349–92.

Pocock, D. and Hudson, R., 1978, *Images of the urban environment*, Macmillan, London.

Porteous, J. D., 1985, Literature and humanistic geography, *Area, 17*, 117–22.

Relph, E., 1976, *Place and placelessness*, Pion, London.

Richler, M., 1964, *The apprenticeship of Duddy Kravitz*, Penguin, London.

Richler, M., 1972, *St. Urbain's horseman*, Bantam Books, Toronto.

Sennett, R., 1973, *The uses of disorder*, Penguin, Harmondsworth.

Smith, R. E., 1985, Activism and social status as determinants of neighbourhood identity, *Professional Geographer, 37*, 421–32.

Soja, E. W., 1989, *Postmodern geographies: the reassertion of space in critical social theory*, Verso, London.

Suttles, G., 1972, *The social construction of communities*, University of Chicago Press.

Tuan, Y. F., 1977, *Space and place; the perspective of experience*, Edward Arnold, London.

Unger, D. G. and Wandersman, A., 1985, The importance of neighbours: the social, cognitive and affective components of neighbouring, *American Journal of Community Psychology, 13*, 139–69.

Walmsley, D. J., 1988, *Urban living: the individual in the city*, Longman, Harlow, England.

Watson, J. W., 1983, The soul of geography, Presidential Address, *Transactions of British Geographers, 8*, 385–99.

Watson, J. W., 1979, *Social geography of the United States*, Longman, London.

Weenig, M., Schmidt, T. and Midden, C., 1990, Social dimensions of neighbourhoods and the effectiveness of information programs, *Environment and Behaviour, 22* (1), 27–54.

Wheatley, P., 1971, *The pivot of the four quarters*, Aldine, Chicago.

Williams, M. R., 1985, *Neighbourhood organizations: seeds of a new urban life*, Greenwood Press, Westport.

Williams, R., 1977, *Marxism and literature*, Oxford University Press, Oxford.

Williams, R., 1981, *Culture*, Fontana, London.

Williams, T. and Kornblum, W., 1985, *Growing up poor*, Lexington Press, Lexington, Mass.

Wolpert, J. et al., 1972, Metropolitan neighbourhoods: participation and conflict over change. Resource Paper No. 16, Association of American Geographers, Washington, DC.

6

Community Development: The Conscious Development of Communities in Cities

Introduction

Community development is not an easy field to summarize or to define, as many reviews (Sanders 1958) and books have shown (Christenson and Robinson 1989). This is partly owing to its relatively recent development as a separate academic and professional field from the late 1940s, and the fact that the major specialist journals are barely a quarter of a century old. For example, in Britain the *Community Development Journal* started publishing in 1965; in the United States the *Journal of the Community Development Society* began in 1970; and, from the Centre for Neighborhood Technology (Chicago) since 1977, the more popularistic *The Neighborhood Works*. However, its biggest problem arises from a diffuse focus due to several factors: its overlap with so many academic disciplines, such as sociology, political science, economics and geography; a tradition of professional practice linked to applied fields, such as planning, administration and social welfare; and a content area that relates as much to Third World rural development as it does to western inner-city and rural area change. Moreover, Sanders (1958) showed that community development can be viewed in four ways: as a *process*, in the sense of a progress between conditions through time; as a *method*, as a means to achieve some end; as a *programme*, in the sense of carrying out some procedures to produce some action; and a *movement*, through the commitment of people to some cause. Not surprisingly, this variety of approaches has meant that the field has been summarized in a number of different ways (Christenson and Robinson 1989, 11–12) but

the variety of options can be crystallized as follows: *community development is the purposeful, locality-based attempt of people — either from inside or outside an area — to initiate some action to improve their local environment, associations, services and other attributes in their area.* These conscious actions not only entail the local satisfaction of needs but also the creation or stimulation of local organizations or delivery systems to provide or monitor these features. This latter issue is the focus of this chapter, in which the emphasis is upon the principles and problems, *not* on case studies of particular examples. The needs that are satisfied are discussed in Chapter 7.

Reasons for Community Development

Participation Chapter 2 has described how the earliest human settlements were based on the principle of self-help, where there was co-operation between individuals. The development of larger, urban-based states, with centralization of authority, led to the loss of local control and participation. The philosophical rationale against this seemingly inexorable trend in the evolution of society, with the conscious development of horizontal or locality-based associations, rather than the vertical links to higher levels of society, can be traced back to the ancient Greeks. Aristotle, particularly, encouraged people in the new polis, or city-state, to join together in fellowship to create a better life (Barker 1969). Downey (1976) observed that Aristotle's use of the term *koinonia* to describe these new communities was confusing, for it can be interpreted as 'partnership' and 'association' as well as community. Yet whatever shade of meaning is implied the *koinonia* of the polis or city-state was considered the best setting in which man, released from complete dependence upon other-worldly abstractions, could attain 'the supreme good' by the enjoyment of mutual association, the fulfilment of basic needs and the addition of meaning to life. In essence, Aristotle articulated the fact that the polis provided another scale of *koinonia*, one beyond the basic association in social life — the household. The city-state community was an entity with dynamic energy, with the ability to transform life to one that was based on reciprocal relationships between residents, with obligations on both sides. However, this entity was never the only one: administrative subdivisions within the city-state and later in cities of the Roman empire were used to organize the political entity or provide functions at a more localized level. The Greek and Roman heritage should *not* be seen as the only case in which people had the right and the duty to participate in urban corporate life. Rather it was the intellectual fountainhead for a set of ideas that intermittently resurface in the western urban tradition, from guild privileges in many west European urban settlements to the late seventeenth-century ideas of political philosophers such as Locke and Hobbes discussed in Chapter 2. This contrasts with the arguments made about urban centres in Asian countries, where subservience to higher levels of political authority was a consistent theme (Murphey 1954; Wheatley 1971). This background may provide a philosophical rationale for the development of communities within cities, in the sense defined above, and illustrates the historic utility of the 'resident participation' factor in the five reasons for community action that have been identified in a recent article by Keyes (1987).

Reaction against change Community development often begins as a reaction against some proposed change in the local area, one that is perceived as having negative consequences in the sense of disrupting the quality of life of the residents in an area. This is the type called 'area or turf-based defence' by Keyes (1987). Plans to build a new highway through a community, resulting in the destruction of homes and adding to noise and pollution has been an important cause of community action. Similar reactions have come from the construction of new office-blocks, shopping-malls, the expansion of sports stadia, exhibition areas, or reductions in the size of green areas. Similarly, the invasion of an area by transients, prostitutes, or other groups seen as undesirables, has often produced reaction from local residents who combine to resist or modify the changes or plans for change that are negatively perceived. This frequently leads to conflict between the various interest groups in the city (Cox and Johnston 1982; Knox 1987, Chapter 7).

Modification of conditions The second set of causal explanations are those attempts to solve, mitigate or at least stabilize the severe social and economic problems of a local urban community. This is the 'local control' argument of Keyes (1987). The best examples can be found in inner-city areas plagued by high levels of poverty, crime, unemployment, obsolescence in housing and other facilities, and environmental degradation in general. Community-based action programmes in the most disadvantaged areas have frequently been used to attack these seemingly intractable problems, although these have often been criticized by those who see the problems as a consequence of the distribution of economic rewards systems in capitalist society (Harvey 1973, 1985; Badcock 1984). These are briefly discussed in Chapter 7: Community Associations and Actions.

Missing needs or resources Community action is often initiated by individuals, from inside or outside the area, who wish to satisfy some need in a local community which is not being effectively provided by private enterprise or government. This is the 'local resources' factor of Keyes (1987). In the suburbs of most North American cities the organization of children's sports teams and many adult recreational facilities has historically been provided by voluntary community groups.

These four major reasons for community development are not always mutually exclusive. Also they need to be extended to include the 'communication of opinion' factor, such as when local associations are consulted in matters of planning policy or changes (see Chapter 7), and the creation of 'liaison networks' with other organizations. Many community development programmes often include elements of all categories, especially in the inner city, although the 'needs and resources' issue may be paramount here. The fourth reason is more typical in middle-class suburbs. In all cases, however, community development occurs because problems, as perceived by the residents of the local area, are not being solved by existing authorities or by private initiative. The stress on 'perceived' problems is deliberate: a problem to a local resident may not be considered as such by a city official or exploitive slum landlord. In other words, some deliberate community-based development seems essential if there is to be a positive improvement.

Alternative Delivery Systems

Community development is usually considered in three different ways: by the *technical assistance, self-help, critical or conflict approaches* (Christensen and Robinson, 1989). However, they were often preceded by *philanthropic endeavour or charity* so it is logical to consider this first. Obviously the methods do not include private enterprise schemes that also provide local services or satisfy needs: these are activities and organizations carried out without reference to the community. In the rest of this discussion the basic features of each approach, together with their key problems and utility will be identified. It will be shown that no single method is suitable for all purposes: indeed the four approaches tend to concentrate on different aspects of community development. Nevertheless, there are also some similarities: the Philanthropic and Technical Assistance approaches both entail change

by outside agents, whereas the Self-Help and Conflict methods depend primarily — though not exclusively — upon the participation of local residents. Hence the last section will endeavour to integrate the various stages, providing a summary of the key issues that have to be addressed in the successful development of communities.

Charity and Philanthropic Assistance

Since time immemorial societies have struggled with the problem of catering for those incapable of caring for themselves, especially paupers, the aged, the homeless, 'fallen' women and orphans. In medieval society many were supported by the church or by feudal barons as part of their obligations to retainers or supporters, whilst they depended upon the philanthropy of the *nouveaux riches* after the commercial and industrial revolutions in Britain (Owen 1964) and America (Bremner 1960). In Britain from the sixteenth century onwards the state developed successive Poor Laws to provide at least the minimum for survival, with workhouses and relief supported by local taxes and delivered by parishes. Nevertheless, these were never enough, for the nineteenth century saw an explosion in the numbers of outcasts in society as Jones (1971) showed in London. Chapter 3 has already outlined how social commentators, as diverse as Mayhew, Engels and Booth, described the growing problems of poverty, crime and housing in the large and expanding cities of the western world. Others went further and attempted not simply to educate the public about these areas but also deliberately to change them through the development or modification of political parties to alter the redistributive basis of society. Such national approaches are beyond this study. Instead the discussion examines the other route to change: that of local or community development.

There is no doubt that Christian churches fulfilled a role in this task of social betterment in local communities, although all too frequently they supported the status quo and acceptance of the conditions in this life by promising a better one in heaven. More radical Christians operated in different ways. For example, The Salvation Army, developed by William Booth as the East London Revival Society in 1865, and renamed in 1878, was an attempt to create a new kind of Christian church, one that was designed to improve the conditions of the poorest of the poor in the slums. In addition, two essentially secular approaches can also be recognized.

The first lay in the establishment of *local charity organizations* to mitigate the poverty and despair in big industrial and commercial cities where new migrants had nobody to turn to in case of distress. Most began with the provision of food, shelter and medical help to residents in poorer areas, and evolved into organizations that paid more attention to the underlying causes of poverty and social conditions, such as insanitary houses, overcrowding, child labour, sweat shops, etc. For example, by 1878 in Philadelphia there were twenty-three charity societies organized in wards within the city, which not only dispensed their own funds in their area but also organized themselves into a city-wide council based on two members from each area (Dillick 1953). Similarly philanthropists, such as Carnegie (Bobinski 1969) in the case of libraries, spent fortunes in the provision of other needs that may not have been satisfied by local co-operation or entrepreneurial activity.

A later device was the creation of so-called *settlement houses* in the slum areas, places which attempted to enlighten and improve local life by example and education, not by charity alone. In many ways they can be seen as an outgrowth of F. D. Maurice's pioneering Working Men's College in London in 1854 which attempted to combat urban degradation through popular education (Lees 1985). Staffed by members of the intellectual or social élite who had sufficient conscience to want to help the impoverished, these houses and meeting-halls obtained money by charitable donations from the rich and professional help by volunteers from the universities or educated classes.

Settlement houses provided courses in social and educational improvement. These programmes were designed to act as moral beacons amidst the dark satanic mills, so eloquently described by contemporary novelists and social commentators. They were designed to spread self-improvement and hope for the impoverished to surrounding areas by enlisting the most fortunate to improve the area. The first of these was Toynbee Hall established in Whitechapel in London in 1884 through the efforts of the parish priest, Samuel Barnett, who invited a group of university students to help improve the area. The idea spread to America (Davis 1967) and the most famous American example, Hull House, was set up by the Adams sisters in Chicago in 1889 (Adams 1910, Lees 1985). By 1900 it has been estimated there were 103 such settlement houses in the United States and 400 by 1910 (Dillick 1953, Hillman 1960). All were designed to help people in deprived neighbourhoods through the relief of poverty, care of neglected children, removal of unsanitary conditions and the sponsoring of a range of activities: day care, playgrounds, public health and public education in general. These activities helped millions of people and provided beacons of hope in a life that was often full of despair and dependency. They were emulated by the development of workers' institutes and libraries in hundreds of communities.

There seems little doubt that many individuals affected by these settlements did attain an improved life. However, many of those who gained the most left the impoverished areas to practice their new skills in other parts of the city. In other words, although these approaches transformed the life of many individuals, they did not necessarily permanently transform the areas in which they were located. The biggest permanent effect of the charity and philanthropic approach may have been to alter the attitude of society and eventually governments to conditions within cities. From the turn of the century most western governments gradually accepted the need to provide many of the health, education, library and welfare functions pioneered by charities and settlement houses. Our emphasis on the English-speaking world should not lead us to discount the role of other nations, for Lees (1985) has described the greater advances made in big German cities and in particular the influence of the Dresden Exhibition in 1907. This growth in municipal effort often led to the demise of the philanthropic organizations as effective agents for intra-urban community change. However, the decline has not been absolute. Some church organizations — especially the Salvation Army — have maintained their historic concern with the outcasts of society, providing meals and shelter for the homeless in the worst slum areas of cities. This is not the last remnant of charity in an increasingly affluent society, as was believed by many in the 1950s and 1960s, or of philanthropic effort. In the last twenty years an increasing number of people have joined the ranks of the unemployed, whilst the number of homeless (Dear and Wolch 1987; Heilman and Dear 1988) has been increasing at the same time. One result has been a revival in charity organizations in many spheres. For example, in Canada there were 292 registered food bank charities in 1991, serving over 2 million people or 7.5 per cent of the Canadian population, a rapid increase from the first example established in Edmonton in 1981 (Oderkirk 1992). With increasing cut-backs in the level of government provision due to the neo-conservative philosophy of the 1980s, and the debt problems of western governments, it is likely that charity organizations will thrive rather than disappear.

Technical Assistance

The technical assistance approach describes the delivery of programmes or services to a local area in a city by the intervention of some higher government authority, such as the municipal authority, state or nation. Essentially it is a type of 'top–down' process, requiring the use of experts — usually with some technical or professional capability — who are introduced to the community to fulfil

some local needs, to provide goods, services or facilities that are unlikely to be provided in any other way.

In the early nineteenth century the prevailing *laissez-faire* philosophy meant that most national or state governments did not intervene in the development of cities. However, the explosive growth of the industrial cities led to crises in public order, public health, housing and poverty, and these problems led to demands for city governments to take a more active role (Hall 1988). Municipalities responded in two ways. *Direct action* led to the provision of infrastructure to eradicate health problems, such as in creating a safe water supply and building sewage facilities, or the organization and maintenance of public order by policing, or the provision of education and welfare services. The *indirect* approach consisted of influencing development by setting standards for housing, education, etc. For most of this century this approach has been the primary method by which local areas in cities have attained needed services. In many cases city or other governments gradually took over functions previously fulfilled by philanthropic effort, so these can legitimately be considered as its successor.

Many governments can legitimately argue that they have tried to respond to local needs and provide the best possible set of facilities and services to localities, given the constraint of finance. Certainly the number and variety of services have created a vast bureaucracy that is difficult to understand let alone influence, and many of the services were simply delivered to the local area and the key decisions were made without reference to the local residents. As such they involve what Littrell and Hobbes (1989) described as *development in the community, not development of the community*. Several problems arising from this approach have been recognized.

First, economic development without community development often leads to an *increase in the gap between the social classes* (Wilkenson 1979). Some people — especially the property-owners — are more likely to benefit from the changes than others.

Second, the absorption of these activities by city governments frequently resulted in the *removal of local community participation or capability*, bringing about an even greater dependency on outside bureaucracies. Indeed it can be argued that the history of municipal provision has seen a virtual trade-off between *efficiency*, in the provision of a service because of the technical requirement to ensure economies of scale through large-scale systems and specialist facilities, and *access*, in the sense of a citizen's ability to influence or be provided with individual service in a local area. Hospitals and policing are obvious examples, where the large, high-technology hospital has replaced local community facilities, whilst car-borne patrols have often replaced the policeman on the beat. At first sight these consequences seem to be the inevitable result of the increasing technical sophistication in the services provided or the training needed to provide the service — whether fire engine, hospital or classroom. These features ensure that professionally qualified individuals from outside the area may be chosen for jobs, whilst the need to service the city as a whole and to provide equity between areas take priority over delivery systems for local areas. However, as Fear, Gamm and Fisher (1989) observed, technology or specialized training, are, by themselves, equivocal in community development. The utility of the technical service or expertise in satisfying local needs or developing community interaction depends on the reason for its development, the delivery process adopted, its use and the consequences of the actions (Kelman and Warwick 1978); these often entail ethical considerations.

The third issue is the question of *whose values influenced development* and whether recipients participated in the choice of objectives. All too frequently it has been the middle-class values of the government bureaucrats and their consultants that are dominant in choosing and locating the services provided by municipal or state authorities. Certainly it is apparent that the final decision appears to rest with the local politicians; however, numerous researchers have shown that many of the real decisions are made by the technical experts in any government or those who weld power behind the scenes (Knox 1987). So it is difficult to argue the case that the 'people rule' or really determine their future through the ballot box.

On a different scale the influence of local values is often seen in the resistance of many middle and upper-income areas to the introduction of what are seen as undesirable facilities, namely social housing projects or half-way homes, in what is seen as the NIMBY (not in my back yard) syndrome. This conflict over location of urban facilities has stimulated many neighbourhood activists and has been of particular interest to geographers (Cox and Johnston 1982; Dear 1992; Knox 1987, Chapter 7).

The fourth problem is the spatial inequality in the distribution of the services provided, as shown by many researchers (Lineberry 1977; Rich 1977; 1982a; 1982b). Suburban hospitals are often in upper or middle-class suburbs because of the influence of medical experts acting as decision-makers who would prefer to live near these facilities. Poorer areas often have less recreational space and lag in the development of schools and other facilities. Certainly the welfare state has attempted to provide services in the poorest areas in a compensatory attempt to counteract the regressive pattern that will be produced if left to dependency upon provision from local property-related financial resources. However, studies of the location of services have shown that there is no simple relation between the most disadvantaged areas and government spending. Pinch (1985) calculated the relationships between a summary index of need in London's administrative areas and various measures of service provision. Not all of these relationships showed strong positive associations, some, such as those concerning the elderly, displayed negative associations. He concluded that it was difficult to generalize, for some low-income, high-need areas such as Camden had high levels of service, whereas others such as Lambeth did not. Financial problems related to the ability to raise money by the local tax, typically based on property valuation, is obviously one of the reasons for the discrepancies in service provision. As important is the political will to change and the capability to do so through leadership, a vital ingredient which is often missing.

Criticisms of the technical assistance approach can also be seen in the urban renewal sector. Large areas of older, obsolescent housing in inner cities were destroyed in urban renewal schemes, yet some could have been saved. The historic network of local social integration in many older areas of the cities, where the residents were close to local shops, entertainment and relatives, was replaced by an often isolated, crime-ridden life on the windswept margins of the city. This alien landscape may have been created by a compassion for social justice — paradoxically it produced greater social alienation for most residents at enormous public expense. Moreover, little attention was paid to those displaced by such schemes, for many of the revitalized areas became commercial or public building complexes. The grouping of large concentrations of these tower blocks created their own ghettos. Equally important was that the success of high-rise living for the wealthy was not duplicated in these council housing projects. The lack of foresight in the spatial layout of the public areas and the failure to provide custodians — such as the porters of the rich — led to the absence of control over space (see Chapter 8).

Another big disadvantage of the technical approach in community development is that the location of the service is often made only in relation to the function concerned, so there may be *little co-ordination* of where buildings are located. In terms of the efficient location of some facilities the scatter approach can be easily justified. For example, in the location of fire stations it makes a great deal of sense to locate fire stations at points of greatest accessibility to potential fire hazards and main roads so that response times can be minimized. Other activities can be located in the same way. The result is a scatter of activities throughout the urban space, given the variety of different threshold values for publicly pro-

vided functions and the restricted number of sites available if residential development occurs before the facility is needed. This scatter fails to provide a basis for local residential interaction. This is particularly apparent in North America where there is almost universal car-ownership outside the biggest cities and decisions on the various parts of a new area — such as houses, shops, schools — are usually made by different developers or different city departments. Libraries, schools, shopping-areas, community recreational facilities have been scattered through areas and transit routes have been planned with little reference to the zones of conflux. Obviously there are exceptions, as discussed in Chapter 8: the 'Neighbourhood Unit Planning' and 'City in the Suburb' concepts. The logic and advantages of single facility location are less easy to see in many other functions provided by city governments and a strong argument can be made for the locational integration of many facilities in locations where public transport can provide accessibility to all. The task is not easy. Different threshold population sizes for individual services mean that there is no necessary coincidence of a set of market or provision areas, whilst the changing needs and provision of individual functions mean the decisions rarely coincide in a temporal sense. When large suburbs or towns are built over a few years the approach is much easier than when the decisions are spread over many years or in areas already built-over.

It has been fashionable in our disaster-hungry media to be critical of the technical or 'top–down' provision of technical assistance by experts from government departments. The number of planning disasters created by this type of intervention certainly provide grist to the mill of criticism (Hall 1980). However, we must not exaggerate. In many cases the criticism is misplaced, for the problems being attacked cannot always be solved at a local level. The urban scourges of poverty and crime cannot be completely solved by locality-based interventions: they are societal issues embedded in the wider problems of inequality, job availability and social behaviour, although the problems may be mitigated by community-based initiatives. Similarly, it is simply unfair to label all such interventions as being disastrous: there are many examples where the provision of advice and services have been either models of efficiency or have reduced if not eradicated local problems. Such positive results are certainly not inevitable; nevertheless, enough cases of successful and unsuccessful interventions exist for authors such as Davis and Salasin (1975) or Zaltman (1983) to summarize the principles needed for the successful introduction of change. The former organized the key elements for success in an easily remembered acronym, A VICTORY, that summarizes the requirements for positive community development by the technical assistance approach (Table 6.1). It is worth stressing that many of the issues identified relate to the resolution of the potential dichotomy between

values, attitudes and knowledge in the community, compared with those of the assisting group. If these two groups can agree on the needs, there is a high probability of success by this method.

In the last generation three trends have resulted in a reduction of the remoteness of the technical assistance approach and attempts to improve the responsiveness of the system.

The first can be seen as a derivative of the general movement to empower the people by the development of local control to achieve neighbourhood government, a case so eloquently made by authors such as Kotler (1969). Many of its principles and problems will be discussed in the next section. Here it is enough to note that real grass-roots government in local areas has still to be achieved, although there has been increasing local community input into the planning process through *citizen*

Table 6.1 Elements for successful community intervention by the technical approach

Key Issues	Elaboration
Ability	Ability of people in the community to evaluate and understand the assistance provided.
Values	The relationship or fit between the values of the community and assisting groups.
Information	Appreciation by the local community of the knowledge and understanding of the assistance.
Circumstances	To what extent does the assisting group understand the community — socio-cultural context and beliefs, particularly those that can or cannot be altered.
Timing	The ability of the assisting group to consider and choose an optimal time to structure change.
Obligation	The ability of the assisting group to consider change from the community, not their own perspective, and to relate it to a definite local need.
Resistance	The myriad forces and factors that resist change — in social and psychological spheres — that should be understood by the assisting group.
Yield	An evaluation and appreciation of the benefits to the community users if change is implemented and differences in impact among different groups in the area.

Source: Revised from Davis and Salisan 1975.

participation. Planners and private developers in most western cities routinely organize information sessions when new housing, transport or other projects are planned and seek local input and support. Many will sympathize with the argument that the results of citizen participation were little more than token changes in original plans. Nevertheless there have been major success stories. Just as important has been the fact that the trend to citizen participation has made criticism of technically derived solutions more acceptable. It has been shown time and time again that the conclusions often presented as 'superior' are based on economic assumptions of dubious value, on values divergent from the norm of a community and, until the birth of the green lobby, have failed to consider environmental effects. In a liberal democracy such challenges to the technical experts are possible. The tragedy of the socialist systems in eastern Europe was that many decisions were taken by a small, isolated élite who could not be challenged, producing poor standards of provision and often disastrous consequences, such as high levels of pollution. The conclusion must be that although the technical approach has many merits, a healthy scepticism and the ability by those most affected to question decisions are necessities that must be incorporated into the process.

The second change lies in the challenge to the system by the use of *advocacy planning and bureaucratic guerrillas*. The first entails the use of technical experts by community groups to help community residents with legal or planning problems. Court challenges or public inquiries demand information be presented in particular ways, so advocates have been employed or used to obtain the technical assistance available to bureaucracies and corporations and put it to work for individuals or community groups. Again the approach was considered almost revolutionary in the late 1960s (Corey 1966), although it should be considered in the same context as the provision of medical services to impoverished areas — another type of technical delivery system: one that is based on the values of the local community. The second challenge to the technical

assistance approach is far more secretive. Individuals in the political or bureaucratic system have often leaked information to the community affected about new plans or potential changes. Not only does this alert the community to the changes but may also provide them with the evidence to challenge the system. It is, however, difficult to evaluate the real utility of this approach.

The third change can be seen in the *mass social protest movements* that were so typical of the late 1960s and 1970s (Castells 1983). Many of these protests, such as the race riots of Watts (Los Angeles) in 1968 or in cities in many countries, were sparked by insensitivity in policing. A new outbreak of arson, pillage and murders in south central Los Angeles in the spring of 1992 was a response to the failure of the justice system to convict a group of police who used excessive force in arresting a black person, a conclusion difficult to deny since the episode was filmed and seen on television around the world. Many will argue that the responses had their root cause in the poverty, discrimination, and the lack of resources for blacks in inner-city disadvantaged areas. They were an almost nihilistic reaction against intolerable conditions. However, in 1992 the victims were often other ethnic groups who had built up businesses in these areas. Many of the European protest movements were linked to more specific causes, to the lack of housing, evictions, or the impending commercialization of older residential areas. There is little doubt that although many authorities have attempted to improve the lot of the disadvantaged by area development schemes, the problems remain as intractable as ever. The conclusions of the British Community Development Project (CDP 1974, 52) designed to study and improve twelve localized pockets of impoverishment are worth quoting: 'They are a central part of the dynamics of the urban system and ... the problems are not going to be solved by marginal rearrangements to take account of their special minority needs'. Not surprisingly, the Conservative central government in power distanced themselves from these conclusions, for they seemed to call for an attack on what the action teams thought of as the real cause: the capitalist system itself.

The Self-Help Approach

The self-help approach is really the opposite to the technical method. It is based on the principle that people should and can collaborate in an area to provide the needs and services they require. In origin, of course, the ideas go back to the beginning of time: to societies based on reciprocal exchange, or in a context where people in the first settlements co-operated to provide facilities from which they could all benefit: whether well, wall or public buildings. As society became more specialized and controlled by élites, the self-help or bottom–up approach decayed and was replaced with the technical approach. Three features have proved particularly influential in the maintenance and modern revival of the approach that is frequently based on neighbourhood organizations (Biklen 1983; Marshall and Mayer 1983; Hallman 1984; Bender 1986).

The first feature lay in the heritage provided by the development of societies in some of the remote and frontier areas where control by an élite was minimal. The classic case lies in the United States of America, where de Tocqueville's classic (1835) *Commentary on America* directed attention to the number and variety of associations found in this society. This was so different from the paternalistic or top–down systems with which he was familiar in Europe, or from colonial regimes in the Spanish possessions where local control was frowned upon.

> Americans of all ages, all stations of life, and in all types of dispositions are forever forming associations ... . In every case, at the head of any new undertaking, where in France you would find government, or in England some territorial magnate, in the United States you are sure to find an association. (A. de Tocqueville 1966, 685)

The result was that Americans grew up to assume that they would have to look after their own interests rather than depending on government provision, thus creating a heritage of independence and associations based on self-help.

The second modern source can be found in co-operative movements, a reaction by the people against the dominant and often monopolist conditions found in the capitalist industrial cities. Although influenced by the Owenite Experiment in utopian communities (Chapter 8) the original Rochdale pioneers of 1844 did not seek such communal aims. They sought only to establish a retail shop to share in the profits of distribution and prevent exploitation by the company shops (Bailey 1955). The idea spread rapidly from these humble beginnings, and now encompasses a large number of different enterprises (Roy 1969).

A third trend can be linked to the 1960s reaction against the technical decisions made by remote bureaucrats who often ignored the most needy areas or imposed drastic change upon inner-city areas. The publicity given to those community-based movements of protest that stopped new motorway developments led to imitators everywhere, and an increasing inability of transport planners to create new transit systems without reference to the areas affected. Inner-city residents also protested against the commercialization of residential areas and the loss of single family homes. Although not all areas were successful in resisting change, there were enough to encourage others. As described in the previous section it led to the modification of the technical approach. In many Canadian cities today it is routine for planners and developers to consult with community organizations before new land-use plans or changes are developed.

These changes, part of an opening up of government to citizen participation in general, also become a community-building exercise, in the sense of both creating and strengthening local interaction and identity (Littrell and Hobbs 1989), and ensuring their subsequent capacity for continuing improvement (Summers 1986). Not only do these relate to long-cherished ideals of community participation in western democratic society (Sayer 1986), but also, as Bender (1986) observed, it is considered to be a vital part of a broader conception of social development in society as a whole. This is true not only in developing countries, but also in depressed areas of big cities in the United States, where the self-help process in community developments has been considered to represent a grass-roots revival of real democracy (Kotler 1969; Williams 1985). It is seen as a return to the fundamental principles upon which the New England communities of the seventeenth century were based, keeping alive the concept that the spirit of 'the people' should be the primary source of power (Perlman 1979, Fisher and Kling 1989). Nevertheless, one must not overemphasize the role of the majority in these self-help endeavours: usually some change agent, an outsider, is a vital catalyst for the creation of self-help local organizations.

Unfortunately for the successful development of communities the approach was not without a large number of problems. In theory the self-help approach seems to be the ideal, satisfying both community needs and building intra-community relationships and associations. In practice a number of critical problems can be recognized which have seriously impeded its development and have drastically reduced its impact. Thirteen major issues can be identified, with the acronym PRACTITIONERS providing a suitable mnemonic summarizing the concepts.

1. *Problems Capable of Local Solution.* Many so-called community problems are not completely capable of solution at the community level — particularly the crisis of inner-city decay and poverty — since they are linked to societal change and the distribution of rewards.
2. *Removal of Fatalistic, Apathetic Attitudes.* These characteristics, typical of many areas in greatest need, play a large role in accounting for the difficulty of generating change because of a corrosive belief in their inability to introduce change.
3. *Acquisition of Leadership.* Few lasting organizations arise from spontaneous mass uprisings so the absence of effective local leaders is a major problem in creating or maintaining change. Williams (1985, 264) and Lassey and Fernandez (1976) have summarized the key works that stress the importance of leadership in local organizations.
4. *Collective Resources.* Sufficient financial and skill resources, are needed to provide the necessary basis for implementing change. This is always a problem of impoverished areas, compared with middle-income areas.
5. *True Objectives of Leaders.* The key role played by leadership means that caution must be exercised as to the real factors that motivated these individuals to improve a local area or create local associations. Researchers have emphasized that activists are motivated either by self-interest (O'Brien 1975) or a concern for others (Henig 1982). Rich's (1980) study of the leaders in eleven neighbourhood organizations in Indianapolis showed that 39 per cent claimed a desire to fulfil civic duties, and the same percentage to serve the neighbourhood interests. Obligations of friendships accounted for a further 15 per cent, whilst the rest (6 per cent) claimed their primary desire was to protect property values. Yates's (1973) study also showed a similar bias in favour of a desire for neighbourhood improvement and maintenance. However, one must be careful of accepting these survey results at face value. At a national level leaders will often clothe themselves 'in the flag' or argue for 'motherhood' resolutions, so political leaders are likely to disguise their own self-interest and egotistical ambitions. In practice, therefore, disguised or latent motivations may be more important than the manifest explanations provided. If these unknown or latent motivations — such as personal gain or power — really are the primary explanations for any leader, a community may be used by such individuals to realize these ambitions at community expense.

6. *Inequality.* Self-help organizations in different areas have access to very different resources, so provision on this basis usually leads to great areal inequalities.

7. *Temporal Changes.* Interest groups maintain themselves through time by changing memberships. Place-based self-help organizations often find it difficult to respond to the changing needs and requirements of people which often come from the *in situ* ageing of the population or the influx of newcomers, leading to clashes in attitudes.

8. *Intra-Community Value Differences.* It is a mistake to believe that people who live in the same area have homogeneous attitudes. In most cases — particularly in inner-city areas — there is usually a variety of lifestyles and points of view which contribute to community tension, not to consensus. The problems are exacerbated when different values are held by change agents and outside authorities.

9. *Objectives and Goals.* It is not easy to derive consensus on particular objectives to be achieved by community action. Most effective community action occurs when there is mobilization owing to a threat to the area, such as the intrusion of a new transport route.

10. *Needs Vary.* Different communities have very different needs based on their economic power, stage in life cycle, degree of obsolescence, etc. Poorer neighbourhoods are more likely to require outside financial support than richer ones and may be subject to far greater pressures than middle-class areas whose inhabitants have the ability to buy their own services rather than having to depend on co-operative endeavours.

11. *Endeavour.* Many self-help organizations become the victims of their own initial endeavour. They cannot maintain the high levels of volunteer commitment, fail to make progress after initial gains, and often become an unresponsive élite group of leaders.

12. *Results.* Self-help approaches frequently work best in areas that have the least problems. Middle-income areas have the money, leadership skills and commitment from residents to assist in implementing change, whereas the biggest problems lie in areas without resources.

13. *Seeds of Dependency.* Few self-help movements are really autochthonous, spontaneous movements. Kotze (1987) observed that most are dependent in many ways on outside experts for the initial stimulus and on governments to provide money for facilities and educational programmes. If the outside resources are withdrawn, the nascent movement frequently collapses. In addition many argue that the provision of food, shelter, etc, never addresses the real problem — the distribution of rewards in society — so the residents who are helped are confirmed in their dependency.

The underlying assumption of the self-help approach has been that people really are *free* to engage in these tasks. In totalitarian societies apparent co-operation may actually be concealed coercion. So self-help is actually another form of dependency upon the state, with high levels of resentment in the service provision: attitudes that rarely lead to adequate provision. Given these problems, it is not surprising that a recent review (Littrell and Hobbs 1989, 66) concluded: 'the self-help approach to community development is a simple concept ... but many more communities pledge allegiance to that philosophy than actually practise it.'

Despite this rather pessimistic conclusion and the seemingly insurmountable problems facing self-help initiatives, three major reviews of different types of grass-roots, self-help organizations in neighbourhood or community studies in American cities attempted to winnow the evidence from successful programmes to identify the kernels of success. Table 6.2 integrates these results even further, summarizing the features under seven broad categories. The acronym COMMUNES seems a suitable and hauntingly apposite shorthand summary of the principles that seem to be needed — so long as the socialistic overtones are not treated too seriously. What must be emphasized in conclusion

Table 6.2 Features of successful self-help organizations

Key issues	Detailed elaboration
Control	*Community participation* (a) Project is community controlled (w)
Origin	*Community Initiation* (a) Clearly defined local needs are present (b) Initiation of action by community (w)

Manpower	*(i) Effective leadership*
	    (a) Executive director with broad skills (m)
	    (b) Management capacity in service delivery (p)
	(ii) Staff Skills
	    (a) Record of achievements in development and neighbourhood issues (m)
	    (b) Advanced issue capability in policy and planning (p)
	    (d) Negotiation, confrontation and lobbying (p)
	    (e) Effective use of volunteers (w)

Money and finance	*Sound Fiscal Management* (a) Understanding financial feasibility (m) (b) Well-developed fund raising (p) (c) High ratio of private to public money (w)
Utility of results	*Tangible benefits* to community in: quality of life, social services, more employment opportunities, better income prospects, better health facilities, and housing (w)
Neighbourhood and community relationships	*Significant co-operation and integration* with other: (a) Community organizations and people (w) (b) Support of umbrella groups (p) (c) Access to technical assistance inside and outside area (p) (d) Effective volunteers (w) (e) Skills in information dissemination and expose (p) (f) High level of local support (m)
Externality	*Access to Outside Support*, such as: (a) Technical assistance action-research, organizer-training schools (m) (b) Coalition-building with one another, public interest groups, labour groups (p) (c) Monitoring and evaluating government programmes (p) (d) Quality of relationships with other local governments (m)
Spur to future	(a) Self-sustaining enterprises or spur to other community programmes (w) (b) Issue growth from neighbourhood to nation (p)

Source: Integrated from (a) p—Perlman (1979, 17); (c) w—Washington Consulting Group (1976); (b) m—Marshall and Mayer (1983) Urban Institute Survey, Washington, DC.

is that the balance between the features identified in Table 6.2 will vary between organization and areas. Moreover, the emphasis upon skills and management demonstrate the Achilles heel of many self-help schemes. Initially they are likely to be amateur efforts, with low probabilities of success, unless there are some extreme, consensus-building issues that integrate the community until the organizations become professionalized and create the necessary skill and financial capacity for success. Even if they are successful, the danger of creating a professionalized and bureaucratic staff may produce the *Gesellschaft* or associational society that they originally resisted — leading to an attitudinal split between the activists and the ordinary people in the community. This is why community initiation, support and control seem to be absolutely vital elements in self-help organizations, whether they are single-purpose or multiple-purpose organizations. Also, the need to maintain the initial impetus and to sustain efforts for the future are of critical importance if the self-help approach is to survive in any area. Finally, it must be emphasized again that although the self-help component may be the primary theme in the provision of services and community organization in an area, there seems little doubt that self-help is rarely achieved without outside assistance in some form or another. Even in Neighbourhood Watch programmes (Chapter 7) there are usually police guidance and monitoring. However, despite its problems a strong element of self-help seems to be essential in any community renewal scheme, particularly in the impoverished inner-city ghettos. Without self-help and participation the culture of welfare dependency from top–down delivery systems seems likely to be perpetuated.

The Critical or Conflict Approach

The fourth approach to planned community development is of much more recent origin. Explicitly recognizing that development in an area entails change, which creates conflict or difference of opinion, its primary focus is upon the deliberate use and even creation of confrontation by professional organizers (Reitzes and Reitzes 1980; Dillon 1984; Robinson 1989). The approach has grown from the pioneering efforts of Alinsky (1969; 1972). Beginning his career as an organizer for the American union of workers called CIO, headed by John L. Lewis, he soon realized that the organization of the work-force and the provision of better wages and working conditions in the workplace did not solve many of the problems experienced by inner-city residents. Alinsky maintained that the poorest areas in industrial cities could not be improved by spontaneous self-help schemes and were obviously ignored or patronized by municipally inspired programmes. Instead he argued for a radical, community-based conflict approach to remove the injustice and imbalance in the distribution of rewards in society which had created these problem areas. His earliest work was in the late 1930s in the notorious 'Back of the Yards' area of Chicago, an area that seemed without hope. Obsolescent housing combined with high levels of poverty and crime created a classic urban slum, in an area dominated by the cattle-packing industry. A key objective was to unify the diverse interests of individuals in these areas to build upon the power of numbers and release the latent energy of the people. Although other radicals of the day believed that only a new communist dawn could create real change, such issues are not considered here. The essentials of Alinsky's method can be encapsulated in seven main stages: Invitation, Research, Power Structure, Organization, Tactical Actions, Self-Perpetuation and External Resistance. The easily remembered term RIPOSTE provides a useful anagram derived from the first letters of these stages, illustrating that the conflict approach to community development can be one type of 'riposte' against local impoverishment. All of these issues, perhaps with the exception of the first, apply almost equally to the grass-roots approach that has been discussed above.

Formal Invitation to Organize

Unlike the nineteenth-century philanthropists, Alinsky believed that concerned outsiders or professional organizers could not just walk into an area and create real change. Indeed, not all areas had the possibility of successful community development. He maintained that a professional organizer should attempt the conflict approach only when a formal invitation for assistance was received — one that was signed by as many local organizations as possible. Local concern and commitment to change were considered as vital precursors for future progress.

Research

The second stage of this activist approach requires detailed research to provide outsiders with a real understanding of the nature, problems and dynamics of community areas. The two key issues normally recognized (Robinson 1989) are succinctly summarized by a series of questions because the answers to the first have been covered in Chapters 3 to 5, whilst leadership questions were discussed in the self-help section of this chapter.

Key Issues	Detailed Elaboration
1. Understanding the Community	Who lives in the area? What are the boundaries? What are their attitudes, needs, and grievances? What are their interdependencies, and previous co-operations? How has the area evolved?
2. Leadership Appraisal	Who are the potential leaders? How many people can clearly see the current problems, future potential, or can communicate their views and have the tact, coverage and enthusiasm to sustain

their vision? Can those people be persuaded, convinced to help the community effort?

Power Structure

Successful change depends upon the identification of the existing power structure in an area if any meaningful change is going to occur. Alinsky believed that many of the problems in any local community area resulted from the feeling of powerlessness of its people: their lack of knowledge of the real power brokers exploiting the area and a feeling of being helpless to effect change. Hence a critical element in the improvement of any area was the identification of the various individuals or organizations — especially politicians, bureaucrats, corporate managers and landowners — whose decisions affect or rather control the area. Even though the existence of democracy gave the appearance that the 'people ruled', the reality was quite different. Most of the work carried out on this question has been done at city level, since this is the major source of power; nevertheless, many of the results can be applied to small areas within cities, such as wards or community organizations. In the 1950s and 1960s evidence from different cities was used to support the view that cities was controlled by an élite (Hunter 1953) or a pluralist bloc (Dahl 1961) so that individual voters had little real influence. It soon became apparent that there was nothing to prevent one of these groups from being dominant in one centre and another group elsewhere, so it could be argued they are end-points on a scale of influence. Further research even questioned the relevance of a single scale of political power, for the application of multivariate methods led to the identification of a series of dimensions of power rather than a single élitist–pluralist distinction. For example, Bonjean and Olson (1964) identified four sources of variation in cities:

1. Legitimacy is linked to the holders of public office.

2. Ideology or Consensus measured the degree of similarity or differences in beliefs among individuals in an area.
3. Visibility is the degree to which leaders are known or unknown in the area.
4. Scope or Influence identifies the way power was exercised, such as by many people in one area, or one group in many areas.

Although there was a correlation between the first and third of these dimensions, the results showed that a city — and by extension a community — could be pluralistic on one scale and élitist on another. Also large, more economically diverse centres were more likely to be pluralist, although those with city managers and having 'at large' election systems were likely to be more élitist.

By the 1970s the real question was seen to be not 'who governs', but 'why', 'how' and 'for whose benefit'. At first the debate was dominated by those who claimed a primary role for the structural mechanisms of society; in particular the capitalist interests that dominated decision-making whether directly through politics, indirectly through influence, or by setting the rules of the state (Bachrach and Baratz 1962; Harvey 1973). However, a recent reviewer observed:

> Structuralists conceptualize the political order as ultimately subordinate to economic structure. They tend to reduce the urban political order to economic imperatives; even social control achieved through political means serves capitalist ends ... This trivialization of the political not only removes a major source for explaining why outcomes vary even though capitalism is a constant; it flies in the face of the state's obvious importance in constituting economics and the contingent nature of outcomes subject to political conflict. (Mollenkopf 1989, 129)

Mollenkopf (1989) proposed the concept of the 'dominant political coalition' as the best way of understanding how political orders are developed, maintained and overturned. Unlike the essentially unstable character of pluralist blocs, which form and re-form, the new school argues that the coalition is able to direct government power on a continuing basis over many issues. Applied to the community level within the city the approach would assign a vital role to the identification, characteristics, strengths and weaknesses of the power structure affecting the area of interest — whether these power sources are inside or outside the area. A vital role of the organizer is to make the community aware of the sources of power and the possibility of change.

Organization

The fourth stage entails the organization or mobilization of the people in an area. Several distinctive principles and approaches have been advocated within this overall category.

The *origin and dissemination* of the issues, the way the community achieves some consensus on the problems it faces is important. Although an organizer could bring problems or issues to a community's attention, it has been argued that it is more productive to adopt different strategies: to arrange meetings to encourage the critics and dissidents to articulate their feelings and problems; to share their criticisms; to disseminate the issues; and to create a majority that are sufficiently interested in sharing the same sentiments and concerning themselves with change. This is far from easy. Many people in the worst slum areas often accept the conditions with a fatalist attitude. They are perceived as a fact of life — not as a situation adaptable to change. To assume that people in any area are homogeneous is also false. There are differences in values, attitudes and behaviour, as well as in age, gender, occupation, ethnicity, etc, and in associations with past events and personal antipathies. So much skill is often needed to elicit a community-wide and coherent response.

The second organizational response is the need to produce, very early on in the organization of a depressed community, a single *winnable issue*, one that represents the heart of the problem in an area. Preferably it is an issue with visibility and is non-divisive so as to have the widest appeal. Occasionally it may be appropriate to start with smaller issues. Neighbourhood Watch programmes and community clean-ups have often been used to provide a small beginning for community action: to encourage people to co-operate, to give them a taste of success, and to provide the dissemination of knowledge about community problems and prospects for change.

Conflict advocates have also stressed the need to concentrate problem issues by identifying an *adversary* — a visible entity to fight against. Large employers who create negative externalities in an area, such as pollution, noise and smells, yet have outside ownership and put little back into the area, provide useful prospects. Alinsky, in his initial community work in Chicago, identified the owners of the meat-packing plants as the real problem for the local community. Direct confrontation was to be avoided — simply because the strength of the adversary would probably be too great in the initial stages. Instead he advocated the indirect approach favoured by military strategists. In the Chicago case he advocated that the community should put pressure on the banks financing the meat-packing moguls. They, in turn, would be reluctant to lend money unless the industry responded to the requests for change.

Linkages within and outside the community were also crucial elements for success. Linkages between the various clubs and associations in the area built vital local coalitions and encouraged the creation of consensus. Developing contacts with outside support groups or agencies — whether resource people, government agencies, or funding sources — are considered essential for future support (Alinsky 1969). This approach was necessary because a local area is unlikely to have the financial or legal power to be able to implement change by itself; for example, the legal responsibility for change in land use or economic policy may be outside the area, such as in the municipal or state government, or in some corporate headquarters. If these power sources cannot be induced to help in the change, then outsiders have to be co-opted into the cause or at least neutralized.

Tactical Actions

Communities have to plan campaigns to implement change. This details the tactics to be followed and the actions to be employed. Both have been the subject of much debate. Although these are as varied as the needs to be satisfied or the range of social groups taking part, Alinsky (1972, 127) identified what he called thirteen power tactics for confrontation in his book entitled *Rules for radicals*. These have been regrouped in Table 6.3, using the acronym PIKET as an appropriate, if misspelt, memory aid for these principles.

Tactics alone are not enough to achieve success. Many different types of actions to achieve change have been employed by community organizers around the world. Kahn's (1982) useful list has been reorganized into three broad areas: Publicity, Action and Pressure. The expectation is that one or all of those specific approaches could be used in particular circumstances, and community organizers should be aware of their strengths and weaknesses (although it is hoped that the approach adopted is not PAP, the acronym produced from the three areas!). It is very difficult to argue conclusively that one or another of the actions identified in Tables 6.3 and 6.4 is adequate: it depends on the problems, the values of organizers and constituents, the strength and intransigence of the opposition. In cases where resistance is high, all approaches may be adopted; in other cases simple publicity may be enough. Repeating the various alternatives in the table is redundant, although it is worth stressing Alinsky's observation that ridicule may be a potent weapon in the armoury of radicals.

External Resistance

An essential part of the knowledge base of community organizers is the prospect of counteracting the inevitable reaction to the confrontation tactics. Those with something to lose by the community's objectives will undoubtedly react against the proposed changes. The

Table 6.3 Principles for confrontation

Key categories	Alinsky's Rules
Pressure	Keep the pressure on adversaries (8) An operation should maintain constant pressure (10)
Illusion	A threat is usually more terrifying than the thing itself (9) Power is not what you have, but what the enemy thinks you have (1)
Knowledge	Never go outside the experience of your people (2) Whenever possible, go outside the experience of the enemy (3)
Enjoyment	A good tactic is one your people enjoy (6) A tactic that drags on too long becomes boring (7) Ridicule is man's most potent weapon (5)
Targets	Pick your target, freeze it, personalize it, polarize it (13) A negative pushed too hard will break through to its counterside (11) The price of a successful attack is a constructive alternative (12) Make the enemy live to his or her own book of rules (4)

Source: Summarized and rearranged from Alinsky 1972, 127. Numbers in brackets represent the original numbers.

Table 6.4 Options available for confrontation

Key Groups	Kuhn's Options
Publicity or Threat	Press Conferences, Advertising, Leaflets, Public Hearing
Action	Existing Channels: Courts, Meetings or Lobbying, Representations, Owners Confrontational: Sit-ins, Strikes, Work-to-rule, Demonstrations
Pressure	Private Organizations: Boycotts on Goods Public or City Bodies: Tax Strike

Source: Rearranged and extended from Kahn 1982.

reaction can come in many forms, although a series of prevention strategies can be identified. Many of the stages already identified in pro-conflict approaches can be used and turned back against the community in a search for weak spots. Robinson (1989, 109), in a summary of previous work on a training programme, identified four major conflict resolution strategies, and these can be extended into additional or related issues — all designed to reduce the impact of the conflict method.

Fragmentation of the conflict into smaller parts is a favourite tactic to reduce the pressure for change. By adopting this approach the outside authority may be able to cope with individual issues, to demonstrate that some change is taking place, thus allowing the movement to run out of momentum and prevent real change. Stalling tactics designed to spin out the discussion or to reduce demands produces the same effects — obviously a favourite tactic used against hijackers.

Community leaders play a crucial role in confrontation. A traditional ploy is to reduce their effectiveness by co-opting the leaders into advisory or committee positions in the existing power structure — although personal threats are not unknown. The former approach is particularly effective when the search for personal power is their main motivation.

A series of different *prevention strategies* may also be followed. The most obvious is the use of force by the outside authority, using existing laws, preventing removal of property rights, or stopping riotous assembly by extra policing or troops. Even though these actions are often successful, there is always the danger that they lead to increased resentment and the seeds of even greater future conflict. Indeed, Alinsky constantly emphasized the need to compromise if community action was confronted with inexorable force to make it possible to regroup to achieve future success. Hence a series of mediation strategies are often favoured, entailing the use of outside experts or those held in high esteem, either to mediate an end to confrontation or to give the mediator the power to coerce a compromise by threatening other actions if a solution is not taken. Alternatively the use of incentives may be appropriate — contingent upon an agreed solution — such as the offer to reduce local taxes or to establish educational programmes to improve the job prospects of people in the local area. After all it has been suggested that: 'education may not be as helpful as some believe. Power usually whips truth in conflict situations, especially in community controversy.' (J. W. Robinson 1989, 110)

There is, of course, no reason why only one of these approaches has to be adopted. All can be used in a concerted effort to prevent or reduce the impact of community conflict. In the last two decades a voluminous literature on the conflict resolution has been produced, although Robinson's (1972; 1989) succinct reviews and summaries of the steps needed for conflict management in communities are

worthy of note. However, it must be emphasized that the ability to act in this context demands a number of skills that usually need a period of training before effective results can be obtained.

Self-Perpetuation or Continuity

One of the biggest criticisms of the conflict approach is that it may not be successful in maintaining the organization through time. The economic and political forces that created the community problems in the first place are difficult to eradicate completely so there is a need for constant vigilance to maintain the initial gains. Unfortunately a series of problems make it difficult to maintain the continuity of a community organization after the initial euphoria of organization or success.

1. *Maintenance of effort.* Once the initial grievance or problem has been solved it becomes less easy to maintain the commitment of effort to deal with what might be seen as subsidiary or less important issues.
2. *External Forces.* Outside forces that are associated with local problems frequently adopt the procedures described in the conflict resolution section; they may bide their time, modify their behaviour to reduce the scale of the problem, or co-opt people in the community to take their side. This may be enough to reduce the tensions that created the initial problem, or buy off the key local leaders — without losing their real grip on power or control.
3. *Burn-out.* Key organizers and volunteer staff are likely to become burnt out after the initial organizational efforts because their commitment — especially if they are part-timers — cannot be sustained. Those who are professionals, particularly the invited community organizers, often move away to other problem areas. The area is left with new leaders who may lack the same experience, knowledge or

negotiation skills in managing future community conflicts.

4. *Loss of Leaders.* Even if the leadership remains in an area, it is very difficult for these individuals to resist the temptation to seek municipal office or other power structures outside the community, whether as advisers to governments or corporations. Then it is only a matter of time before they lose touch with the needs of the community that they once served. This means the community organization can easily fall prey to ineffectiveness, or fall under the control of professionals who lack the burning commitment of the initial organizers.

5. *Finance.* A community seeking to maintain its commitment to change cannot exist without a reliable source of finance. Local communities in cities do not have the taxation powers of higher government levels or real access to the funds obtained from the area. In the early stages of community action money may be raised quickly if there are sufficient resources in the area and the desire for change is high. Once the initial problems of a community are solved, volunteers lack the motivation for continued door-to-door collecting. The revenues from local dances or bingo sessions — the most frequent source of independent community funds — are limited. Government grants are episodic and unreliable. Hence the financial capability for sustaining old or creating new community ventures are extremely limited. Indeed, sustained community action may be inhibited by the very success of the organization. Local area improvements will probably increase land and property values, making it more difficult for the organization to buy property for local community ventures. The result is that sustained local area community action may be spoiled by its own success.

Studies of successful community development efforts have, however, demonstrated that there are ways of sustaining the dynamics of community action. The first two problems identified above can be partly solved if there is a concerted push to identify and extend the needs of the area in the early stages of community effort, and to create some organization or committee with a mandate to monitor the forces that create problems, in other words some early-warning system. This type of organization may be easier to sustain in inner-city areas where there are many pressures for change. The third and fourth problems can be mitigated if a training programme for future leaders is implemented and if democratic procedures, designed to incorporate as many people as possible in the organization, are used. The last problem is more intractable. It entails the search for permanent money sources and is a difficulty that can only be conclusively resolved if a local area has the authority to levy taxes or legitimate access to part of the tax revenue. The British system implemented after the local government area changes of 1972 provides one of the rare exceptions. Local community organizations that are legally defined can use 1 per cent of the locally collected taxes for community projects (the taxes were formerly the rates based on a tax on property or businesses and are a poll or head tax since 1989). Unfortunately the amounts realized are too small for more than cosmetic changes in the landscape. This tax is a successor to the ancient parish charge which has its own origin in the medieval tithe or tax used to support the established church. Contemporary churches as diverse as the Latter Day Saints (Mormon) or the Jehovah's Witnesses still maintain themselves by a tax on members, unlike the voluntary financial approach of most others. In many jurisdictions, even those with a range of effective community organizations, most finance is raised from local fund-raising efforts or from government grants. Unfortunately these are limited and episodic respectively. This is why so many of the neighbourhood organizations in the impoverished inner cities of the United States in the late 1960s came to the conclusion that it was vital to establish local community corporations (Hallman 1984). These were non-profit-making organizations designed to improve the economic development of areas, to achieve social goals and retain local control.

Problems

There seems little doubt that the conflict approach has been successful in creating more effective communities in those areas where it has been applied, although the continuity of success once the initial problems are solved is still problematical. Even so, the method has two main problems.

Within-group tension. The deliberate use of the conflict approach can result in a series of negative consequences. It may provoke bitterness and intergroup tension in an area. In an extreme case it may even lead to bloodshed or disrupt the normal lines of communication between people in the area and adds to its probably already stressful lifestyle. So attention should be paid to the resolution of conflict, using the same methods that were discussed earlier in the previous section.

Ethics. A second issue is that the approach assumes that the change agent, the professional organizer, cannot be neutral since it requires the deliberate manipulation of people in the area. This creates the real problem of which ethical principles should be followed. The key issues have been succinctly stated by Laue and Cormick (1978, 218) in their observation that three basic goals should be sought: 'empowerment, justice and freedom are ends in themselves so long as all individuals are equipped to advocate their interests to similar degrees.' This means that organizers should concern themselves with community disputes only if the object is to seek to maximize the ability of powerless individuals to determine their needs, subject to the common good of the city or the region in which they are located. Such a goal would not, however, be considered to be relevant to a slum landlord determined to maximize his gain from a building. Inevitably,

therefore, there may be struggles between the residents of the area and those who control property or businesses in the community for their objectives will often be different.

Conclusions

This review of the alternative methods that have been used for community development and of their respective utility has taken an analytical approach, treating each option as if it were entirely separate. In practice there can be much overlap in individual developmental endeavours. For example, the self-help method is often dependent upon some change agent — either a seconded government employee or an independent professional organizer. The principles used in creating confrontation in the conflict approach can be equally used by self-help organizations. The technical assistance approach now routinely consults with affected community organizations in many cities, though perhaps not as much as many areas would like. Indeed, it could be suggested that each approach concentrates on one part of the range of possible community developmental options. Table 6.5 combines the features of successful organizations, using the three main organizational or delivery types. The summary shows that many of the key features are found in all the types, although the financial and managerial problems of the self-help and conflict approaches contrast with deficiencies in the extent of participation in many technical expertise approaches. Nevertheless, there is a great deal of similarity in the issues that have to be addressed if community development, in the sense of conscious endeavour, is going to be successful. There are few empirical studies which measure the effectiveness of community associations but Oropesa (1989) showed that community wealth and stability are only weakly related to effectiveness. Member activity is the more important factor, but it must be remembered that the local community area is still only part of a complex system of modern society, with limited financial resources and usually no legitimate political role

Table 6.5 Integration of key issues in community organization

A Technical Expert	B Self-Help	C Conflict	D Integration
	2. Origin	1. Invitation to organize	1. Community initiation of project
		2. Research on community	2. Community character, values, context
2. Values 3. Information 6. Obligation			
		3. Power structure	3. Power relations
			4. Resources in area and outside
	6. Neighbourhood relationships		
1. Ability	3. Manpower 4. Money 7. Externality	4(b). Outside links	
			5. Neighbourhood mobilization —Meetings
		4. Organization (a) Issue discussion (c) Effective issue (d) Adversary	—Issues —Adversary
			6. Implementation —Circumstances —Timing —Tactical Actions
4. Circumstances 5. Timing		6. Tactical (a) Publicity (b) Pressure (c) Action	
		7. External resistance	7. Knowledge of: —Conflict Resolution —Resistance
Resolution 7. Resistance			
8. Yield	5. Utility 1. Community control		8. Product —Results —Local control
Mnemonics	8. Spur to future	5. Self-sustainment or continuity	9. Self-sustainment and growth
A VICTORY	COMMUNES	RIPOSTE	PINPRICKS

in the democratic process. If the local community areas were the basic building block of the political system, with the ability to use some of their locally generated tax funds, then intra-urban communities might have a more positive role in urban life. As yet most are still dependent upon higher levels of authority. So decisions taken elsewhere — such as in board-room or legislature — have major effects in these local areas. Local community associations at best modify the basic conditions.

References

Adams, J., 1910, *Twenty years at Hull House*, Macmillan, New York.

Alinsky, S., 1969, *Reveille for radicals*, Random House, New York.

Alinsky, S., 1972, *Rules for radicals*, Random House, New York.

Bachrach, P. and Baratz, M., 1962, Two faces of power, *American Political Science Review, 56,* 947–52.

Badcock, B., 1984, *Unfairly structured cities*, Basil Blackwell, Oxford, England.

Bailey, J., 1955, *The British co-operative movement*, Hutchinson's University Press, London.

Barker, E., 1969, *The politics of Aristotle*, Oxford University Press, London.

Bender, E. I., 1986, The self-help movement seen in the context of social development, *Journal of Voluntary Action Research, 15,* 77–84.

Biklen, D., 1983, *Community organizing: theory and practice*, Prentice-Hall, New Jersey.

Bobinski, G. S., 1969, *Carnegie libraries*, American Library Association.

Bonjean, C. and Olson, D., 1964, Community leadership: directions of research, *Administrative Science Quarterly, 9,* 278–300.

Bremner, R. H., 1960, *American philanthropy*, University of Chicago Press, Chicago.

Castells, M., 1983, *The city and the grassroots*, University of California Press, Berkeley.

Christenson, J. A. and Robinson, J. W., 1989, *Community development in perspective*, Iowa State Press, Ames.

Community Development Projects, 1974, *Interproject Report*, Information Office, London.

Corey, K. E., 1966, Advocacy in planning, *Antipode, 4,* 46–63.

Cox, K. R. and Johnston, R. J., 1982, *Conflict, politics and the urban scene*, Longman, London.

Dahl, R., 1961, *Who governs?*, Yale University Press, New Haven.

Davis, A. F., 1967, *Spearheads for reform: the social settlement and the progressive movement: 1890–1914*, New York.

Davis, H. R. and Salasin, S. E., 1975, The utilization of evaluation, in H. R. Davis and M. Guttentag (eds), *Handbook of evaluation research*, Sage, California.

Dear, M. J., 1992, Understanding and overcoming the NIMBY syndrome, *Jnl. Amer. Plng. Association,* 58 (3), 288–300.

Dear, M. J. and Wolch, J. R., 1987, *Landscapes of despair*, Princeton University Press, New Jersey.

De Tocqueville, A., 1966, *Democracy in America*, Harper and Row, New York. Originally published in 1835.

Dillick, S., 1953, *Community organization for neighbourhood development: past and present*, William Morrow, New York.

Dillon, B., 1984, The change agent: a radical perspective, *Community Development Journal, 19,* 246–51.

Downey, G., 1976, Aristotle as an expert on urban problems, *Ekistics, 253,* 316–21.

Fear, F. A., Gamm, L. and Fisher, F., 1989, The technical assistance approach, in J. A. Christenson and J. W. Robinson, *Community development in perspective*, Iowa State Press, Ames, 69–88.

Fisher, R. and Kling, J., 1989, Community mobilisation: prospects for the future, *Urban Affairs Quarterly, 25,* 200–211.

Hall, Peter, 1980, *Great planning disasters*, Weidenfeld and Nicholson, London.

Hallman, H. W., 1984, *Neighbourhoods: their place in urban life*, Sage Publications, Beverly Hills, California.

Harvey, D. W., 1973, *Social justice and the city*, Edward Arnold, London.

Harvey, D. W., 1985, *The urbanization of capital*, Basil Blackwell, Oxford, England.

Heilman, J. and Dear, M. J., 1988, Homelessness: a comparison of national experiences. Working Paper 5, Department of Geography, University of Southern California.

Henig, J. R., 1982, *Neighborhood mobilization*, Rutgers University Press, New Jersey.

Hillman, A., 1960, *Neighborhood centers today*, National Federation of Settlements and Neighborhood Centers, New York.

Hunter, F., 1953, *Community power structure*, University of North Carolina Press, Chapel Hill.

Jones, G. S., 1971, *Outcast London*, Oxford University Press, England.

Kahn, S., 1982, *Organizing: a guide for grassroots organizers*, McGraw-Hill, New York.

Kelman, H. C. and Warwick, D. P., 1978, The ethics of social intervention, in G. Bermant, H. C. Kelman and D. Warwick (eds), *The ethics of social intervention*, John Wiley, New York.

Keyes, L., 1987, The shifting focus of neighbourhood groups, *Policy Studies Journal*, 16, 300–6.

Knox, P., 1987, *Urban social geography*, Longman, Harlow, England.

Korten, D. C. and Klauss, R., 1984, *People centered development*, Kumarian Press, West Hartford, Connecticut.

Kotler, M., 1969, *Neighbourhood government: the local foundations of political life*, Bobbs Merrill, New York.

Kotze, D. A., 1987, Contradictions and assumptions in community development, *Community Development Journal*, 22, 31–5.

Lassey, W. and Fernandez, R. R., 1976, *Leadership and social change*, University Associates, La Jolla, California.

Laue, J. and Cormick, G., 1978, The ethics of intervention in community disputes, in G. Bermant, H. Kelman and D. Warwick (eds), *The ethics of social intervention*, John Wiley, New York, 205–2.

Lees, A., 1985, *Cities perceived*, Columbia University Press, New York.

Lineberry, R. L., 1977, *Equality and urban policy*, Sage, Beverly Hills, California.

Littrel, D. W. and Hobbs, D., 1989, The self-help approach, in J. A. Christenson and J. W. Robinson (eds), *Community development in perspective*, University of Iowa Press, Ames, 48–68.

Marshall, S. A. and Mayer, N., 1983, *Neighbourhood organizations and community development*, Urban Land Institute, Washington, DC.

Mollenkopf, J., 1989, Who (or what) runs cities, and how?, *Sociological Forum*, 4, 119–37.

Murphey, R., 1954, The city as a centre of change: Europe and China, *Annals of American Association of Geographers*, 44, 349–63.

O'Brien, D. J., 1975, *Neighbourhood organization and interest group process*, Princeton University Press, New Jersey.

Oderkirk, J., 1922, *Food banks*, Canadian Social Trends, Statistics Canada, Ottawa.

Oropesa, R. S., 1989, The social and political foundations of effective neighbourhood improvement associations, *Social Science Quarterly*, 70, 3, 723–43.

Owen, D. E., 1964, *English philanthropy: 1660–1960*, Cambridge University Press, Cambridge, England.

Perlman, J., 1979, Grassroot empowerment and government response, *Social Policy*, 10, 16–21.

Pinch, S., 1985, *Cities and services*, Routledge and Kegan Paul, London.

Reitzes, D. C. and Reitzes, D., 1980, Saul Alinsky's contribution to community development, *Journal of the Community Development Society*, 11, 39–52.

Rich, R. C., 1977, Equity and design in urban service delivery, *Urban Affairs Quarterly*, 12, 383–410.

Rich, R. C., 1982a, *The politics of urban public services*, Lexington Books, Lexington, Massachusetts.

Rich, R. C., 1982b, *Analysing urban service distribution*, Lexington Books, Massachusetts.

Rich, R. C., 1980, The dynamics of leadership in neighbourhood organizations, *Social Science Quarterly*, 12, 383–410.

Robinson, J. W., 1972, The management of conflict, *Journal of the Community Development Society*, 3, 100–205.

Robinson, J. W., 1989, The conflict approach, in J. A. Christenson and J. W. Robinson (eds), *Community development in perspective*, Iowa State Press, Ames, 89–116.

Roy, E. P., 1969, *Co-operatives: today and tomorrow*, Interstate Printers, Danville, Illinois.

Sayer, J., 1986, Ideology: the bridge between theory and practice, *Community Development Journal*, 21, 294–303.

Sanders, I. T., 1958, Theories of community development, *Rural Sociology*, 23, 1–12.

Summers, G. F., 1986, Rural community development, *Annual Review of Sociology*, 12, 347–71.

Wheatley, P., 1971, *Pivot of the four quarters*, Aldine, Chicago.

Williams, M. R., 1985, *Neighbourhood organizations*, Greenwood, Westport, Connecticut.

Wilkenson, K. P., 1979, Social well-being and community, *Journal of the Community Development Society*, 10, 5–16.

Yates, D., 1973, *Neighborhood democracy*, Lexington Books, Lexington, Mass.

Zaltman, G., 1983, Theory in use among change agents, in E. Seidman (ed.), *Handbook of Social Intervention*, Sage, Beverly Hills, California.

7

Service Provision and Communities

Introduction

Local services have always been provided in communities within cities. Places of worship were among the first facilities to have a community role, with medieval European cities being divided into separate parishes, each served by a local church. The Protestant religious schisms meant that their role was selective and did not necessarily cover the whole population. In non-western societies local religious centres frequently retain an important role. In Japan, for example, most neighbourhoods have one or more Shinto shrines providing local identification and cohesion for different groups, for the religion is linked more to propriety, prosperity and daily life than other-worldly concerns. Many shrines are small and unobtrusive, for they are usually attended by a group representative, rather than the whole family as expected by churches of the Judaeo-Christian tradition. In non-western countries local community provision is best seen by the street traders and local markets; in historic cities by the stores around medieval squares; or in the nineteenth-century industrial city by stores clustered at central points in housing areas. These commercial establishments fulfilled an important community role, apart from their basic function of providing goods and services. The stores, as well as the cafés, drug stores (pharmacies) or pubs in French, American or British cultures respectively, assumed significant roles as sites for the exchange of information. Education, health care, recreation and other facilities are also locally delivered, enhancing the local interaction that created the 'urban village' (Gans 1962).

This chapter contrasts with the 'delivery orientation' of Chapter 6 by providing selective examples of services that are provided locally in intra-urban areas. Although four alternative types of provision can be recognized — philanthropic, private, public sector and grass-roots — in practice there is a variety of combinations of these basic types (see Hallman 1984), such as in the many investment partnerships found in impoverished US inner cities where community groups and private enterprise have both committed resources and jointly run the activity. This chapter does not attempt to explore these issues. It is enough to note that there is nothing necessarily fixed about the way local services are delivered by individual agencies: considerable differences exist between western cities and countries in the number of local services and the mix of provision. These can be contrasted with the high levels of local community activity in welfare provision in totalitarian countries such as China (Leung 1990). However, it is worth noting that the local area is the first bastion of party control, so the apparent grass-roots activity may be a function of party 'encouragement', in the same way that the Nazi party created Block-Overseers to monitor local areas.

Provision of Retail Goods and Services

Community areas are not alike in their attitudes to the introduction of new facilities as Smith (1980) has shown (Figure 7.1). Results of a survey of attitudes towards the introduction of over twenty different types of facilities in six

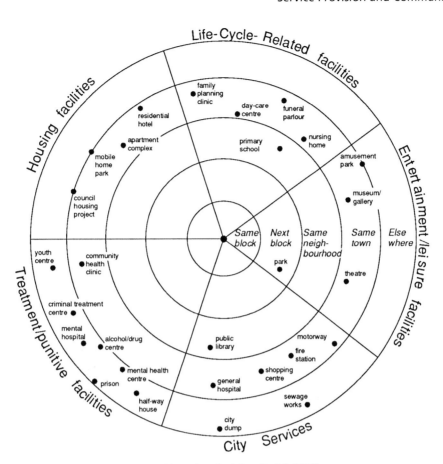

Figure 7.1 Acceptability of facilities in neighbourhoods (after Smith 1980)

different areas in Los Angeles (Banerjee and Baer 1984) (Table 7.1) shows that four facilities (food store, drug store (pharmacy), library and street lighting) were favoured by people in all areas, whereas other areas differed in their attitudes to the various facilities, although the most disliked included utility lines (electricity/telephone cables), billboards (hoardings) and night clubs. The differences based on the social class of the areas is particularly striking: the high-income white areas were intolerant to sixteen of the facilities, the lower-income white to only four. In another section of the same survey, residents were asked to reflect on aspects of neighbourhood quality which provided sources of dissatisfaction. Middle-income areas cited smog, noise and crowding, whereas the list in low-income areas was longer and included lack of privacy, incivilities, insecurity, dirt and ugliness.

Local retail units provide what central place workers call *lower-order functions*, the provision of daily or weekly needs of food and basic household items, whereas the central business district increasingly concentrated on higher order or less frequently purchased goods. Many of these local stores have been replaced in contemporary western society, except where cultural preferences, such as the French desire for freshly baked bread or rolls for breakfast, sustain local bakeries. In the modern city the notion of local service delivery has undergone substantial change in the second half of the twentieth century owing to changes in threshold size and range. Increases in the scale of retailing have affected local stores, for larger and specialized stores have cheaper prices and more choice. A more mobile clientele is able to travel quickly and easily by car to alternative locations, hastening the decline of many small

Table 7.1 Facilities **not** wanted in neighbourhood by 50% or more of residents

Neighbourhood type:	Upper-income white	Middle-income white	Middle-income Hispanic	Middle-income black	Lower-income white	Lower-income Hispanic	Lower-income black
	1	1	2	1	2	3	2
	2	2	3	2	3	12	4
	3	3	7	3	4	13	5
	4	4	11	4	12	15	7
	5	5	15	5		17	15
	6	7		7			17
	7	8		8			
	8	12		11			
	9	13		12			
	10	15		15			
	11						
	12						
	13						
	14						
	15						
	16						

1. amusement park
2. telephone/electricity cables
3. hoardings
4. nightclubs
5. bus station
6. bowling alley
7. zoo
8. arena
9. technical school
10. ramp access
11. marina
12. bar
13. thrift shop
14. skating-rink
15. alleys
16. department store
17. liquor store

(Facilities *most favoured* – pharmacy, food store, library, street lighting.)

Source: Banerjee and Baer 1984, 136.

shopping-centres. In North America, the growth of suburban planned shopping-centres and highway-orientated ribbons linked to passing trade, together with rigid planning restrictions that keep suburban areas residential, except for the designated shopping-area, has helped limit the number of retail areas in suburbs. In many British cities the trends have meant the diminution in the number of 'corner shops' and lower-order shopping-centres and a recent trend in retailing towards large suburban out-of-town centres and hypermarkets combined with scattered corner shops (Thomas 1989). Yet over the same period, the volume of retail sales has increased steadily as new methods of selling and new trading has led to a change from the independent store-owner to the large corporate chains, franchises and superstores with a major move towards out-of-town shopping-centres. Several repercussions of these trends for neighbourhood and community shopping can be noted.

All surveys show that there have been shop closures and a decline in numbers of independent traders. Dawson (1983) estimated that the number of shops in Britain had declined from 530,000 in 1950 to an estimated 300,000 in 1980. Much of this decline has been linked to the growth of supermarkets, replacing a number of local food stores. Yet Jones (1988) noted the rapid growth of a new breed of franchised convenience stores, such as Mac's, 7-Eleven and Quick Mart. They are relatively small (up to 300 square metres), trade in a limited range of convenience goods and have benefited from the removal of constraints on late-night or 24-hour shopping. Jones (1988) has estimated that these stores grew from 2,500 to 58,000 between 1960 and 1985 in North America, and there are likely to be approximately 6,000 such stores in Britain by the mid 1990s. Although these may have added a new *local* component to retail geography they are externally controlled and come nowhere close to replacing the size of the losses since the 1950s.

The pattern of local provision has changed. In Britain Davies (1984) showed an urban hierarchy of shopping centres still survived, of which the two bottom tiers were neighbour-

hood centres and local centres/isolated stores. Both had been subjected to recent change, however. Neighbourhood centres serving around 10,000 people had changed from clusters of fifteen to thirty-five shops to a large supermarket and about six other shops. The lowest order altered from the traditional mixtures of corner stores and small parades or strip malls of shops to a single modern convenience store of the mini-market type, often integrated with a petrol station and with a catchment of up to 2,500 people. Many of the new style convenience stores are located on highways and are as much geared towards passing traffic as they are to the needs of the locality. This bottom end of the hierarchy is still dominated by independent retailers or franchise operations and with a strong service, rather than goods-selling, component.

The diminution in the amount of local provision has led to the rise of 'disadvantaged consumers', placed at access and cost disadvantage by the changing pattern of retail trade. The elderly, and those on low income, such as single-parent families or disadvantaged ethnics, who lack the mobility to extend their shopping range, have to tolerate higher prices in more local stores. This disadvantaged group is of growing dimensions in the inner city and in some peripheral public housing estates.

The exception to the trend for local retail losses may be found in some new ethnic neighbourhoods. Many, although not all, of the new ethnic groups have lower income and mobility and also have some culture-specific consumer demands and preferences, particularly for convenience goods and services. In British-Asian communities today the language of transaction may be that of the local immigrants, so such stores may fulfil historic neighbourhood roles as a point of conflux and interaction. This goes beyond the way many immigrants occupied certain commercial niches in the past, whether the ubiquitous Chinese restaurants and laundries of North America, or the Italian cafés and Jewish jewellers/watchmakers of industrial South Wales. In many North American cities ethnic communities have a longer history and play a role in cultural retention and assimilation. Yet Chinatowns, in particular, have specialized in food retailing and restaurants, creating a distinction between ethnic neighbourhood stores and the speciality ethnic outlets catering for the increasingly cosmopolitan tastes of non-residents.

It is clear that new local shopping facilities in the suburban areas have provided a means of delivering local services to residential areas, although it is doubtful if this has ever amounted to a replication of the community-bonding role of local stores in the inner urban areas. Many of these families have two wage earners and freezers, so there is less frequent food purchasing with less time for socialization. Many customers arrive by car and the area caters to a larger population, thereby reducing the number of repetitive personal contacts that create the neighbourly feeling. In any case planning restrictions mean there are far fewer stores.

Many authors, from Jacobs (1961) onwards, have condemned the sterility of suburban residential areas that lack the vibrancy of the city. Much of the criticism is directed at rigid land-use or zoning policies designed to preserve the exclusivity of residential suburbs where commercial and workplace activities are restricted. Many favour the contemporary policies, although it is clear that there are variations in the acceptability of different activities and in different types of neighbourhoods as Figure 7.1 and Table 7.1 have shown, highlighting the need to exercise caution in applying blanket criteria. However, temporal changes must also be noted, for the electronic revolution has helped return some work and service activity to many residential communities. Although normally city by-laws exclude home-based businesses, the increasing demand for them and the difficulty of tracking down the small and mainly service-based workplaces have led to policy changes. The municipality of Mission in British Columbia, 50 miles from Vancouver, changed its by-laws in 1987, allowing small, home-based businesses in all residential areas, except for retail and auto-repair, both of which are prone to neighbourhood complaints. Such changes go some way to modifying the typical 'bedroom' suburb.

Schools

The introduction of compulsory education in western societies led to the construction of primary or elementary schools in neighbourhoods. Frequently these were used as basic building-blocks in planned neighbourhoods (Chapter 8). Schools can be regarded as highly significant points of community contact where parents share a common concern for the welfare and education of their children and are interested in the quality of the school and its staff. Interaction among parents at school meetings or events frequently spills over to the more general socialization and sharing that contributes to local community cohesion. Other schools, such as secondary schools, comprehensive and high schools, can fulfil a similar role, though since they cater for older children they have larger catchments, which do not correspond with local neighbourhoods. The notion of the 'neighbourhood school' has been powerful as a creative and perpetrating force for a local community which goes beyond the specific concern for the education of their children. Historically, teachers along with doctors, preachers and shop-keepers, were people of some status in the local community and they often assumed the roles of local organizers and leaders. Schools also have an emotive presence. Where communities have aged, proposals to close schools owing to reduced numbers of children has often met with opposition. In addition there is a widely-held belief in the 'school effect', where children from affluent schools know more, stay in school longer, and find better jobs than those from schools attended by mostly poor children. However, the research evidence is ambiguous. Variation in educational attainment is clear by social class, and to some extent by residential area, though the latter may in fact be a surrogate for social class. The school effect is obvious in the extreme case, the disadvantaged ghetto. Wilson (1987, 57) showed that there were only 9,500 graduates (grade 12) of the almost 25,500 ninth-grade (14-year-old) black and Hispanic students in segregated inner-city schools in

Chicago in 1980, and only 2,000 of these were able to read at, or above, the national average. These shockingly low levels of attainment help to perpetuate the cycle of poverty in the black ghettos.

The importance of schools as one of a set of neighbourhood services has been increased by modern trends towards greater community influence, if not control, in the United Kingdom. Now there is greater autonomy for boards of governors of individual schools and an opportunity to opt out of local authority control. In many ways this is reversing the centralization of the past forty years, for local schools were often originally provided and monitored by locally elected boards, not by the virtually anonymous professionals in the contemporary bureaucratic local state. These new trends combine to reinforce the local community roles of schools. Nevertheless, as with all locality-based schemes the problems discussed in Chapter 6 must be noted. In the area with the most local control, the United States, there are huge contrasts between well-supplied schools in affluent suburban areas and impoverished ones in ghetto areas. Similarly, small jurisdictions may be taken over by small-minded groups with a possible reduction in educational standards. Monitoring of educational standards by outside agencies seems essential if local control is not to descend to intolerance and nepotism. Attempts to reduce the locality significance of schools, such as desegregationist bussing and parental choice, rather than allocation to the nearest school, have not achieved marked changes in local achievement rates in poorer areas.

The last generation has seen a spectacular increase in the number of two-income families throughout the western world. For example, only 23.3 per cent of Canadian husband and wife families in 1991 were headed by a single wage-earner. This has led to a growth in demand for day-care facilities and co-operative pre-school centres. Major employers are also creating child-care facilities, whilst they are standard in collaborative communities (see Chapter 8). Hofferth and Phillips (1991) estimated that there are 80,000 regulated child-

care centres in the United States which have a capacity for 5.3 million children. In the English-speaking world most have been accommodated in local church basements or community halls, rather than in purpose-built facilities, for the state has been reluctant to take on this extra responsibility. When cultural issues are at stake, action is more likely to be taken. For example, the demand for Welsh language education led to a national organization of nursery schools (Mudiad Ysgolion Meithrin) in 1971 which, mainly through government grants, had established 433 small nursery schools throughout Wales by 1985 (Williams 1986, 124).

Leisure and Social Facilities

Historically, the church and its associated hall often acted as the venue for many social events in inner-city communities, whilst philanthropic efforts provided many services in nineteenth-century cities (see Chapter 6). Some of these, notably libraries, were later taken over by municipalities. Two related trends can be seen in the provision of leisure and social services, especially in the last twenty years: the first is the development of neighbourhood-based leisure facilities by municipal or state agencies; the second is the grass-roots provision of services.

At the turn of the century, the provision of leisure facilities was restricted to the development of parks, part of the 'greening of cities' linked to reactions against the squalor of the industrial city and the City Beautiful and Garden City movements (see Chapter 8). Later it led to the municipal provision of children's playgrounds, sports fields, swimming-pools, etc. as well as open space. Table 7.2 shows the historical changes in standards proposed by the city of Calgary, illustrating the delivery of more recreational facilities and the way in which a hierarchical areal framework is used for the calculation of open space (Reinson, 1992). These facilities are complemented by sectoral parks in the four quadrants of the city and a series of golf courses

Table 7.2 Calgary Parks, Open Spaces and Facilities Standards, 1962–88

Open spaces	1988	1976	1962
Subneighbourhood	1/500–1000 pop.; $^1/_3$ hectare minimum	no standard	no standard
Neighbourhood	1/5000; 2.4 hectares minimum	no standard	no standard
Community	1/15,000; 5 hectares minimum	5.5 acres/1000	within 1 mile of 2,000 families; 10–15 acres minimum
Regional rec.	1/50,000; 20 hectares minimum	2.6 acres/1000 20 or more acres in size	1/district (about 30,000 people)
Natural areas	Must be reserved (1977 Act)	20 acres or more no locational or service area standard	encourage dev. as available
Special-purpose — golf courses	1/30,000 (18 holes)	4.3 acres or 0.55 holes/1000	2 × 18–27 holes for city;
— athletics parks	1/45,000; 12–16 hectares	1 acre/1000; 20 acres minimum	1/major segment of city; and less comprehensive field as supplements
Pools — indoor — outdoor — wading	1/15,000 pop. 1/70,000 1/125,000 (1 per quadrant)	1/45,000 – no standard	no standard
Arenas — municipal — community — community rink	1/15,000 pop. 1/3,500 –	1/25,000 1/12–15,000 1 set of boards/1,500	included as part of 'regional recreation centre' (athletics parks)

Source: Revised from Reinson 1992. N.B. This list is not comprehensive.

and river-bank green areas to produce an exceptionally well-favoured set of recreational opportunities for the city. It must also be remembered that affluent areas in most North American cities have their own private sports and social clubs with membership limited to those who can pay substantial entry fees and be approved by existing members, although the YMCA–YWCA (Young Men's/Women's Christian Association) provides accessible alternatives in many centres. Within the last decade the 'fitness boom' has led to the addition of many health clubs, but most are privately provided or contained in apartment complexes.

Part of the new emphasis upon leisure activities is that leisure itself has been a recent 'growth industry'. In Britain, Gershuny and Jones (1987) undertook a diary survey which showed that for all groups studied, there were substantial gains in leisure time between 1981 and 1984. In 1980, 88 per cent of workers had four weeks' holiday or more per year, compared with only 20 per cent in 1970. During a normal week a combination of less time spent at work, changes in family life and the roles of women, all contributed to a greater amount of leisure time. Yet British people were generally not prepared to travel long distances for leisure. Veal (1974) showed that three-quarters of library-users travelled less than one mile, as did half of the users of swimming-pools and one-third of the users of indoor sports centres. A Sports Council for Wales (1986) survey also showed sports centres are mainly used by people within 15 minutes' journey time. However, there are often considerable differences in levels of provision. In Wales computer models have been used to compare the supply of facilities with the demand which might normally be expected from the resident population. One model had three principal components of; demand, supply and catchment area, and was used to identify localities in which there was an unsatisfied demand or a lack of adequate facilities. The way in which the model might be used is shown in Figure 7.2. Two swimming-pools, A with a capacity of 10,000 one-hour visits in peak time per week and B with 5,000, are located near the city centre. The catchment areas based upon typical travelling distances show that they serve limited areas of the city and that much of the urban area has an unsatisfied demand for swimming-pools. A strategy of providing locality-based pools, such as C, D and E, would meet unsatisfied demand and would also give a policy of community-based recreation services. The same rationale may be applied to other forms of recreation such as bowling, indoor sports halls and tennis courts, although as with all provisions based on services with different threshold sizes a pattern of scatter is likely to result. Many believe that these activities would be better centred on one location which recognizes what the Sports Council for Wales (SCW) termed 'the limits of many people's mobility and the access benefits of proximity' (SCW 1986, 23). In the United Kingdom, although the earliest multi-purpose leisure centres were large, being conceived on national or regional scales, there was a shift in the 1970s and 1980s towards smaller centres with more localized catchments that included more resident participation in the planning process (Torkildsen 1983). It has been argued that the school is in essence a community leisure centre in embryo. With some modifications and a proper management strategy, schools can be made available for community use in out-of-school hours, for they possess high visibility and ease of access (Torkildsen 1983). Dual-use or optimum-use has become a major component of policies designed to improve local sports and recreation provision. In Wales the Sports Council has strongly promoted the idea and has invested money to improve facilities in local schools with the expectation of large community use. This enables the school to take on a wider role as a community facility, bringing together local residents who are not necessarily parents of children attending the school. Not everyone benefits, however. The concept of 'recreational deprivation' (Glyptis 1989) has been developed to define groups of people and areas of residence which have constraints upon their ability to participate in various forms of leisure activity. This type of approach extends the welfare approach to planning with neighbourhood services used as a base for delivering a range of services designed to minimize recreational deprivation. This approach, of course, is far more common in the United States where the inner cities have seen a wide range of initiatives designed to provide services and jobs for disadvantaged people, stressing public and private partnerships, and the active participation of community residents as part of the empowerment process.

The origin of grass-roots provision of social and recreational services lies in the parish halls of local churches, where attempts were made

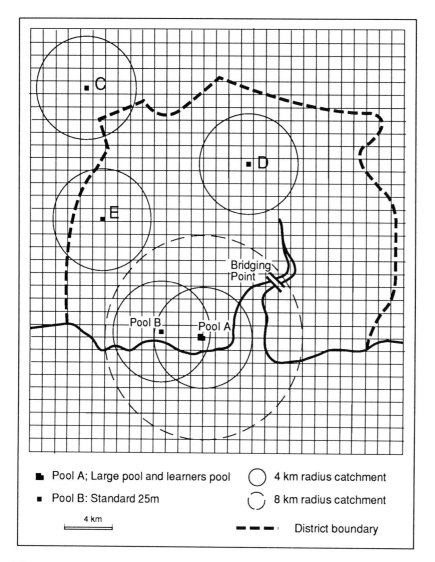

Figure 7.2 Modelling recreation facility locations (Sports Council for Wales 1986)

to improve the quality of working-class life. One of the garden city principles was to secularize this idea and add community centres to planned residential areas. Chapter 8 has described how the idea is being increasingly adopted in contemporary planned residential developments. However, the principle of a grass-roots approach to the building of local meeting-places and the organization of recreational facilities is growing. It is particularly prominent in many Canadian suburban areas where local community organizations in cities have built local meeting-halls with a combination of locally raised funds and loans from various levels of governments. By the 1990s some had evolved into million-dollar complexes with extensive indoor sports centres such as hockey rinks and pools. Calgary has a particularly extensive system of community halls with the larger buildings in the post-1950 suburbs. At the same time many of these communities run many recreational and social programmes (some co-sponsored by the city's Parks and Recreational Department), although

Townshend (1992) has shown that there are considerable variations in the level of activity between the communities (see Figure 7.3).

Health Care Systems

Medical services are also widely distributed throughout the urban area and since they are often privately provided they are often taken as analogous to retailing, although market rules are by no means the only guidelines for location. In the past, surgeries were randomly scattered, for most were single doctors in converted rooms or in a room of the residence. In England, the number of single-doctor practices declined from 5,337 to 2,925 between 1961 and 1986, whilst large practices of six or more doctors increased from 450 to 4,539. As group practices have replaced individual surgeries, the logic for locating a new clinic in, or close to, a shopping centre has become stronger. Phillips (1981) studied surgery attendance in Swansea and showed that high-status groups used local surgeries, though not necessarily those entailing the shortest journey. Lower-income groups either used the nearest surgery, or retained allegiance to a practice in the city centre close to their previous place of residence. This latter situation typified people who had moved from older neighbourhoods in the inner city to peripheral public sector estates.

In the United States the fee-for-service basis of health care delivery gives it a stronger link with market forces, so most physicians are located in commercial centres. The 'general practitioner' in the traditional sense of a single all-purpose physician is becoming uncommon. There are more group practices and doctors who specialize, often resulting in a locational shift to higher levels in the hierarchical status of commercial centres and thus creating greater distances between home and doctor. This has also been the trend in Canada despite its universal health care coverage. An important feature of many community-level shopping-centres in western Canada in the last decade has been the development of walk-in

clinics, often called Medi-Stops, which are open for long hours, where individuals can simply turn up and wait for service, rather than being subject to the increasing delays through the appointment system in traditional practices.

Changing city-wide locations of physicians over time tend to follow the changing social geography of the urban area. De Vise (1971) showed the rapid decline of physicians from 475 to 76 between 1950 and 1970 in the inner suburbs of Chicago as the communities changed from middle-class white to low-status black. In these situations, some low-status areas become denuded of medical care. Local hospitals, through their casualty departments, assume the roles of neighbourhood clinics. De Vise (1973, 1) concluded in the early 1970s that in American cities: 'if you are average poor, under 65, female, black or live in a low-income neighbourhood, ... you are a disenfranchised citizen as far as health-care rights go.' These observations were confirmed in the 1980s, for Whiteis and Salmon (1987) noted some 150 community hospital failures in the United States between 1980 and 1984. The combination of hospital closure, which showed a strong correlation with ethnic communities, and the growth of private health care, ensured that many poor neighbourhoods in cities such as Chicago, Philadelphia, St Louis and Atlanta, were denied access to welfare hospitals. Changes also affected the *quality* of primary health care in poorer neighbourhoods. Knox (1987) described a situation in inner-city areas, where a residual, marginalized population with high health care needs was being served increasingly by elderly doctors, often working in ill-equipped, single-handed practices. During the later 1980s and 1990s there was evidence of a new American policy towards health care in the community. Nevertheless, Farrant (1991) argued that although the locally provided community health movement had grown rapidly, it was greatly under-funded. Other health care professionals show similar trends to doctors. Dental and optical practices are also found in close proximity to local shopping-centres, whilst the growing use of chiropractic services in North American cities has meant that these professionals are now typical of the lowest level of neighbourhood service centre in the suburbs.

The Caring Community

Historically the provision of care outside the family or kinship group, was a responsibility of the church in western society, supplemented by the role of neighbours. Medieval churches and abbeys took on the role of ministry to the body, as well as to the soul. Gradually the state, through Poor Law legislation and the provision of work houses took over responsibility for those unable to help themselves, although this was usually paralleled by the development of hospitals and homes funded by philanthropic efforts. In recent years two trends can be seen. The growth of purpose-built communities for the retired able to afford such residences will be discussed in Chapter 8, whilst the 'community delivery' model has been favoured for formal 'health care'. Targeted at disadvantaged groups such as the mentally ill and the elderly, it has been supplied within the ambit of bureaucratically structured agencies of the local or national state (Bulmer 1986).

The community delivery approach goes beyond the provision of specialist medical services discussed earlier and has been based on the concept of the 'caring community'. Bulmer's (1986) review of the work of the late Philip Abrams showed that he softened his initially sharp antithesis between the formal and informal sectors and saw neighbourhood care as: 'Becoming a meeting ground for the informal values of reciprocity, mutual defence, proximity exclusion and internal social control and the formal values of provision, coverage, distance, accessibility and external social control' (Bulmer 1986, 230). However, Walker (1986) has argued that in the final analysis it is not usually the neighbourhood community *per se* which provides care for the elderly, but the family, and more accurately, the women relatives who act as lone carers. Similarly, Stoller

and Pugliesi (1988) show that the informal networks of most older people were dominated by kin; where they have to rely on neighbours, the elderly tend to receive a more limited range of help. Also Philip Abrams was clear that the role of kin was a fundamental component of neighbourhood care, demonstrating that 90 per cent of informal community care was in fact provided by kin, almost all by women. Walker (1987) further argued that informal support networks within the community were insufficient unless backed by good levels of state provision. From this it follows that neighbourhood care based upon the availability of relatives is that most assured of success. If any policy for informal care is to be realistic, it must begin with relations, and with the problems and possibilities of supporting the bonds of kinship. Altruism and reciprocity, the two main reasons for informal care (see also Chapter 3) develop most strongly within the world of kinship. Philip Abrams argued (see Bulmer 1986) that the ideal of domiciliary care proclaimed by the vast majority of those in need is, in effect, a blunt preference for the family. Most of the work of others, agencies and individuals, can be viewed as supplementary. For those without kin, or with few members in the locality — the increasingly typical pattern of modern cities — the options were institutionalization or a package of care entailing the fine division of labour among many helpers. In such circumstances the emotional association between giver and recipient may be lost. The reversal to the historic kinship ties of the earliest human communities may still be viewed as the favoured model, in the same way that most people in society still assume that parents should be primarily responsible for the nurturing of their young. Even so, we must recognize that this is not a feeling found in many communal colonies, where children spend most of their time with specialist helpers, or even in upper middle-class western societies where children are sent away to boarding-school to be educated in the mores of their class and establish linkages with their classmates from similar backgrounds.

Two examples of groups that have been subject to the new ideas of the caring community — the mentally ill and the elderly — provide further evidence of the approach, although similar arguments can be provided for other care-related facilities at a local community level.

The mentally ill

Through most of this century, and for many decades before, medical opinion advocated the isolation of the mentally ill in specialist institutions, part of the specialization and segregation of modern society described in Chapter 2. Increasingly, however, the potential role of neighbourhood or community care for these groups gained favour as national policies of deinstitutionalization led to the progressive discharge of patients from long-stay institutions. In the United States, the process began in the early 1960s and the Community Mental Health Centres (CHMC) Act was passed in 1963. The aim was to minimize the amount of care provided in institutional settings, and the resident population of state and county mental hospitals declined from about 560,000 in 1955 to 125,000 in 1981 (Shadish, Lurigio and Lewis 1989). By 1980 over 700 CHMCs had been established and outpatient attendances increased from 379,000 in 1955 to 4.6 million in 1975. The approach has been paralleled elsewhere: for example, deinstitutionalization in England and Wales caused the resident population of mental hospitals to fall by 28 per cent between 1951 and 1970.

Deinstitutionalization worked best for the acutely ill who remained in less crowded institutions and for those, often with manageable conditions, who could return to home and family; it worked worst for the chronically ill. Shadish et al. (1989) stated that most of the chronically ill in America were either still in institutions or in community settings characterized by poverty, stigma, social isolation and poor care. In the early 1980s the CHMC Act was repealed. Funds now went to states, rather than directly to centres; the future of the com-

munity health movement had become uncertain and an era of innovation had come to an end. Although the pragmatic cost-cutting objectives for deinstitutionalization must be clearly recognized, the Community Health Program did have welfare and redistributive aims and the hope that the chronically mentally ill would lead a normal life in the community. These were wildly optimistic hopes, based on what Smith (1980) described as idealized traditional roles for the community (Table 7.3). The *locational* role of neighbourhood would give the mentally ill an 'address' within the city, a place in the 'normal order of things'. The *structural* role provided both a liveable built environment and access to the range of services which are delivered at the neighbourhood level, including mental care facilities. The *humanistic* role would provide the more subjective qualities of neighbourhood life, with an emphasis on 'sense of belonging' and neighbourhood as 'haven' or 'anchoring space' within the larger urban area (see Chapter 5).

Research has revealed that there has been very limited success in assimilating the chronic, mentally ill patients into neighbourhood or community care. Shadish et al. (1989) estimated that 15 per cent of this group in the United States are still in hospital, 10 per cent are with families and 7 per cent are homeless. Warner (1989) estimated that only half of the non-institutionalized mentally ill were in anything resembling a 'domestic environment', the rest were homeless, in gaols, boarding-houses, nursing-homes or a range of other arrangements such as sheltered care. Although patients do best where they fit into the social fabric of the community, as with other forms of care, it is the presence of kin which makes the integration most likely. For many that route to neighbourhood integration and care is not available, and Warner (1989) estimated that between a quarter to a half of the men on America skid rows suffered from severe mental illness, excluding alcoholism. This simply reconfirmed the classic ecological study by Faris and Dunham (1939) which demonstrated the high correlation between the incidence of most mental disorders and several

Table 7.3 Attributes and elements of neighbourhoods

| ATTRIBUTES | ELEMENTS | | SERVICE |
	Spatial/Physical	Social	
HUMANISTIC	Home, haven (unselfconscious awareness of place)	Belonging, psychic identity	Participation, involvement
LOCATIONAL	Address, residence, security	Social status, trackability, encapsulation	*Formal service provision:* (a) housing, recreation, education, transportation, etc. (b) Services (counselling, information and referral, etc.)
STRUCTURAL	Physical stimuli (physical, ecological, geographical, demographic) — evaluative effects — responsive effects		Service provision (natural support systems) — informal *services* from kin and kith *access* functions — *context* or climate for helping

Source: Smith 1980.

indicators of stressful social and environmental attributes in Chicago.

The first point to emerge in any evaluation of the neighbourhood care approach is that small proportions of the mentally ill actually return to stable residential neighbourhoods. Those with kin support are most likely to assimilate. However, many end up in those parts of the inner cities where although facilities may be accessible, the general living conditions are likely to accelerate rather than ameliorate their condition. Smith (1980) confirmed that many of the residential areas in which the mentally ill are found are dilapidated and disorganized, arguing that neighbourhoods can be regarded either as part of the solution to mental health problems or as part of the problems themselves. Giggs (1986)

has explored the respective utility of two hypotheses for the concentration of schizophrenics: the breeder (increase due to the stressful environment); and drift (downward to the poorest areas). His analysis in Nottingham provided support for the former, although he was careful to emphasize the restriction of the conclusion to the specific cohort studied and the case study area — for Britain has not been subject to such a rapid and massive deinstitutionalization as the United States. Another point in the evaluation of deinstitutionalization is the acceptability by neighbourhoods of mental health centres. Whereas people are very happy to see a park in the next block, and a library or school as part of their neighbourhood, mental health centres, along with city dumps and prisons should be 'elsewhere'. Taylor (1989) argued that community exclusion was a predictable response to the deinstitutionalization of mental health care, for territorial prerogatives were challenged when neighbourhoods were identified as potential locations for mental health care facilities (the 'not-in-my-backyard' syndrome discussed in Chapter 6).

> Community exclusion of the mentally ill emerges as a manifestation of individual and collective desires to protect territory with the aims of maintaining the use and exchange values of home and neighbourhood, and on a deeper, but related level, as a component within a process of reproduction which perpetuates the uneven distribution of life changes and advantages. (Taylor 1989, 317)

Hence it is not surprising that other facilities with the same negative aura, such as shelters for the homeless or battered women, or halfway homes for convicted prisoners, are viewed in the same way. However, although opposition to the siting of mental health facilities is widespread, it does vary. Dear et al. (1985) indicate that whereas higher-status groups are more tolerant of mental illness, they are considerably less tolerant on issues of facility location if home and neighbourhoods are threatened. Resistance is strongest in suburban localities, so facilities have tended to be located in low-income and inner-city neighbourhoods. Where such resistance is overcome, host communities are likely to show grudging acceptance, not positive support (Taylor 1989). Again, increasing numbers of the elderly are present in most western cities, not owing to any deliberate policy but mainly to natural demographic trends (see Chapter 3). The elderly have always made high demands upon both the health and social services care systems. With the growth of the nuclear rather than the extended family, increasing longevity and greater mobility, which has meant children no longer live in the parents' locality, there has been extra pressure on institutional care.

Old people

Chapter 3 (Classifying Communities) has already described the huge increase in the number of elderly people in western society. In Britain, Bebbington and Davies (1980) showed that between 1948 and 1975 the permanently supported elderly patients in Britain rose from 50,000 to 120,000. However, this has done little more than keep pace with increases in numbers of especially vulnerable old people since the late 1960s. This group of the elderly retain hospital-bed priority because of their frailty and infirmity and tend to be long-stay patients. In 1968 some 14 per cent of the average daily occupied hospital beds in the United Kingdom were taken by geriatric and chronically ill patients (Social Trends 1970), and cuts in the British National Health Service led to a decline to between 10 and 13 per cent by the end of the next decade (Social Trends 1981). Between 1971 and 1978 when the average daily bed occupancy decreased from 435,000 to 381,000, other forms of care have been substituted and there has been a spectacular growth in residential care homes. Phillips and Vincent (1986) identified five categories of institutions that care for the elderly: sheltered homes, local authority homes, private residential care homes, nursing homes and voluntary homes. In 1986 there were just over 231,000 elderly residents in care homes in Great Britain, with about half of these in the public sector. Whereas the numbers in local authority homes remained constant from 1982 to 1986, those in private residential care homes had increased at an average rate of over 21 per cent per year (Social Trends 1990). Overall, it has been estimated (Warnes 1982) that the demands of old people on health and social services are five times as high as those of the average adult citizen.

Less reliance on traditional institutions and more use of smaller-scale community-based homes for the elderly give one dimension to a new emphasis upon neighbourhood care. However, as the numbers of the 'old-old' (over 75 years of age) increase, so the role of community care in its various forms become critical, for the institutions cannot cope with the influx. Rowles (1978) has shown that old people become increasingly dependent on local space: home and neighbourhood assume dominance in their lives (see also Chapter 5: Extending the Sense of Place). Most old people still live in their own homes, often alone or with a spouse, and are dependent on others. Doctors, preachers and social workers all have key roles, though again, kin is a central consideration. Good neighbours also seem to be essential if the personal well-being of the elderly is to be sustained, for many prefer to remain in their old and familiar environment as long as possible. Unfortunately the trends discussed in Chapters 2 and 4 demonstrate the decline in neighbourly contact — although there are exceptions — whilst the increase in distances to even minimal shopping and services due to post-war spatial rationalization and suburbanization have created a huge problem of isolation for the elderly and immobile. This explains why there has been such an expansion of domiciliary services designed to care for old people in their homes. In Britain, the 'home-help' service is the most important. Although started for maternity cases, by 1953 one-half of its clients were old people and this has risen to almost 90 per cent by the 1990s. Complementary to home-helps is the meals-on-wheels service which began on a voluntary basis and was taken over by local authorities following the National Assistance Act of 1962. Again it is a service which has become dominated by the needs of the elderly. The problems of the elderly explain the growth in private residential communities in North America (see Chapter 8: Retirement Communities).

Crime and Policing

Historically only the rich could afford to guarantee their safety and the security of possessions by the employment of private bodyguards. Policing became one of the earliest municipal concerns as the nineteenth-century cities increased their level of services,

replacing the medieval pattern of voluntary sharing of night-watches. Hence, in most western countries the policing of communities passed into the hands of increasingly professionalized police forces based on large regions or cities, usually subject to national guidance and standards, and with only limited local input from lay membership in consultative commissions, a pattern that can be found in related services such as fire prevention. The United States provides the real exception, where police chiefs are often subject to election, and many local forces still exist, although they are paralleled by state forces. The typical decrease in local control has been matched by an apparent decline in local police presence, due to the use of cars in place of foot patrols, and the increasing bureaucratization and specialization of the forces. Within the last twenty years there has been increasing academic interest in the relationships between communities, crime and policing (Evans, Fyfe and Herbert 1992), in which three themes can be recognized: areal or community variations in crime; areal control by police; and community participation.

Community Context of Crime

It is clear that the incidence of crime in both the residence of offenders and occurrence of criminal events is subject to area variations. As some 'neighbourhoods' within the city contain disproportionate numbers of criminals and delinquents, so also are there 'vulnerable neighbourhoods' which suffer disproportionately from victimization. The notion of crime areas or delinquency areas has been extant since the nineteenth century and can be supported by a considerable amount of empirical evidence, as well as being fictionalized in Dickens's classic descriptions of London's crime 'rookeries', where people were habituated, even bred, to a life of crime. The most recent research into urban communities and crime (see, for example, Taylor 1991) confirms the relevance of the local community as a context for the study of crime. Research shows that situations of poverty and relative deprivation are linked to crimes of violence and to other crimes such as theft. Poor and ethnic inner-city neighbourhoods in American cities are particularly at risk for these conditions are prevalent. Wilson (1987, 25) has described how the four-square-mile, largely black, Wentworth Avenue police district of South Chicago, which contains the notorious Robert Taylor public housing project of twenty-eight high-rise towers, was the site for 81 murders and 1,691 aggravated assaults in 1983. These were 11 per cent and 13 per cent of the city's total respectively, although the area only contained 3.4 per cent of the city's population. The British Crime Survey has also revealed strong area variations in the incidence of crime and showed clear concentrations in poor areas, both in the inner city and in more problematic public sector estates. Research has shown that public housing projects may become stigmatized at an early stage and persist as foci of criminality (Gill 1977). For example, a study in Chicago found that public sector housing projects which were vulnerable initially, were made more unstable by placements of rehoused population, and this produced higher delinquency rates (Bursik 1989).

Another line of research has developed the idea that communities move through 'life cycles' or 'careers' in their experience of criminality. Bottoms and Wiles (1986; 1992) analysed public sector housing projects in Sheffield, England, and showed the effects of managerial decisions, sales of houses and their changing status on criminality. Schuerman and Kobrin's (1986) study was based upon the twenty-year histories of some of the highest crime-rate neighbourhoods in Los Angeles. They found that rising crime-rates were associated with a number of changes which signalled neighbourhood deterioration, such as shift to multiple-family dwelling, greater mobility, more broken families, more children and minority ethnic groups. Several recent studies have developed these ideas, stressing the significance of 'incivilities' such as signs of vandalism, graffiti and abandoned cars, as indicators of neighbourhood decline. Taylor

and Gottfredson (1986) regarded physical incivilities as signs of community breakdown which indirectly influenced the attitudes of residents and offenders' perceptions of risk. The association between high-rise accommodation and anti-social behaviour was highlighted by Coleman (1985) and will be discussed in Chapter 8. Herbert (1992) recently demonstrated the links between levels of incivilities, perceived level of crime and fear of crime in intra-urban areas.

A recent advance in explaining the incidence of crime is that of the 'community-career' concept, namely changes that take place in the demographic composition of the neighbourhood (see the discussion in Chapter 3: Classifying Communities). The peak crime-offending years are the teens and early twenties, so when the area 'life cycle' reaches the stage at which there are large numbers of youths in these age categories the local level of crime is likely to rise. Taylor (1991) suggested that the 'age change–crime change link' was underpinned by worsening economic prospects. The force of this observation is clear in neighbourhoods where large numbers of youths face very limited employment opportunities. A more general thesis on neighbourhood change was advanced by Bursik (1989) who argued that rapid change, regardless of its direction, was linked with increasing levels of disorder. Parts of many poor inner-city neighbourhoods, for example, have experienced 'gentrification' (see Chapter 3: Classifying Communities). Since this has increased the opportunities for some kinds of criminal behaviour, the local crime-rates have risen.

Area Control

If community, as locality, provides a significant context within which crime can be studied, then it is rational to assume that policing and other crime control strategies can usefully adopt a similar community base. Police resources are traditionally allocated by areas or territories within the city: both car and foot-patrols have 'beats' or similar areas for which they are responsible. Two recent initiatives in this area have attempted to improve area control. The Kansas City Preventive Patrol experiment is one of the most commonly cited strategies of crime prevention, and was based on the assumption that a more *visible presence of police* or patrol cars would prevent crime in public places, particularly the saturation patrols of the worst areas. A second approach is the intensive application of *information technology* to crime events and a quicker policing response so that the perpetrators may be caught in their crime. Remote burglar alarms that ring in the local police station or surveillance cameras provide the most obvious examples.

Some research (Smith 1986) has indicated another component in areal policing. Although the pattern is not simple, police patrols do vary their use of their discretionary powers in different types of neighbourhoods. They tend, for example, to be more active in racially mixed neighbourhoods and there are higher probabilities of *being* arrested in lower-status areas. Although police decisions on whom to arrest appear to be independent of race, sex and neighbourhood, there are highly publicized criticisms of prejudice against blacks, Hispanics and natives in American cities. This has led to calls for the inclusion of more minority groups to reduce the racial imbalance in police forces. In an areal context Sherman (1986) advocated a mix of police initiatives which could include: differential police responses to different types of neighbourhood; saturation patrols to suppress disorder; foot-patrols in high-density areas; and occasional pro-active strategies. Although few will admit to such a policy, there seems little doubt that some areas of cities are almost 'no-go' areas where the level of policing is at least minimal and perhaps restricted to major crimes in day-light hours. In western cities that have identifiable 'red light' areas, the police will often tolerate a wider range of behaviours, except in the case of major crimes. The response of the populace should also be considered in the context of areal control. Jones, McLean and Young (1986) argued that aggressive policing in low-income ethnic areas had the effect of alienating large sections of those communities. Moreover, since the police relied upon residents within the communities for much of their information about crime, aggressive tactics were effective in cutting-off an important source of knowledge.

Community Policing

Ekblom (1988) made an important distinction between the type of policing described above, which can cause friction with local residents — what he called *uniformed policing* — and *community policing*. The latter builds up contacts and understanding, and is relevant to the broader issues of community and social policy. Community policing is a new strategy of the last decade (Tuck 1991) which seeks to integrate individual officers as normal and accepted members of a specific community, and to encourage the local community to help in the control of crime. This is not seen as an interventionist, vigilante-style approach; but as promoting the notion of trust, and a willingness to confide in, and pass information on to officers. Tuck (1991, 34) argued that the new community approach consisted of ways in which the general public could be arranged to discourage crime. The strategy encouraged the joint practice of living together in a community with the aim of learning necessary *social norms* and habits of *virtue*. Although these may be considered rather idealistic given the changes in social mores in the past forty years, they include a set of measures based on local residential communities. Three trends can be recognized.

In the United Kingdom, *police consultative committees and crime prevention panels* are recent policy initiatives to increase the participation of the police in the local community. They can certainly claim some success in achieving citizen input, but they rarely reach the most disadvantaged members of community and the marginalized youth with whom the need for contact is greatest. This is why the next strategy has been favoured.

A second approach can be called the creation of *trusting relationships* to turn potential or actual criminals from a life of crime. Whether the initiative comes from a community police officer or a community participation officer, it is clear that much of the success depends upon the personality of the individual in establishing the initial trust to help turn the person's life around. As with any 'agent', be it police, priest, social worker, friend or teacher, in the end it is the quality of individual relationships which is critical in this approach. This is why so many voluntary, church or charity-based organizations have been established in the inner-city transient areas most prone to crimes and homelessness. Trained or experienced social workers try to help those who have dropped through the state's social security net, those who may turn to crime, or wish to leave the 'street-life', especially those without homes or those engaged in prostitution. Many of these agencies deliberately restrict themselves to donations and endeavour to distance themselves from the state apparatus. The 'top–down' process of provision for people in the most transient and disadvantaged areas of cities has failed to eradicate poverty and crime, so a number of street-based philanthropic or charity-funded organizations have tried to fill the gap.

Increasingly it has been recognized that a wide range of crime control strategies, particularly those involving crime prevention, rest upon *citizen participation* or *citizen collaboration*. Many believe that people must help themselves. The typical twentieth-century model of the professional, publicly provided 'top–down' system of policing is not enough. Public police officers need to interact with the range of private police, security guards and citizen volunteers in the common concern with safety in the community. A number of different programmes can be identified. In Canada, local Crime Watch television programmes that re-enact crimes have led to a positive and continuing citizen response and the solving of many crimes. More general is the Block Parent programme which entails placing a 'safe house' sign in the window of participating households. The occupiers are investigated by the police to ensure that the sign is justified, and

that responsible individuals are taking part. The house can then be a 'haven' for children who are being followed, bullied, or have mislaid their keys, or the mentally ill who have become lost, or individuals who simply need help; the occupants have received training in how to respond to requests for help and whom to contact. In 1990, 5,000 households, out of 262,000 in the city of Calgary, participated in the Block Parent Association in 1990. Another example can be seen in the Neighbourhood or Block Watch programmes that have become a new community-based strategy for crime prevention in many North American cities, one that it is spreading to other countries. It is based on reviving the principle of neighbourly co-operation, virtues that have been decreasing in our mobile, specialized and individualistic society. Groups are formed within communities which collaborate with police officers who establish codes of behaviour, and offer advice on ways in which crime can be reduced, such as the placing of signs in windows which declare the person to be a member of 'Neighbourhood Watch'; alertness to the safety of neighbouring dwellings and the establishment of reciprocal practices among others; the identification of strangers or individuals with suspicious behaviour in areas; and the adoption of security practices in their own homes. Again, although the measurable success of such efforts to reduce crime rates is difficult to assess, such schemes seem to have positive effects upon the quality of neighbourhood life by increasing interaction. These schemes demonstrate the move to prevention rather than post-crime reaction. The police accept that their own role in noticing a crime is minimal and it is the public who can best act as eyes and ears in the guardianship of a community, especially in sprawling suburbia. Sadly, Neighbourhood Watch is least adopted in those neighbourhoods which most need it. As Chapter 6 has pointed out the real 'problem areas' frequently have no social fabric or co-operative tradition upon which to build. By contrast, middle-income areas grasp it with fervour! As in the promotion of democracy by Locke and the seventeenth-century property-owners (Chapter 2: The Enlighten-ment), it is the threat to security of possessions which has stimulated action.

Another type of policing strategy which requires community participation of a different nature can be described as *target-hardening*. This may be the selection of specific neighbour-hoods to mark property, improve window and door locks or to improve street lighting (see Herbert and Moore 1991). Such programmes are often part of the Neighbourhood or Block Watch approach and can be extended by the design recommendations made by Newman (1972) and Coleman (1985) for decreasing crime and incivilities.

All the police initiatives targeted at commu-nities in the attempt to control crime are diffi-cult to evaluate. The results are not always clear because the danger of displacement of crime to less protected communities is always present. In addition, there is the ambiguous nature of crime-rates themselves. All official rates have 'dark areas' of unrecorded crime, and it is difficult to untangle inroads in the 'dark area' from inroads into real crime-rates. It must be stressed that crime afflicts different residential areas in different ways, and strate-gies to control crime can recognize this fact. In the 'historic' community, the police officer was an integral and recognized member of the locality, with a normal and accepted presence: in Britain the 'bobby on the local beat' was con-sidered to be a real deterrent in cities. Community policing is in some ways an attempt to return to that sort of relationship and to recognize that mobile policing has widened the gap between police and commu-nity. The police have the multiple roles of pre-venting crime, of apprehending criminals and of enforcing the law, and undertake these in conjunction with others. In dealing with offenders, they are part of a network which includes probation and other social service agencies; in dealing with victims, they must increasingly co-operate with victim support services, and in dealing with crime prevention their allies are the resident public. Many of these approaches have a local community base. Policing will be more effective if it gives proper

weight to the place of local community, encouraging local interaction to replace some of the bands of local solidarity that have been lost in western society.

Community Associations and Action

Chapter 6 has already noted that one of the major changes in the 1960s in North America was the growth of grass-root organizations in many cities (Kotler 1969; Williams 1985). However, many are of recent origin. For example, Kotler (1979) claimed that three-quar-ters of American organizations were created since 1970, and Logan and Rabrenovic (1990) showed that only 8 per cent of the organiza-tions in the New York Capital region existed before 1960, compared with the 70 per cent founded between 1975 and 1985. Examples of three major types of community development in intra-urban areas are discussed below. One is associated with the provision of needs, and is suburban-based. Another is linked to the cre-ation of area-based organizations in the inner city designed to fight against unwanted change, based on grass-roots action alone or by expert activists (Chapter 7). Through time this distinction has become blurred as even the suburban areas fight against unwanted devel-opment. To these essentially grass-roots devel-opments must be added a third example: the government-directed inner-city policy initia-tives which entail community action.

Needs

A good example of the first trend is provided by the city of Calgary, which has one of the most extensive series of community organiza-tions in North American cities (see Figure 7.3). These organizations started to develop in the 1920s in order to provide recreational and beautification programmes. By 1940 forty com-munities formed the original Federation of Calgary Communities financed by contribu-tions from the local areas. It was reorganized under the Societies Act in 1961, elected a Board

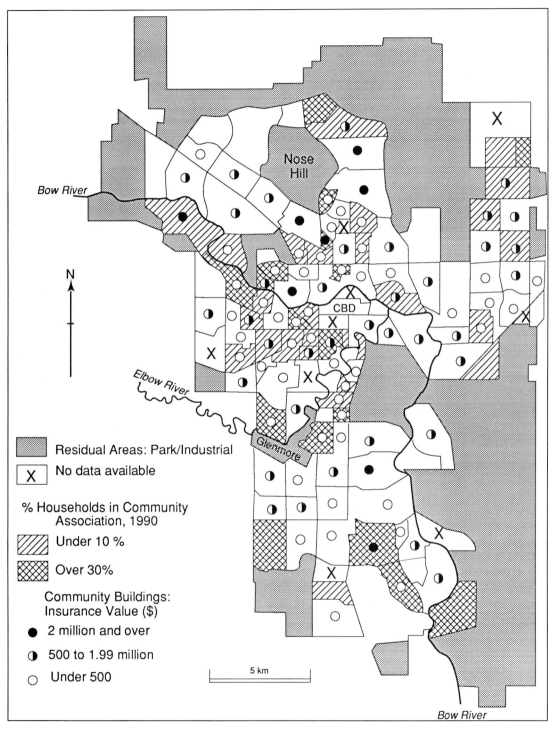

Figure 7.3 Community associations, community centres and membership levels; Calgary (adapted from Townshend 1992)

of Directors and started to provide consultative services for its members to help them survive, influence, even fight against development in their areas, whether from City Hall, Province or private developers. In 1978 the sports facilities split from the federation and formed an organization for Minor Sports. By 1992 there were 136 community associations in a city of three-quarters of a million population, each with its own Board of Directors and annual budget (see Figure 7.3). The proportion of households that are members of their local association varies considerably between the communities, with a city-wide average of 19 per cent, yet ranging from two cases with over 70 per cent membership (Scarborough and Parkdale), to five below 4 per cent (Bridgeland, Richmond, Elboya, Banff Trail and Capitol Hill).

Six communities have annual budgets of over $500,000 per year in 1990, although the average for the city associations is $152,000. The number and type of activities performed also show considerable variation, with four communities in the suburbs of the late 1960s providing over forty different activities, compared with the city community average of thirteen. Most community activities are still based on leisure pursuits, even though there has been a major change in the role of these areas in the last twenty years. Community associations have become the focus for citizen improvement projects, particularly in traffic control, where they advise or pressure city planners to close roads or limit exits so as to exclude through-traffic. There are also many examples of communities stopping or modifying plans for new shopping-centres, delaying the north-west leg of a light rail transit system for the city, preventing development on environmentally sensitive areas and supporting the preservation of Nose Hill as the largest urban park (2,600 acres) in Canada. The new political clout of these communities is seen by the fact that they are routinely consulted by City Hall planners and private developers before major land-use decisions are made in existing areas, although the final decision still rests with the elected city council. Moreover, 'structure

plans' that define land-use patterns for each community have to contain citizen input.

Unwanted Change

The inner-city community of Hillhurst-Sunnyside in Calgary provides an example of the second trend, where local activists fought against the development pressures for high-rise residences and offices spilling over from booming downtown in the 1970s. They managed to preserve much of the area for single-family residences, although it has been gentrified and the shopping-centre has been transformed into a zone of restaurants and boutiques. In addition, the community association for this area provides a series of unique services from its budget of $256,000 in 1990 with several fulltime and part-time paid staff, as well as claiming the occasional use of over 300 volunteers. It provides some housing for senior citizens and also runs a series of care facilities, such as day-care and pre-school activities. Neighbourhood help is also provided, such as assisting senior citizens with their yards and sidewalks. Meetings on issues of local and environmental concern are also held. In the last year pressure for the recycling of garbage, especially paper, glass and metal, led the city to establish one of its pilot community drop-off recycling facilities in the area. To complete its role as a distinctive community, the association runs an annual festival, to promote its image as much as an occasion for fund-raising and enjoyment.

Government Community Development Initiatives

The third example is that of government attempts to improve the quality of life, job opportunities, and environmental conditions of impoverished and obsolescent inner-city areas. It has already been noted in the objectives of this book that the topic is too broad to be dealt with in detail here: not only does it deserve its own treatment but also it goes beyond strictly community issues. What is worth noting is that in the 1950s and 1960s a series of top–down government policies aimed at inner-city areas were initiated. They included schemes such as urban renewal, housing improvement, environmental clean-up, and the provision of a range of social services (Wilson 1987; Pinch 1985). To these must be added a variety of philanthropic and church-supplied services. Also, many results were far from expectations. The poorest were often pushed out of the renewed areas and large council housing projects became the home for new squalor and hopelessness. The level of unemployment increased because of the flight of goods-producing jobs from the inner-city at a time of increasing unemployment and the creation of a new service economy, which either provided low-paid jobs or employment demanding high educational skills. In addition, a veritable jungle of bureaucratic control from a large number of overlapping programmes and agencies increased the level of dependency.

In the 1980s the nature of area policies changed from improvement of social conditions, such as in housing, social services and education, to an economic base, entailing public and public partnerships in economic development, job training and renewal, and investment strategies (see reviews in Williams 1985, 265). Governments, developers and academics in most western countries now agree on the need for a high level of local resident participation and job creation, to eradicate, or at least mitigate, the welfare dependency, the unemployment and the frequently violent local sub-culture. New programmes such as Enterprise Zones and Urban Development Corporations (Church and Hall 1989) were enacted in Britain; in America programmes such as the Urban Department Action Grants used federal funds as a leverage for private investment to revitalize older urban areas (Eyles 1989). It is difficult to evaluate the effectiveness of area policies. Those with Marxist leanings see all these local initiatives as palliatives, not cures (Harvey 1985; Badcock 1984) Some local area initiatives have improved the quality of life of residents,

becoming an exemplar for other areas. Others have been unsuccessful. To assume societal conditions are dominant in explaining behaviour implies an economic determinism with no possibility of escape.

Conclusions

This chapter has examined the ways in which the local community has participated in the provision of services. It is not exhaustive and several of the themes overlap, although it does demonstrate several issues: examples of how the local community or neighbourhood is used as a base for the provision of services; how the efficacy of that base has varied over time and from one kind of community to another; and how community associations can respond to the services provided and act as provider. However, as the example of the mentally ill demonstrates, community-based programmes are not a universal panacea: there is a need to distinguish between myths and realities, to recognize the limitations as well as the potentials of the use of local areas and the harnessing of local community groups (see also Chapter 7). Nevertheless, the increasing role of local community organizations must be acknowledged. In part this is a new grass-roots empowerment, a reaction against the top–down provision from the local municipality. Even so, it must be recognized that the functions performed are still limited, both legally and in their financial ability to find enough money to undertake local tasks, for they have a subordinate political role in municipalities reluctant to give up control. There are variations in service provision by local area and from 1994 in the United Kingdom a set of performance indicators have been proposed which will monitor the effectiveness of provision over the set of local authority areas in services such as education, housing and public utilities. The Audit Commission will undertake to provide data in order to measure the extent to which value for money is being achieved. It should be possible to extend this kind of monitoring of performance down to local community scales.

References

Badcock, B., 1984, *Unfairly structured cities*, Basil Blackwell, Oxford, England.

Banerjee, T. and Baer, W. C., 1984, *Beyond the neighbourhood unit*, Plenum Press, New York.

Bebbington, A. C. and Davies, B., 1980, Territorial need indicators: a new approach, *Journal of Social Policy*, 9, 145–68.

Bottoms, A. E. and Wiles, P., 1986, Housing tenure and residential community crime careers in Britain, in A. J. Reiss and M. Tonry (eds), *Communities and crime*, University of Chicago Press, Chicago, 101–62.

Bottoms, A. E. and Wiles, P., 1992, Housing markets and residential community crime careers: a case study from Sheffield, in D. J. Evans, N. R. Fyfe and D. T. Herbert (eds), *Crime, Policing and Place*, Routledge, London, 118–44.

Bulmer, M., 1986, *Neighbours: the work of Philip Abrams*, Cambridge University Press, Cambridge.

Bursik, R. J., 1989, Political decision-making and ecological models of delinquency: conflict and consensus, in S. F. Messner, M. D. Krohn and A. E. Liska (eds), *Theoretical integration in the study of deviance and crime: problems and prospects*, SUNY Press, Albany, New York, 105–17.

Church, A. P. and Hall, J. M., 1989, Local initiatives for economic regeneration, in D. T. Herbert and D. M. Smith (eds), *Social problems and the city: new perspectives*, Oxford University Press, 345–69.

Coleman, A., 1985, *Utopia on trial*, Hilary Shipman, London.

Davies, R. L., 1984, *Retail and commercial planning*, Croom Helm, London.

Dawson, J. E., 1983, *Shopping centre development*, Longman, London.

De Vise, P., 1971, Cook County Hospital, bulwark of Chicago's apartheid health-care system, *Antipode*, 3, 9–20.

De Vise, P., 1973, Misused and misplaced hospitals and doctors: a locational analysis of the urban health-care crisis, *Annals, Association of American Geographers*, Resource Paper 22.

Dear, M. J., Taylor, S. M., Bestvorte, D. and Breston, B., 1985, *Evaluation of the information and action program*, Department of Geography, McMaster University, Hamilton, Ontario.

Ekblom, P., 1986, Community policing: obstacles and issues, *Policy Studies Institute*, Discussion Paper No. 13, 126–30.

Evans, D. J., Fyfe, N. and Herbert, D. T. (eds), 1992, *Crime, policing and place*, Routledge, London.

Eyles, J., 1989, Urban policy? What urban policy? Urban intervention in the 1980s, in D. T. Herbert and D. M. Smith (eds), *Social problems and the city: new perspectives*, Oxford University Press, England, 370–86.

Faris, R. E. and Dunham, H. W., 1939, *Mental disorders in Chicago*, University of Chicago Press.

Farrant, W., 1991, Addressing contradictions, health provision and community health action in the United Kingdom, *International Journal of Health Services*, 21, 423–39.

Gans, H., 1962, *The urban villagers*, Free Press, New York.

Gershuny, J. and Jones, S., 1987, The changing work–leisure balance in Britain 1961–84, in J. Horne, D. Jary and A. Tomlinson (eds), *Sport, leisure and social relations*, Routledge, London, 113–38.

Giggs, J. A., 1986, Mental disorders and human ecological structure, in W. K. D. Davies (ed.), *Human geography from Wales*, Part III, Cambria, 13, 151–80.

Gill, O., 1977, *Luke Street*, Macmillan, London.

Glyptis, S., 1989, What do we mean by recreational deprivation?, *Sport and Leisure*, 2–4.

Hallman, H. W., 1984, *Neighborhoods: their place in urban life*, Sage Publications, Berkeley, California.

Harvey, David, 1985, *The urbanization of capital*, Basil Blackwell, Oxford, England.

Herbert, D. T., 1992, Neighbourhood incivilities and the study of crime in place, *Area* (forthcoming).

Herbert, D. T. and Moore, L. A. R., 1991, *Street lighting and crime: the Cardiff project*, British Parliamentary Lighting Group, London.

Hofferth, S. L. and Phillips, D. A., 1991, Child-care policy research, *Journal of Social Issues*, 47, 1–13.

Jacobs, J., 1961, *Death and life of great American cities*, Random House, New York.

Jones, P., 1988, The geographical development of convenience stores in Britain, *Geography*, 73, 146–8.

Jones, T., Maclean, B. and Young, J., 1986, *The Islington survey*, Cowe, Aldershot.

Knox, P. J., 1987, *Urban social geography*, Longman, London.

Kotler, M., 1969, *Neighbourhood government: the local foundations of political life*, Bobbs-Merrill, New York.

Kotler, M., 1979, A public policy for neighbourhood and community organizations, *Social Policy*, 10, 37–43.

Leung, A., 1990, The community based welfare system in China, *The Community Development Journal*, 25, 195.

Logan, J. and Rabrenovic, G., 1990, Neighbourhood associations, *Urban Affairs Quarterly*, 26, 68–94.

Newman, O., 1972, *Defensible space: crime prevention through design*, Macmillan, New York.

Phillips, D. R., 1981, *Contemporary issues in the geography of health care*, Geo-books, Norwich.

Phillips, D. R. and Vincent, J. A., (1986), Private residential accommodation for the elderly: geographical aspects of development in Devon, *Transactions, Institute of British Geographers*, 11, 155–73.

Pinch, Steven, 1985, *Cities and services: the geography of collective consumption*, Routledge and Kegan Paul, London.

Reinson, K., 1992, *Recreation and community planning in Calgary*, unpublished Masters thesis, University of Calgary.

Rowles, G. D., 1978, *Prisoners of space: exploring the geographical experience of older people*, Westview, Boulder, Colorado.

Social Trends, 1970, 1981, 1990, HMSO, London.

Schuerman, L. and Kobrin, S., 1986, Community careers in crime, in A. J. Reiss and M. Tonry (eds), *Communities and crime*, University of Chicago Press, Chicago, 67–100.

Shadish, R. R., Lurigio, A. J. and Lewis, D. A., 1989, After deinstitutionalization: the present and future of mental health long term care policy, *Journal of Social Issues*, 45, 1–15.

Sherman, L. W., 1986, Policing communities: what works? in A. J. Reiss and M. Tonry (eds), *Communities and crime*, University of Chicago Press, Chicago, 343–86.

Smith, C. J., 1980, Neighbourhood effects on mental health, in D. T. Herbert and R. J. Johnston (eds), *Geography and the urban environment*, 3, John Wiley, Chichester, 363–415.

Smith, D. A., 1986, The neighborhood context of police behavior, in A. J. Reiss and M. Tonry (eds), *Communities and crime*, University of Chicago Press, Chicago, 313–41.

Sports Council for Wales, 1986, *Changing times: changing needs*, SCW, Cardiff.

Stoller, E. P. and Pugliesi, K. L., 1988, Informal networks of the community-based elderly, *Research on Ageing*, 10, 499–516.

Taylor, R. B. V., 1991, Urban communities and crime, in M. Gottdiener and C. G. Pickvance (eds), *Urban life in transition*, Sage, London, 106–34.

Taylor, R. B. and Gottfredson, S., 1986, Environmental design, crime, and prevention: an examination of community dynamics, in A. J. Reiss and M. Tonry (eds), *Communities and crime*, University of Chicago Press, Chicago, 387–416.

Taylor, S. M., 1989, Community exclusion of the mentally ill, in J. Wolch and M. Dear (eds), *The power of geography: how territory shapes social life*, Unwin Hyman, Boston, 316–30.

Thomas, C. J., 1989, Evolution or revolution? Retail change in greater Swansea, *Geography*, 74, 201–13.

Torkildsen, G. E., 1983, *Leisure and recreation management*, E. and F. N. Spon, London.

Townshend, I., 1992, *Community associations in Calgary*. Unpublished Master's thesis, University of Calgary, Canada.

Tuck, M., 1991, Community and the criminal justice system, *Policy Studies*, 12, 22–37.

Veal, A. J., 1974, Estimating demand at urban recreational facilities, *Planning Outlook*, 58–74.

Walker, A., 1986, Community care: fact or fiction, in A. Walker, P. Ekblom and N. Deakin, The debate about community. Policy Studies Institute Discussion Paper, No. 13, 4–15.

Walker, A., 1987, Enlarging the caring capacity of community, *International Journal of Health Care Services*, 17, 369–86.

Warner, R., 1989, De-institutionalization: how did we get where we are? *Journal of Social Issues*, 45, 17–30.

Warnes, A. M., 1982, *Geographical perspectives on the elderly*, John Wiley, Chichester.

Whiteis, D. and Salmon, J. W., 1987, The proprietorization of health-care and the underdevelopment of the public sector, *International Journal of Health-Care Services*, 17, 47–64.

Williams, C. H., 1986, Bilingual education as an agent in cultural reproduction: spatial patterns in Wales, in W. K. D. Davies (ed.), *Human Geography from Wales*, Part III, Cambria, 13, 111–29.

Williams, M. R., 1985, *Neighbourhood organizations*, Greenwood, Westport, Connecticut.

Wilson, W. J., 1987, *The truly disadvantaged: the inner city, the underclass and public policy*, University of Chicago Press, Chicago.

8

Physical Design and Communities

Introduction

Although community development may be an essentially social process, it also has a physical or design component. The social segregation, social interactions, cognitive and affective relationships described in Chapters 3 to 5 take place in specific areas and some of these places have been deliberately designed to enhance community interaction or provide services. Such developments imply a high degree of control over the construction of building. This control was rare throughout urban history, for most cities have grown by piecemeal and uncoordinated housing additions. Gradually attempts were made to enhance or accommodate community development until it has become a key principle of physical planning in the contemporary western city. Before briefly tracing these developments through time, four initial points must be made. First, most of these earliest examples relate to the urban area as a whole, not to the individual residential subdivisions usually described as community designs. This difference between the part and the whole is not as profound as may be initially assumed: most ancient towns were smaller than the five or ten thousand people accommodated in contemporary residential subdivisions. Second, a persistent theme has been the way that many features in plans originally adopted for the rich filtered down to the less wealthy classes. Third, the designs are not static morphologies; they are the visible expression of particular social values, such as the rural imagery behind the garden city ideas or contemporary ecological worries. Finally, space constraints mean this discussion is restricted primarily to the two-dimensional aspects of urban morphology in western cities: the plan.

Origins of Community-Based Designs

Perhaps the first conscious attempts to accommodate, or even to channel, community behaviour can be seen in the attempts to provide a central focus for the nascent cities. The centres of most pre-industrial towns from the fourth millennium BCE onwards were dominated by the palace and temple complexes of the élite that were usually restricted to the ruling classes and their retainers. Perhaps the best example seen in the modern world is the walled Forbidden City of Beijing, built by a Ming Emperor in the fourteenth century CE to house the Imperial household and government. Since the forms of these complexes are culture-specific and vary from society to society, there is little point in dwelling on their precise morphological details (Mumford 1961; Wheatley 1971). Instead it is enough to note that most of these complexes contain one or more open areas outside the primary temples or palaces, places that were left vacant or deliberately designed to act as a gathering-place: an area for assembly to honour the gods or rulers. In interaction terms, these places can be regarded as points of conflux in which the social solidarity of the community, as manifested in the urban unit or state, is reinforced by participation in, or at least observation of, the announcements, celebrations and rites carried out by the élite on behalf of the people.

The second major planning design adopted with community enhancement in mind was the gridiron plan. Today it is the simplest way of subdividing areas so that the location of each lot can be easily identified. However, it is probable that the grid was first used by Asian geomancers as a cosmologically inspired planning device to symbolize order on the profane space of the earth (Wheatley 1971; 1975). In other words it can be considered as a morphological metaphor to ensure harmony between earthly and celestial forces, both propitiating the gods and impressing the populace with the ruler's ability to order the earth. Hence the grid had a behavioural significance.

The development of town planning in the Greek city-states of the fifth century BCE led to the merger of those two morphological elements into a single integrated design, formalizing in western professional practice the tradition of deliberately planning a central area for the use of the urban community as a whole and controlling the development of the residential areas. Hippodamus's plans for the rebuilding of Miletus after its destruction by the Persians (Mumford 1961; Bacon 1974) shows the deliberate attempt to impose the rigid grid on a sloping site and its organization around a central open space, the agora, which also contained the public buildings of the settlement. The agora can be seen as symbolizing one of the key features of the outpouring of rationality and creative ideas in the Greek city-states: democratic participation in urban government and development. It provided sufficient space for the assembly of citizens to fulfil many functions: to participate in government; to join in festivals; to worship at the collective shrines; and to obtain the necessities of life from the daily markets that were also held in the area.

Although the initial popularization of the open central space must be attributed to the Greeks, the credit for the persistence of this planning principle in western civilization must be given to the Romans who adapted many of these ideas. Their extensive conquests provided the opportunity for a diffusion of these planning concepts throughout their domains, fulfilled by their rather rigid and mechanical approach to urban design formalized by Vitruvius (Morgan 1960), which left a repetitive heritage of gridiron towns centred on a forum throughout their empire. Figure 8.1 illustrates this form with the town of Pompeii, a settlement of 20,000 residents. Although certainly the Roman forum was much more enclosed and surrounded by more public buildings and specialized space than the Greek agora, its guiding principle was the same (Bacon 1974). In bigger cities, such as Rome, the single focus was replaced with a series of specialized areas that were scattered around the city centre: various baths, the race tracks, amphitheatres, and several fora associated with different emperors. This example illustrates how the single focus of community interaction for the settlement as a whole becomes lost in the bigger cities: with the growth of cities, space in the centre becomes partitioned into places for specialized uses.

Two developments within the church demonstrate how the increasing prosperity of medieval life left its mark on the urban fabric. Monasteries and abbeys adopted the traditional Roman warehouse design of an interior open space bordered by stores and residences, which became a green central area surrounded by cloisters, or residences in the cases of the college quadrangle. Additional churches — usually fronted by an open space — were also added to the urban fabric, each of which had its own dependent area, the parish, the area from which the worshippers and taxes were drawn. The result was that in the larger prosperous Italian city-states the churches in their urban parishes became a series of mini-city centres, for the church square attracted local shopkeepers and artisans, thereby providing additional points of local conflux in the cities, perhaps the archetypical medieval city neighbourhood around which daily life revolved. The larger medieval cities also were alike in developing an increasing amount of functional specialization, created by the desire of many trades and activities to cluster together, as well as the development of secular or ecclesiastical administrative areas around the palaces and

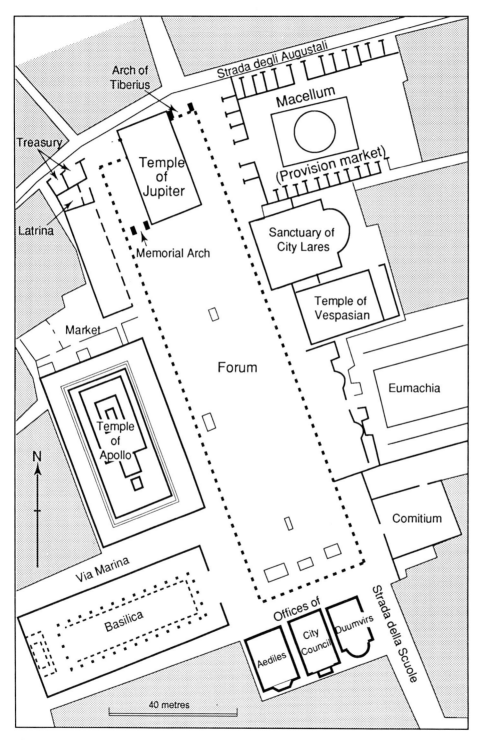

Figure 8.1 Pompeii; elements of morphology and plan (after Morgan 1960)

churches — such as the royal quarters or cathedral closes. In addition there were various degrees of ethnic segregation, caused either by the desire for different groups to reside among their own kind or by deliberate discrimination against certain ethnic or religious groups — as often happened to the Jews. Hence it is clear that the medieval city was separated into many functional or social areas, each with its own particular character or flavour (Mumford 1961), the very essence of intra-urban communities.

In Italy, however, these areas were more than places of peaceful spiritual or commercial interaction: they were often the locale of bitter intra-urban rivalry that spilled over into active violence. This situation was created by the feudalization of Italian cities (Vance 1977). Many Italian cities required the feudal landowners to maintain residences in the cities. The magnates built their palaces, often with distinctive towers to act as look-outs and defensive redoubts, endowed or built churches and surrounded themselves with their retainers, many of whom lived in adjacent dwellings. The result was the creation of a series of miniature feudal areas, each owing allegiance to different lords. Through time each faction, based on its lord's palace, church and square, developed its own patron saint, livery and flag, creating the morphology and symbols for an intra-urban rivalry that expressed itself in bitter competition for influence and power, often in allegiance to other city-states or powerful external patrons, such as the Holy Roman Emperor or the Pope. Sometimes the intra-urban rivalry became sublimated into sporting competitions: the horse-race for the *palio* of Sienna is one of the most spectacular modern survivals. Even today the annual race retains the historic rivalry among the various factions, each of which is still based in part of the old town. Birth into a particular family conditions one's allegiance to the various *contrada* based in urban neighbourhoods, as much as any tribal clan. Indeed contemporary members of the rival groups still express varying degrees of fear, contempt, or at least, a lack of comfort with rival members. These survivals clearly show that territorial behaviour and pride in one's group in the city is of ancient origin and not a phenomenon of modern inner-city gangs.

Within the cities, increasingly absolutist monarchs and prelates left their mark by creating new churches and palaces. The bold new approach was to set these focal points within squares or circles to enhance their visibility — as brilliantly executed in Berlini's setting for St Peter's Church in Rome, although only half of the planned circle of colonnades was built (Bacon 1974). However, it was the new, wide straight avenues, slashing through older residential areas or open fields, which became the planning symbol of the new age. These avenues were as much a sight line between ceremonial arches, palaces or churches, as they were an easier route for the new wheeled vehicles or processional ways to display the new armed might. They also became a convenient killing-ground for authorities armed with cannons when unruly mobs challenged the absolutist power of the monarchs. Indeed many of the new urban design elements that typified the Renaissance and the Baroque can be thought of as symbolizing the average citizen's increasing subjection to the absolutism of the élite through an increasingly inhuman scale of monumental design. Another important trend was the construction of new towns for the monarchies outside the existing city, Versailles being the most splendid example.

In eighteenth-century Georgian England some new elements of intra-urban community planning can be identified. The influence of the geometrical extravagances of the Baroque can be seen in the use of sinuous curvilinear designs and circles to complement the more mundane terraces of town houses which was one of the major trends of the period (Mumford 1961; Vance 1977). However, another popular design, the residential square, centred what the contemporary writer John Evelyn (quoted in Summerson 1962, 41) called a 'little town' within the developing urban fabric. The square was not unique to England or original. Medieval planners of new towns had used the morphological form and it can be seen in both the cathedral close and the collegiate quadrangle, both derived from the walled compound house of antiquity or the bigger atrium of classical Greek and Roman days. On a larger scale the residential square made its appearance in northern Europe in Paris in 1605 (Reps 1965) with Henri of Navarre's Place Royale (renamed Place des Vosges after the revolution). The square was also used in many European and colonial towns from the sixteenth to the nineteenth century, owing to the influence of Phillip II's 'Laws of the Indies', or James Craig's winning plans for the new town of Edinburgh in 1767 (Bell and Bell 1972), or in the planned colonial centre of Savannah (Reps 1965).

These developments began with Carolingian developments in Covent Garden (1636) and perhaps climaxed in Bedford, Russell and Tavistock Squares (1800–14). Even so, the square did not mimic either the paved Italian piazza, or its origin as a meeting-place in the Greek agora. Instead the square was usually occupied by gardens and was designed for the use of the residents in the great houses around. Most of the original squares were deliberately designed in grandiloquent Baroque fashion (Summerson 1962), as a setting for the mansions of the élite who had commissioned the square. However, no aristocrats were prepared to commission substantial buildings on leasehold land so the squares became surrounded with a number of large houses, not by man-

sions set back off the open area. Piecemeal development over many years became the norm, although by the end of the eighteenth century more rapid building and greater control over development led to greater architectural harmony in individual buildings along the sides of some squares — usually to mimic a large palace — again illustrating how a design has filtered down to lower, although still wealthy, groups. However, our concern is not only with the buildings associated with the focal point of the square. Figure 8.2 shows that minor streets were built in close proximity to the squares to attract the servants and artisans needed to service the big houses, and these often had a church and a market nearby to satisfy both spiritual and bodily needs. The markets were increasingly complemented by a row or a close of fixed stores: eventually the development of shops for the élite led to the creation of covered arcades in narrow passages between streets, such as the famous Burlington Arcade. This means that the area should be looked at as a whole: the square and garden forming a core for the élite, surrounded by streets and functions for the lower classes. The repetition of these squares through the northwest part of London created a series of residential areas fixed by the major squares, each having its own character and a cross-section of the classes in the areas around. Cockerell's remarks about his plans for the redevelopment

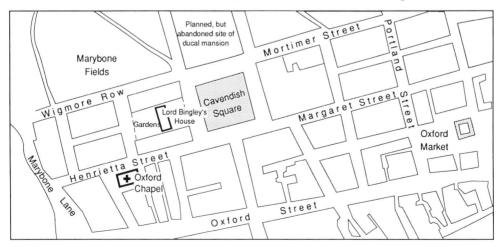

Figure 8.2 The Cavendish-Harley estate, London *circa* 1717 (after Summerson 1962)

of the Foundling Hospital show that the design eventually became deliberate, for the squares should have 'subordinate parts so as to comprise all classes of Building' (quoted in Summerson 1962, 167). Nevertheless, the creation of these residential microcosms must not be attributed to the social concern or altruism of later periods: the limited transport of the day meant that the large army of servants, coachmen and tradesmen needed to support the élite had to live in close proximity. Hence the social microcosm that resulted from these designs was almost a necessity to ensure the functioning of these large ducal houses and those of the lesser gentry and wealthy merchant classes. The similarity of the street plan is due to adherence to common principles and constraints, not to planning by seigneurial dictate.

Upper-Class Segregation in Romantic Rural Suburbs

By the beginning of the nineteenth century, attempts to plan distinctive communities within the city had undergone yet another transformation. In the pioneering designs of John Nash for the development of Regent's Park in London (Figure 8.3) can be seen the creation of some new principles that led to a more determined attempt to segregate the élite, even though there were still elements of the standard Georgian terraces and circles and the desire to include houses for the lower classes in close proximity (Summerson 1962; Bacon 1974). Nash's plans for this Crown Estate were government-approved and contained two distinctive parts: a park and its surrounds to house the rich and improve the quality of their environment; and an avenue of large houses to connect it to the seat of government in Westminster, the modern Regent's Street. Nash planned his avenue to separate Mayfair and Soho, providing a 'boundary and complete separation between the Streets and Squares occupied by the Nobility and Gentry, and the narrow Streets and meaner Houses occupied by mechanics and the trading part of

the community' (quoted in Bell and Bell 1972, 87). This social division still exists today and Nash's design deliberately attempted to exclude access to the area from the lower-class housing developments that lay to the northeast, using cul-de-sacs and eventually the line of a canal to provide barriers to intercourse between the areas. However, the principle of segregation of the classes must not be exaggerated because included in Nash's designs were a succession of small streets to the east, which consisted of a working-class area containing stores and markets, with a canal to bring fresh vegetables into the area, and what can only be described as two small garden suburbs (Park Villages) comprising a series of small, yet picturesque houses.

From the mid-nineteenth century onwards large houses for the upper class were developed outside all western cities that contained sufficient numbers of the wealthy. However, the new roads and transportation links spawned by the industrial age meant the residents of these 'exurbs' were still able to be in daily contact with their workplaces. In most cases no overall planning was at work, the area simply had a concentration of houses for the élite. Again this was not new: the Roman élite had fled Rome for the villas to the south (Vance 1977). By the middle of the nineteenth century residential subdivisions for the wealthy were developed with plans for the whole unit. Reacting against the rigid geometry of the Baroque and the rationalism and mechanism of the Industrial Revolution, the designs of previous periods were rejected in favour of the emerging Romantic belief in the need for art in life and the desire to achieve harmony with nature. These new upper-class suburbs were laid out as imitations of nature — or rather an improved, idyllic and sanitized nature. The single large residences of the élite on large lots were scattered along curvilinear roads to preserve their isolation and maximize their sweeping vistas over woods, streams, lakes and hillsides, although the latter were carefully rearranged to enhance their naturalistic qualities. Some of the best examples are seen in the United States, such as F.L.

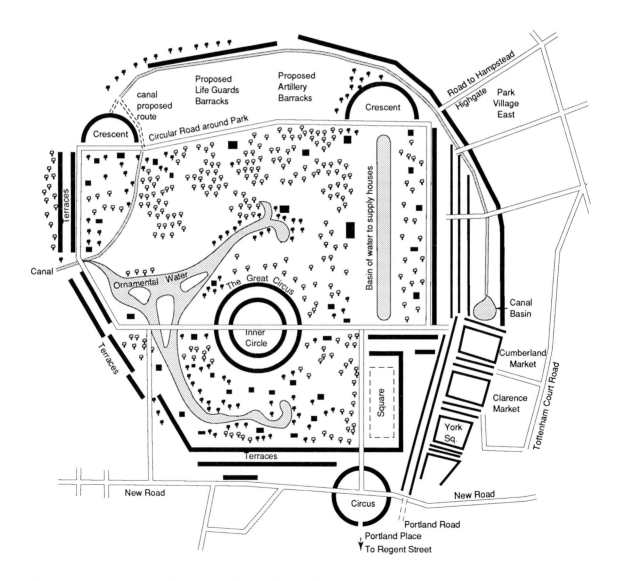

Figure 8.3 Nash's plan for Regent's Park (after Bacon 1974)

Olmsted's plan for Riverside in Chicago or Llewellyn Park in New Jersey, the latter deliberately sited on a terrace to preserve its distinctiveness (Reps 1965). Again the basic elements in the plans were not new, even if the influence of predecessors such as Nash were downplayed. These naturalistic ideas also profoundly affected the growing demand for large urban parks. They led not to the complicated geometries of Baroque Versailles but to the naturalistic designs of Olmsted in Central Park (New York), which created an improved rural setting. However, it should not be forgotten that the plan contained a central focal area, a Grand Parade, and segregated pathways for different modes of circulation together with sunken routes for the limited access roads that crossed the park (Reps 1965). In this design can be seen the two elements, focality and traffic segregation, which were eventually translated to residential area designs to improve community interaction. By the early twentieth century such residential designs had spread throughout the western world and the style diffused down the social hierarchy to the upper middle-class estates. Increasing numbers were now able to escape the city along the new tramways and electric underground railway systems. The obvious need to increase the density of houses in these areas frequently meant that only the curvilinear road pattern and pavement trees survived the downward filtering through the social classes, although the use of restrictive covenants preserved their residential character by preventing the addition of commercial activity.

Model Towns and Garden Cities

From Plato's New Republic to the sixteenth-century ideas of Thomas More's Utopia and beyond, visionaries have designed new types of communities to solve the perceived ills of the day. However, few were built and even fewer specified precise design elements. From the late eighteenth century onwards the desire to counteract the overcrowded, noisy, diseased and crime-ridden industrial cities led to a

number of model communities that were actually built (Bell and Bell 1972; Cherry 1974; Hall 1988). A common thread running through these schemes was the addition of open space and trees, features which were no longer confined to the higher-income estates. One of the earliest of these was constructed by David Dale and Robert Owen at New Lanark. Owen believed he was involved in an experiment to shape character — 'the character is formed *for* and not *by* the individual — society now possesses most ample means and power to well-form the character of every-one' (Bell and Bell, 1972, 251).

The creation of model towns became an increasingly popular approach among enlightened industrialists as the nineteenth century wore on, although the bolder attempts to transform society were dropped in favour of an increasing attention to achieve societal ends by the design of the urban area, not by the addition of needed facilities. Industrialists, such as Titus Salt at Saltaire (1853–63) outside Bradford, or Pullman at his town of the same name in Illinois (Reps 1965), planned towns that were representative of many in the last half of the nineteenth century. They illustrated the three principles of moving factories to the country, providing decent housing for their workers, and separating residential areas from industrial plants. Saltaire contained gymnasia and schools, churches as well as communal laundry facilities, the last because Salt seems to have had an aversion to seeing washing hanging outside homes — a simple illustration of how individual paternalistic beliefs could affect the content of the model towns.

As more and more model communities were developed, they increasingly adopted the upper-class preference for rural or at least open space, not simply because trees and lawns were aesthetically pleasing and noise levels were reduced, but also because of the practical realization that gardens provided a food supply. On both sides of the Atlantic these features stimulated similar movements, such as Frank Lloyd Wright's plans for a low-density and treed environment for Broadacre City in the United States (Johnston 1990) and the

Garden City movement in Britain (Purdom 1949). However, in the latter there seems to be a much more conscious admiration for the social cohesion of the English village and the social and aesthetic ideals of nineteenth-century reformers, such as William Morris and John Ruskin, who stressed the interdependence of aesthetics with art and architecture (Thompson 1991). Ruskin, in particular, saw the need for decent surroundings which included plenty of green space, the creation of well-built houses and the avoidance of environmental pollution. Many of the specific design principles used in garden cities had been anticipated by the model suburb at Bournville in 1894 and the village of New Earswick in 1902, built for the Cadbury and Rowntree families respectively, both Quakers and engaged in the manufacture of chocolate (Creese 1966; Jackson 1985).

In Ebenezer Howard's garden city of Letchworth these imitations of a naturalistic approach with curvilinear roads and a desire for the intimacy of the village, were combined with a high quality of housing and common facilities, the separation of residential and industrial spaces, and the provision of a green belt to contain sprawl; these features achieved a new and world-wide impact (Purdom 1963; Miller 1990). Although Howard was a visionary, not a physical planner or original thinker, his slim volume, *Garden cities of tomorrow* (Howard 1902) proved to be one of the most influential books of the next century. Rejecting the centralized social management of the socialists, the *laissez-faire* world of capitalism, or the industrial paternalism that had produced the model communities, he envisioned the creation of a new co-operative social order to build a series of new towns in the 25–30,000 population range, combining the best of town and country: in Howard's words 'a new civilization based on service to the community, and not self-interest' (quoted in Miller 1990, 11). Letchworth was initially developed on this principle: a group of people borrowed the money to buy a large enough tract of land to develop a new town. From the increase in land prices produced by the conversion of this

land to urban uses, money would be returned to the investors with enough left over for future development and the addition of community services. This process would create a set of self-generating new towns around the big cities, leading to the decentralization of society. These co-operative ideals can be traced back to the book *Fields, Factories and Workshops*, by the anarchist Kropotkin (1899), which supported decentralized economic decision-making and self-government.

The social ideals behind Howard's scheme were never realized, although the foundation of the Garden City Association in 1899 led to the acquisition of enough money to buy a site north of London near the old coaching town of Baldock in 1903. Raymond Unwin and Barry Parker were employed as the principal architects for this venture (Jackson 1985; Miller 1990). The halting nature of growth, the constant change of plans and the need to sell, not lease lots, meant they did not have complete control over the planning detail, although they established the principal roads, the separation of the industrial areas and the provision of a Green Belt. Industrial areas were zoned in their own section and screened by foliage, whilst the attempt was made to maintain low densities of ten houses per acre (Jackson 1985, 76). Houses were organized in groups, set back off the road or placed at angles to it in order to reduce the angularity of junctions and avoid the monotony of the grid. Main traffic roads were located on the edges of the residential areas, whilst cul-de-sacs or groupings around small greens were used to increase the social intimacy of the dwellings. The use of cottage styles, sloping roofs, gables and porches, gave variety to individual dwellings, which contained coal sheds and bathrooms, whilst many groups of houses were either joined by linked walls or designed as a cluster to further create a sense of togetherness. Playgrounds and community buildings were added for the same reason, whilst abundant trees, green spaces and generous gardens created the feeling of the country. Figure 8.4 shows the estate at Bird's Hill in 1906. This evolved into what we would describe as a self-centred neighbour-

Figure 8.4 Bird's Hill estate, Letchworth 1905 (after Jackson 1985)

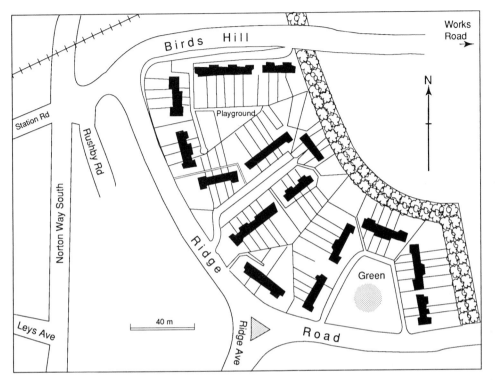

hood in nearby Pixmore 1907–9, with the addition of a community institute which is now a school. Obviously many of these features foreshadowed the neighbourhood unit ideas to be discussed below, although they were never formalized in a concise body of principles, perhaps in part because they were always developing.

Even so, the gradual success of Letchworth, another at nearby Welwyn, and imitations all over the world were not translated into Howard's dream of the creation of a series of adjacent self-developing garden cities relieving the congestion of big cities based on co-operative principles: the planning concepts used are more often found in a series of new garden suburbs on the edge of existing British centres (Jackson 1985). Hence Howard's dream degenerated into plans for residential settings, admittedly ones with marked improvement, which lacked the social processes that underlay the original ideas.

Rival Approaches: Cities of Towers and Neighbourhood Unit Planning

By the 1920s two other new planning ideas began to dominate the design of residential areas — again linked to the need to eradicate both the anonymity and sterility of the growing cities and the squalid, physical conditions of so many working-class areas. However, they produced vastly different plans. One of these, associated with the ideas of the Swiss-born architect who took the pseudonym, Le Corbusier, was dominated by large-scale tower blocks; the other the Neighbourhood Unit design of the American, Clarence Perry, can be seen as a development of the British tradition of village-inspired residential units.

Unité d'habitation and Tower Blocks

Le Corbusier (1929; 1933) rejected the growing tendency to solve the problems of urban places and the absence of community by a return to the low-density conditions of rural or village life or the romantic ideas of Ruskin as shown in the garden city movement or the co-operative worker towns of Kropotkin (1899). He proposed radical solutions to house a new society, based on the emerging technology of his time, calling for 'a style for an age', one dominated by machines and industrialization. The late nineteenth-century development of skyscrapers for offices had solved the technical problems of building at high densities, and in the growing cities of the western world large apartment blocks were increasingly making their appearance. Le Corbusier, however, did not reject these new trends and higher densities. His city was composed of large, 60-storey residential tower blocks scattered in a zigzag form across a landscape of parks. Perhaps the late nineteenth-century preoccupation with the need to add green space remains in these plans: indeed, less than 5 per cent of the area was built-up, and the recommended construction of the towers on stilts enabled the open space to 'flow through' the buildings.

It is important to understand the social values that motivated his designs. He criticized the financial problems of suburban home-ownership, the repression of women marooned by house-keeping tasks and the low levels of co-operation found in new city subdivisions. He envisaged a new urban form that sought to channel the trends linked to his own ideas for a new community form. The basic module he eventually proposed was the *unité d'habitation*, perhaps best described as a 'machine for living', not just a concentration of housing spaces, where individual freedom would be balanced by the necessary collective organization. The latter was considered to be important, for Le Corbusier was profoundly affected by the Syndicalist movement whose members believed that the means of production should be owned and managed by the workers, not the state. In these residential complexes a central floor would be devoted to easily accessible shopping, whilst a variety of types of units would cater for the traveller, the singles and the family, thus creating a mixed

community that is very different from the dominantly nuclear family plans of Unwin and others. On the roof would be gardens for recreation as well as communal facilities such as a nursery, gymnasium, theatre and running track. The individual apartments extended through the building so that balconies on both sides would enable the inhabitants to commune with nature, not only by its views but by the observation of sunrise and sunset, thereby illustrating the proposed use of nature, not its removal. Nevertheless, large blank exterior walls and floor-to-ceiling windows produced a starkly modern effect, especially if concrete was used in construction, in contrast to the picturesque image of the garden cities.

Despite Le Corbusier's indefatigable enthusiasm and designs for many cities, few of his plans, apart from individual buildings, were ever translated into reality. Although, the stark modernity of the ideas undoubtedly offended many, a more important reason was that considerable public investment in housing was required and this was rarely available in the pre-war Depression. Le Corbusier's impact on the design of new residential areas is best seen in the post-World War II reconstruction of many bomb-damaged western cities, and a new concern for social welfare which led to the rehousing of people from slum areas. The need to build at high densities seemed obvious to a generation of architects if sufficient green space was to be provided. The result was that one of Le Corbusier's modernistic principles — tower blocks set in a landscape of parks — became a standard design for many public housing projects in both Europe and America.

Unfortunately the creation of a satisfactory living environment was rarely achieved in the new high-rise estates. Le Corbusier's underlying social philosophy that stressed the need for community provision and mixed development was forgotten as the new designs concentrated solely on the provision of family housing units. Few services were provided. In Britain the first real high-rise block was built in Harlow New Town in 1951, followed by 5,000 others in the next twenty years. The open space was rarely maintained to park standards: it often became a derelict wasteland of uncut grass, broken glass and wind-blown rubbish. The towers themselves were often poorly constructed by prefabricated methods that did not work and were badly maintained. The essential elevators were often out of service owing to vandalism or mechanical failure. Within the towers the new social order envisaged by Le Corbusier turned into a nightmare of high crime-rates, graffiti and rubbish-strewn corridors and what can only be euphemistically called anti-social behaviour. Oscar Newman (1972), in a penetrating analysis of some New York high-rise projects, coined the term *defensible space* to describe a basic failure of the social order: the absence of a resident's control over the new created public spaces. Newman identified three basic features in many of the new designs that encouraged crime and created a community of fear and vandalism.

1. Increased *anonymity* was produced by the sheer size of many estates and high-rise buildings, the number of people using the same entrance and halls and the amount of common as opposed to private space. This increased the impersonal nature of areas and made it difficult for individuals to identify those exhibiting anti-social behaviour or to control them.
2. Decreased *surveillance* over public and private spaces was produced by plans which decreased the extent to which residents could see what was going on in areas, such as the trend to have screened or secluded entrances to houses, winding streets or clumps of bushes.
3. Increased *escape routes* were produced when there were many unmonitored routes out of the high-density complexes.

Helped by the failure to incorporate these characteristics many public sector towers rapidly degenerated and attracted rather than repelled further vandalization. Many of these units — particularly if they were inhabited by frustrated individuals whose teenage rebellion or unemployment led them to take every opportunity to break up or deface their environment in response to a society that had rejected them — became bastions of anti-social behaviour, as bad as some of the festering crime rookeries of Dickensian London. The respectable working class were either terrorized into silence or moved out. Researchers in other countries (such as Coleman in Britain, 1985) also documented the increased incidence of anti-social behaviour in these high-rise units. Intensive work by social welfare agencies often failed to produce any improvement. The result was that many cities, beginning with St Louis and the Pruitt-Igoe Towers in 1972, gave up the fight, simply moved the residents out, and demolished the towers — another failed social experiment of residential living.

Not all took such drastic measures. In other parts of America many private high-rise units have produced a successful living environment, with selected tenants, caretakers and security systems. In Britain recent reports (Housing and Planning Review (HPR) 1987) have documented the problems of high-rise units and shown how some towers have been rehabilitated by the provision of three basic improvements: *warmth*, by the addition of effective heating and insulation; *security*, by the addition of caretakers, new security systems, improved lights and access routes, as well as greater attention to the micro designs to provide surveillance; promotion of *co-operation* through the provision of community facilities, environmental improvements and regular tenant–landlord consultations. The influence of design has attracted much attention in recent years, and Coleman (1985) maintained that specific features should be incorporated or avoided to reduce crime. Many of these improvements can be traced back to Newman's (1972) recommendations, and should also include his suggestion of careful tenant selection to avoid overconcentration of problem families. In addition it is worth noting the growing feminist commentary on the need to take women's problems and needs into account in the design of buildings (Bowley 1990). Even the more socially controlled society of Singapore, which has rehoused much of its population in a high-rise landscape, has not been without its problems. In this case the government's constant attempt at social education has led to the introduction of surveillance cameras in elevators and public places in order to eradicate the problems of vandalism and defecation, and to the immediate prosecution and publicity of violators to shame them into changing their behaviour. All these examples demonstrate the constant battle to remove the negative consequences of the high-rise experiment. In more general terms it is dubious that the increased density of the units has brought about any increase in community spirit within them. Increased density does not usually lead to more interaction — rather it leads to the avoidance of others. However, the addition of swimming-pools, roof gardens and exercise rooms, even restaurants in the more expensive of these units from the late 1970s onwards, could all be said to have been anticipated by Le Corbusier, as could the construction of interior shopping-malls — although these are in downtown office towers, not residential complexes.

Today, it seems inexplicable that the potential problems of such high-density units were not anticipated by the residential developers of the 1950s and 1960s. To take one example, the inter-war social problems in the high-rise tenements of Glasgow, described in novels such as *No Mean City* (McArthur and Long 1957), must have provided a glimpse into a potential future, whilst the absence of a caretaker, such as the *concierge* so familiar to the residents of France or readers of Simenon's Inspector Maigret novels, seems inexcusable. In addition was the oft-repeated finding that families with small children did not like high-rise units, whilst the elderly often felt marooned, being afraid to venture out into a crime-ridden landscape. The idea that traffic-free interior corridors within and connecting the towers would provide a social centre for mothers and a safe environment for children to play was too idealistic. It ignored the increasing trend of female work participation, the noise, and dreary, badly lighted environments of corridors constructed of bare concrete walls. Architects with

middle or upper-class values created environments based on outmoded or impractical ideas for classes about whom they knew little. Moreover, the movement of people to these areas meant the breaking of old social ties, support systems and informal constraints on behaviour, thus creating a fertile ground for the development of alienation and disruptive behaviour that seemed so obvious in the growing cities of the early twentieth century. Nevertheless, in seeking explanations for the failure of some of these high-rise units must be added the unpalatable fact (at least to those who see only the good in people) that there are anti-social individuals in society who seem bent upon its destruction or at least dereliction. If these are concentrated in a building or area, without any adequate security, a poor situation can rapidly get out of control. Few can stand up to the resultant bullying and violence. Perhaps it is unfair to blame Le Corbusier for the subsequent problems of many of these public sector projects that seem to have been at least partly inspired by his designs. What is clear is that buildings alone — even those based on a new technology — do not guarantee a successful residential environment or the enhancement of community feelings.

Neighbourhood Unit Planning

The second major tradition in twentieth-century residential planning is usually linked to the work of Clarence Perry (Perry 1929; 1939), although his ideas were derived from many of the same principles that had inspired the garden city and model town movements. Perry had carried out research for the Russell Sage Foundation in 1909, in which he tried to identify the factors that conditioned success in the growing community movement in cities (Rohe and Gates 1985). Growing out of the philanthropic Settlement House developments in poor areas, the community centre movement (Chapter 6) was essentially a self-help movement designed to bring social and recreational facilities to the middle-class areas — activities which were not provided under the typical piecemeal building practices of the turn of the century. Although Perry was certainly aware of the design of British garden suburbs — he lived in Forest Hills Gardens (Queens, New York) which had been built in this style — he considered that there was a much more explicit need to reduce the tendency to anonymity in residential areas by the deliberate adoption of design principles to enhance intra-community behaviour. Figure 8.5a shows the plan he suggested in which there was to be a definite central focus and the exclusion of unnecessary traffic. Six principles (summarized from Perry 1929) were proposed to achieve community enhancement and provide a safe and satisfactory environment for the residents of the planned neighbourhood units.

1. *Size.* A residential unit will vary in size according to density, although it should provide housing for a population that will support an elementary school.
2. *Local Shops.* Shopping districts should be laid out on the edges of the unit at traffic junctions and opposite areas from neighbouring districts.
3. *Open Spaces.* Small parks and recreation spaces for the area should be provided.
4. *Boundaries.* Arterial streets should bound the area and be able to accommodate flows.
5. *Institutions.* The school and other facilities serving the area should be grouped around a central point or common.
6. *Internal Streets.* Highways should be designed to discourage through-traffic, facilitate circulation within the area and be proportional to their traffic load.

Perry's original proposals for the annexation of private land and its sale to a development corporation, who would design the whole area and provide facilities out of their profits, were dropped in favour of co-operation among individual landowners. Moreover, his specific ideas were modified by his many imitators. Figure 8.5b shows one of the best-known, the layout for Radburn (New Jersey), much more explicitly designed as a town for the new motor age (Stein 1951). Begun in 1928 and planned for a population of 25,000 (it is curious how this population size keeps resurfacing in community plans), it fell victim to the Depression and was not completed as projected. However, its design proved influential for its individual cells retained the essential character of the neighbourhood unit approach: their separation, planning as a whole, and location of major roads on the periphery. This plan called for traffic segregation by specialized roads, the use of cul-de-sacs, and the separation of pedestrian traffic through walkways. In addition there was a conscious reversal of many of Perry's ideas. Houses were reorientated to face gardens, with the lanes turned into service routes. Shopping was removed from the periphery to become a central community focus, creating an area of common buildings which was linked to the housing areas by a number of pedestrian paths. Few of these ideas were original, for many had been anticipated in the design of garden cities. Nevertheless, Perry's Neighbourhood Unit and the Radburn variation extended and integrated existing principles into a coherent philosophy of design based on behavioural needs in a new transport setting.

Many other variations of the initial Neighbourhood Unit principles can be identified in cities throughout the world, for the approach was extensively adopted in the suburban boom of the early post-World War II period as well as in the British new towns. However, an accelerating chorus of criticism led to the abandonment of the method as an integrated planning device. Five issues in particular must be noted.

First, studies showed that the design failed to usher in a new dawn of intra-community cohesion: the interaction and co-operation in areas designed on neighbourhood unit principles were often little different from those in other areas, except for the micro differences in cul-de-sacs etc.

Second, no provision was made for the ageing of areas. Since the unit was composed of new single-family houses, it only took a gen-

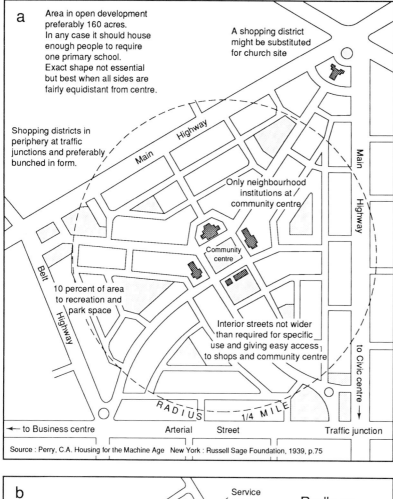

a

Area in open development preferably 160 acres. In any case it should house enough people to require one primary school. Exact shape not essential but best when all sides are fairly equidistant from centre.

A shopping district might be substituted for church site

Shopping districts in periphery at traffic junctions and preferably bunched in form.

Only neighbourhood institutions at community centre

Main Highway

Main Highway

Belt Highway

Community centre

10 percent of area to recreation and park space

Interior streets not wider than required for specific use and giving easy access to shops and community centre

to Civic centre

RADIUS 1/4 MILE

← to Business centre   Arterial   Street   Traffic junction

Source : Perry, C.A. Housing for the Machine Age   New York : Russell Sage Foundation, 1939, p.75

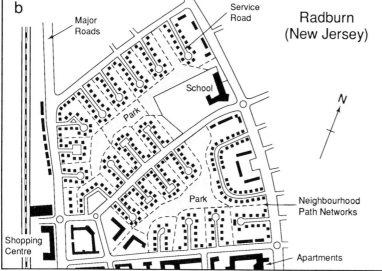

b

Major Roads

Service Road

Radburn (New Jersey)

School

N

Park

Park

Neighbourhood Path Networks

Shopping Centre

Apartments

Figure 8.5 Neighbourhood unit planning (after Perry 1939)

eration for the children to grow up and move away, leaving an underutilized elementary school and recreational space. Similarly, community hall facilities designed for young families would become redundant in an area of empty-nesters or aged people. Added to this was the lack of recognition of the increase in family breakdown and the formation of single-person households

Third, the approach did not anticipate changes in society. One was the growth of supermarkets and suburban shopping-malls which destroyed the vitality of many of the neighbourhood shopping facilities. Another was that the enormous growth in the number of cars — two or three per family — meant that people could spend far more of their time in social and commercial trips outside their area of residence. This decreased the possibilities of local neighbourhood social interaction and often clogged the residential streets with cars since there was too little provision for garages. In addition the explosive growth of single-parent families and single-person households, due to ageing, divorce, or young people leaving home, was not anticipated by this growing fascination with designs for nuclear families. The result was that an increasing proportion of the general populace were ignored by these designs.

Fourth, the plan lost favour because of the increasing tendency of both cities and individual entrepreneurs to develop the various elements in residential areas as individually planned features: houses by builders, shopping-centres by commercial developers, schools and clinics by various branches of city administration, etc.

Finally, the principle of land-use segregation was criticized by exponents of the vitality of big city life, most prominently by Jane Jacobs (1961). She stated that planned neighbourhood units were boring, and that anti-urban areas lacked the excitement and vibrancy that were the essence of cities. The reasons can be succinctly summarized. Most of their streets excluded everything except houses, by-laws banned street entertainers and hawkers, whilst the low-density and the car-borne population

driving to stores and work meant that the local chance encounters that encouraged personal relationships were lost. Adherents of this view pointed to Greenwich Village, Montmartre, or Soho as being the real 'villages' in cities where social and land-use mixture as well as local festivals, and meeting-places, such as cafés and squares, created the ingredients for the unexpected and interesting encounters of the truly urban experience. The introverted, nuclear family bastion of similar social classes in the neighbourhood units could never attain the vibrancy of the real city experience: they are based on privacy and similarity, not mixture and difference.

Contemporary Design for Suburban Residential Units

These criticisms of the neighbourhood unit have a great deal of merit and have led to the demise of the original neighbourhood unit planning approach. Nevertheless, many of the ideas that inspired the plans have not died in contemporary residential area planning. They have been transformed in five rather different ways that can be summarized as: influence; modified neighbourhoods; mini-centres; recreational communities; sustainable communities. In addition the use of micro designs to reduce the impact of crime must be noted.

Influence

The influence of the integrated neighbourhood approach, although not the specific designs, can be seen in the fact that most western cities have adopted planning procedures in which developers of single-family residential areas are required to produce the design for complete subdivisions in which guidelines set minimum standards for recreational and school spaces as well as allowances for commercial development. Similarly most suburban layouts routinely design internal roadways to exclude through-traffic, with peripheral roads acting as the major transport arteries, whilst many include cul-de-sacs and even pedestrian routes. This influence also extends to the modification of existing residential areas. Community groups in many cities have pressured city-planning officials to block off through routes to prevent non-local traffic filtering through their area, thus limiting traffic circulation in their residential areas. Also, large noise reduction barriers have often been added along main roads, producing a curious medieval wall effect in some cities. Moreover, many privately developed suburban areas leave enough land for community reserve, an area that can be used to develop social or recreational centres if the residents so desire.

Modified Neighbourhood Units

The second trend can be seen in the creation of new integrated developments conforming to some overall plan in which many of the traditional ideas have been incorporated or modified. One of the best-known British examples is found in New Ash Green in Kent, built in the 1970s, which contains 2,300 dwellings divided into twenty-two neighbourhood groupings separated by green corridors to preserve access to open space and their individual identity (Elson 1991). The developers also introduced the community management concept. Each homeowner has to buy a share in the local Residents Society which organizes the maintenance of the common green space by an annual tax and sends representatives to the Village Association. The association employed five fulltime and three part-time staff in 1991, manages the village hall donated by the builder, raised a quarter of the capital cost of the youth and community centre, and completed a sports field and pavilion development from grants and loans. The new town expansion for Peterborough in England initiated in 1967 was also based on the concept of residential areas: townships of 25,000 each which were to be self-contained in everyday needs. However, the plans for the newest township (Brown 1991, 59) shows their subdivision into four neighbour-

hood units, each with its local shopping-centre and primary schools, although the shopping areas in the new units are much bigger than in the previous expansion phases. In addition the facilities are more scattered around a large open space in the manner of a village green. Transport routes and a leisure belt provide sharp definitions for the individual areas.

The growing and explicit use of behavioural research in the design of residential areas is particularly well exemplified in the new resource town of Tumbler Ridge in north-eastern British Columbia, which was developed to exploit a new coal resource and reached a population of 4,500 in 1987. The design of the nine residential neighbourhoods and the town centre was based on the so-called 'pattern language' of Christopher Alexander and his co-workers (1977), where design solutions are linked to behavioural outcomes, not so much associated with older concerns about interaction as with crime and the affective domains described in Chapter 5. Gill (1989) has described how there was a conscious desire to create a 'sense of place', a physical environment that was distinctive in character, and a town that was appreciated as a 'people-place', one that engendered feelings of security and permanence. A series of specific designs were employed to achieve these results. For example, strong boundary demarcations were used (pattern 15) to define neighbourhoods (pattern 14) in which street names have a common theme and through-traffic is deterred by looped roads and cul-de-sacs (pattern 52). In the town centre a concern for a humaneness of scale (patterns 95 and 96) and the need to incorporate shared values led to the use of low two-story buildings, and citizen participation in community decision-making. The three main buildings, Town Hall, Health and Social Services, and Community Centre, were placed as anchors to define the extremities of the town centre, with a winding street designed principally for pedestrian use which was complemented by outdoor benches and distinctive lamps to create a clear 'sense of place' that may otherwise take centuries to evolve. The alignment was used to maximize sunlight and create views whilst overhanging canopies linked buildings together and provided shelter.

The utility of these designs in the eyes of the residents were also evaluated by Gill (1989). She found that residents exhibited a positive attitude to their town centre and found it distinctive, although they did not appear to understand the symbolism that it was supposed to identify. Similar positive attitudes were expressed about the residential environment, although these were about the town as a whole, rather than their specific neighbourhood unit. Almost a third had no name for the unit in which they lived, and many could not define the boundaries of their areas. Only 12 per cent maintained they made friends on the basis of residential proximity and 21 per cent because of community activities, compared with over a third from work-related activity and a fifth from friendships in previous locations. Gill concluded that the design could not be considered negative, even if it did not appear to enhance local social interaction, warning that the small size of the town, its cold climate and a resource-based economy dominated by young families and shift-work have provided individualistic characteristics that may have modified the social relationships and should have been taken into account in the planning. However, the fact remains that the study indicates that design has not produced all the intended behaviour, implying that design should be considered for its own sake rather than for some necessary behaviour.

The winners in a recent British competition for New Communities described in a recent issue of *Town and Country Planning* (February 1991) and in an American survey of new planned communities (*Urban Land* 1991) show that the use of rural themes and the integrated planning of communities is as vibrant as ever. This latter source concluded: 'Compared with suburban sprawl, new communities are generally successful in reducing automobile traffic, provide a higher level of aesthetic control, do a better job of paying for their own infrastructure and are better able to provide affordable housing' (*Urban Land*, March 1991, pp. 41–3). Even so, there are few signs of the social values

of co-operation which inspired Howard in commercial schemes, unlike the collaborative housing to be discussed below. There are exceptions, such as the 500-unit Tircoed Forest Village Development (north of Swansea), where the financial gains of building on low-cost land would be returned to the community to pay for the community and leisure facilities and subsidize the housing for the less able. Nevertheless, the halting nature of this example does not make one hopeful that a revival of some third way to the alternatives of capitalist or state control domination is really going to occur in the near future, despite the optimism of recent writers such as Thompson (1991).

Mini-Centres

The third direction in which neighbourhood unit planning has affected contemporary development has been in the creation of some larger-scale nodes in the repetitive sprawl of residential suburbs. It is worth remembering that the earliest new towns were small, so needs could be satisfied in local or neighbourhood units and the city centre. Today many of the cities are far bigger, so there is a need for intermediate levels of provision. In North America, Carver (1962) advocated the mini-city concept, or 'cities in the suburbs', as an antidote to residential sprawl. Not many examples of this approach exist, for large-scale suburban malls are planned by different developers from the residential areas. In Edmonton (Canada) new residential subdivisions planned in the south-east of the city have been deliberately anchored around what amounts to a major mini-town centre which contains municipal offices as well as recreational space and a planned shopping-centre. In the larger British new towns and in Europe there is a high degree of central direction and control by the city planning departments, and they have traditionally designed township centres with a wide range of services to serve a number of neighbourhood units.

Recreational Communities

A fourth derivative from the neighbourhood unit idea can be seen in the trend to centre the residential unit with some active or passive recreational area linked to the accelerating use of leisure-time and the desire to live an active life. Instead of providing a focus with a shopping-centre, community centre, or school — activities often controlled by shopping-centre owners and city authorities respectively — some developers have built new units around golf courses, given the increasing number of people who participate in the game. In origin the heritage comes from the desire of the upper class for sylvan views over parks, undeveloped rural areas, or sea and river-scapes — with the difference being that the area is now actively used by a popular sport. The advantage to the home-owner of this leisure-centred development is not the provision of recreation on one's doorstep, but the fact that golf courses provide a sanitized green setting for houses that overlook an essentially open area. For the developer the advantage is that houses sell for a premium price and the course may use ravines or gullies that may otherwise be undeveloped or are increasingly protected by environmental legislation.

The same attraction for exclusivity and the creation of a distinctive community focus lie behind designs that have used man-made lakes as the centre of their area. Although most of these early developments were in California and the sun-belt states, the idea has diffused to Canadian cities such as Calgary, where five lakeside communities have been built since the late 1960s in the south-east of the city, namely Lakes Bonavista, Bonaventure, Midnapore, McKenzie and Sundance. The lake at Bonavista is open to canoeing and swimming, is stocked with fish, has a community centre and play-grounds, and contains sculptured hills from the materials dredged to create the lake. The hills are turned into toboggan slides in the winter, whilst the lake becomes a skating rink. Obviously houses on the lake collect premium prices for a view that has been as manufactured as the landscape gardens created for

England's stately homes in the seventeenth century (Jarrett 1978). The constraint for residents of the city as a whole is that these facilities are located within fences that keep out people who are not members of the home-owners association. Membership of this association is usually mandatory for all purchasers of houses through restrictive covenants. By contrast the membership of the community associations and their facilities is voluntary. Not all these lake communities are operated in the same way. In the case of Bonaventure only the houses that front the lake have access to it. This creates an exclusivity of use that is often found along shore-lines or riverbanks, or in the estates of the very rich in American cities, where the separation of the community from the rest of the city may be completed by a wall. Figure 8.6 shows the plans for the latest lake community in Calgary, Lake Arbour, where a 13-acre lake is set in among 700 acres of development containing sixteen different subunits with distinctive names set back from a winding master road network and bounded by major arterials. The whole is pierced by recreational land use and some of the major entrances have a distinctive walling or building to give definition to the entry point. The Regional scale shopping centre is still in the planning stage although a series of supermarkets and smaller malls have opened in the area; links to the light rail transit is a distant prospect.

This type of recreation-centred area is of course more familiar in tourist areas where developments can be identified. In winter sports areas the ski resort contains a series of specialized facilities, and the unit often doubles as a mountain-hiking centre in the summer. On coasts the seaside resort became the nineteenth-century successor to the spa built around a mineral spring, a development that can be traced back to those inveterate bathers, the Romans (Mumford 1961). Moreover, the availability of personal transport and jet travel has meant that many free-standing and isolated tourist complexes have been constructed in environmentally attractive areas. Since they do not cater for a permanent residential group but depend on a throughput of people on a

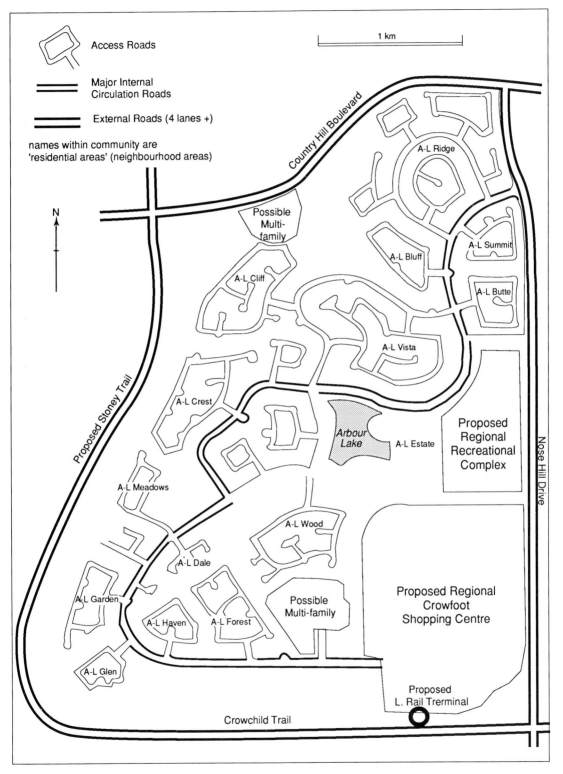

Figure 8.6 Modern neighbourhood design in suburbia; Arbour Lake, Calgary

seasonal basis they are not really planned intra-urban communities in the sense described here.

Sustainable Communities

Contemporary interest in the development of green or sustainable communities can be seen as one of the most recent manifestations of the garden city ideal of living with, not obliterating nature. During the last two decades concern over man's negative impact on the environment and the fear of an increasing scarcity of resources has led to even greater criticism over continued urban sprawl and the need for radical alternatives. Signs of change in attitude came after the energy crisis of the 1970s, which led to the widespread adoption of greater insulation in houses and the pioneering use of solar panels to generate an individual source of heat. In addition the 'winter cities' movement in northern climates (Gappert 1987; RUDAT 1986) directed attention to the need for interior shopping-malls, the creation of opportunities for community activity in the winter, or to use new designs to maximize adjustment to the environment, such as by orienting houses to maximize potential solar heat in areas of limited sunlight. Of course such climate-related design was not new. Prehistoric monuments were often orientated towards the cardinal directions and interiors of tombs such as New Grange north of Dublin (O'Kelly 1982) were illuminated once a year at the solstice. All the palaces in the Forbidden City of Beijing face south because the cosmological belief that good influences come from this direction, unlike the evil that stems from the north — a set of ideas that may have their origin in climatological considerations — with the east–west axis to follow the orientation of the sun. The Roman planner, Vitruvius, of course, also recommended such alignments (Morgan 1960). Indeed, in Mediterranean and tropical climates traditional houses were always orientated away from direct sunlight to reduce heat, whilst houses in windy, westerly climates have frequently been located in sheltered spots.

These environmental considerations, developed over centuries of vernacular adaptation, were often ignored in the last two centuries; the transport of energy made it possible for heating and eventually air-conditioning to modify the effects of climate. Certainly there were costs entailed in overcoming the local climate; however, until recently these were quite low. After the Brundtland Report sustainable and environmentally friendly development have become the new buzz-words of the 1990s. Recent reviews (Steeley 1991; and Stren, White and Whitney 1992) have described how planners and developers are searching for new ways of creating planned communities to fulfil these new demands. These can be seen to require several interrelated features.

Greater land use efficiency and flexibility is a common theme. Increased density is recommended to increase the possibility of public transit use and to reduce land needs. Mixed and linked land uses are needed to reduce monotony and create interactions. Flexibility in building design stresses the multiple use of buildings, such as using school buildings in the evening for community recreation needs.

Reduction and recycling in resource use is a more definable target. The growth of suburbs has been linked to the use of cheap energy that has allowed low-density sprawl. Many other externalities exist whose cost is really counted. Eliminating the need for extensive land consumption, barely used roads, and lengthy telephone and electricity cables, can lead to a reduction in resource consumption. In addition a more holistic view of the inputs and outputs of the traditional residential units demonstrates the way power and other utilities are brought in and increasing amounts of waste are dumped. The emphasis is now to separate waste and recycle it, not to throw it away, thus providing a source of paper and metal, compost for gardens, even local power from the waste gases. Also the water disposal system should avoid the multiple use followed by main highway patterns; it should follow the 'segregation of paths' approach, such that rain-water run-off is separated from the sewage, whilst lawns are watered by a separate system not fed by expensively filtered water designed for household use.

Ecologically sound and friendly actions are the core of the new ideas. Varied local food production should be encouraged. The use of powerful herbicides should be prohibited to avoid damaging the soil and killing off the insects, wild flowers and birds that can embellish the local environment. Trash should be removed on a regular basis and open spaces maintained. In one critic's pungent prose: 'even public utilities do not have to municipalize their land with security fencing, weed killer, gang mowers and battleship paint, nor do estate managers have to plan with sole reference to their boundaries and business objectives' (Steeley 1991, 78).

Exchange, in the sense of the range and variety of informal and formal contacts, has always been the core of urban life, so effort should be devoted to improved community interaction through local organizations, information exchange, demonstration projects, technology transfer and business linkages, perhaps by using the new technologies by some central 'information port' in addition to personal electronic devices. Added to this must be the capacity for citizen input and control, not the domination by outside municipal, state or corporate interests.

New communication technologies may allow the substitution of contact for travel. The use of cheap and often personalized electronic communication devices make it possible to substitute car journeys with electronic contacts, thereby reducing congestion and resource use. Actually it is doubtful that the number of movements are reduced in total, because social and leisure visits may replace the business associations, despite the absurdly hopeful forecasts of a return to the home-centred workplace. However, it certainly leads to more, even global, contacts by electronic means, and perhaps a slower growth in the increase of movement during the rush hour.

As yet many of these five major principles — which can be summarized in the acronym of Green! — are still in the experimental phase, although individual parts of these approaches are being tested in the more futuristic new community designs. Nevertheless one critic has warned that 'green planning requires resource management to be its core decision-making focus, with a rate–rent mechanism based on the use of land ... with real resource cost-benefit methods etc' (Steeley 1991, 79). The economic planning of most new communities is based on individual costs of each commodity used in the area at one time or at best in the short term, so the long-term, integrated effect of the consumptions or subsequent maintenance costs to consumers or society are rarely understood. Although this may lead to a gloomy view of the creation of many really sustainable communities in the near future, there seems little doubt that in the middle and upper-income areas at least, many of the trends described separately in these five sections are gradually being integrated into new community designs.

Niche Communities

Finally, a group of rather different contemporary residential developments can be recognized, which are not based on the idea of a residential community as a cross-section of society, but upon a group of people with some shared interest or problem who decide to live in close proximity to one another in a deliberately designed complex. A useful summary term may be the 'niche community', one that refers to the creation of housing projects planned as a whole which are designed for a specialized group of people who have something in common. Similarly, urban development entrepreneurs have catered for the needs of groups who have a set of specialized requirements, for example, belonging to existing groups with particular social differences, such as age, ethnic background, lifestyle or religious affiliation, etc. By making the decision to live in close proximity and excluding others, they create the segregation that separates them as a distinctive community in the sense described in Chapter 3. The concentration has to be a voluntary one and is linked to the creation of a residential complex to be considered as a planned community in the context of this chapter. As such they are different from the entertainment areas such as theme parks or Disneyland, etc., which do not have permanent residences and are based, like resorts, on a throughput of people. In capitalist societies the construction of such complexes requires money and the persuasion of people to buy into the project. This usually entails advertising the project frequently, persuading potential members that they have common, collective needs that can be satisfied in the planned community. Three broad types of these planned residential units can be recognized: collaborative, retirement, and lifestyle communities.

Collaborative Communities

Fromm (1991) has summarized the variety of the new arrangements of this form, pointing out that unlike communes they have no common social ideology; instead they have some communal aims that are shown in the design of residential complexes with private living-spaces and some common areas. Scandinavia has proved a pioneer in the creation of these areas with the Swedish term *sto-familj* referring to a residential community formed by unrelated people. The 1981 Fristad community in Stockholm provides an example of collaborative living, with 133 apartments and an adjacent complex of 175 units for elders set in a forested area in which there are play-spaces for children and allotments for gardeners. Woodward (1987) has described how the residents are characterized by their greater valuation of the quality of their life than their possession of material objects, implying that the community works because of some shared goals. A different example can be seen in the Settedammen co-housing project where residents have their own units but share common

facilities that meet everyday needs — such as cooking, child-care, outdoor maintenance — features that are reflected in the design of the units. Again it is worth noting that although social reformers in the past had advocated similar ideas, the pioneering and increasingly widespread adoption of the idea had to wait until women had not only been emancipated from their domestic role but also shared similar problems. Similar concentrations of people from a particular ethnic or religious background may correspond to this type, such as the floors for francophones in some Toronto condominiums. However, since they rarely have co-operative living-spaces, they are not collaborative communities in the sense described here — enhanced with some common design feature.

Retirement Communities

The second example is best seen in the deliberate creation of new residential complexes for the elderly or retired. Unlike nursing-homes, or hospices for those near death, where residence is necessary because of an inability or potential inability to look after oneself, these areas attract people who voluntarily join the planned residential unit and are not restricted to it. The creation of new residential areas for the retired has gone much further in America where new towns, such as Sun City (Fitzgerald 1987, Chapter 4) outside Tampa (Florida), were designed for the increasing numbers of people who had the pension funds to leave the winter behind and live in sunshine. Many are deliberately designed to provide an attractive environment, with golf courses and lakes.

Retirement communities are not unique to environmentally attractive areas. Smaller versions of the concept are advertised in most cities and regions in North America. Some are no more than high rises or a cluster of low rises with some common facilities such as restaurant, gym or pool but create an exclusivity by only allowing seniors or restricted age groups to reside. The most common form may be the *sheltered housing complexes* that are so common in contemporary cities in which the elderly have their own apartment, but have access to common lounges or even dining rooms and frequently have a resident warden and staff (Rose and Bozeat 1980). These units fulfil the elderly's need for housing, protection, caring and even self-help and shared interests — the creation of some of the basic ideals of place community life. Others go further and 'provide a campus approach to meeting the needs of fellowship, security, meaningful activity and health care for its residents' (1991 Brochure of the Elbert A. Smith Retirement Centre of Independence, Missouri, run by the Reorganized Church of the Jesus Christ of Latter Day Saints). Many other North American cities are seeing new communities designed for the still active retired. These residences are separated by a wall or fence around the unit's property, whilst a single gate controls access, although these are more psychological than physical barriers. The popular retirement area of the Okanagan Valley in British Columbia contains a number of these developments, derisively called 'walled cities' because they are fenced off. For example, Sandstone City, Kelowna, is one of the eight areas developed by Canadian Adult Communities in the Okanagan. Building began in 1989 with 190 lots on 14 hectares sold to buyers who had to choose between nine single-storey house designs, each with two bedrooms and bathrooms, co-ordinated in beige colours and set along a meandering road. The landscaped grounds and gardens are maintained by the company for an extra fee, whilst the large club-house has pools, meeting-halls, sports facilities and bar. Most people are retired or semi-retired, although the only real rule is that children under 16 are not allowed. Major selling-points for many people are the down-sizing of homes, the limited amount of maintenance that is required, the security and opportunity to travel knowing the house will be looked after, as well as potential interaction with people of similar interests or problems yet with independent living. More importantly, the units combine the comforts of privacy with the security of a managed complex and fellowship with people of one's own age, and none of the

aggravations of noisy neighbours or children. However, the colour conformity and bans on such things as large pets, recreational vehicles and hanging washing (incidentally also a pet peeve of Titus Salt in Bradford!) do not appeal to all. Nevertheless, the concept is spreading rapidly in North America and is becoming a familiar sight in many cities. It is a curiosity that the attempt to wall off the area takes one back to pre-industrial societies where real walls and curfews were used to separate different ethnic or tribal groups within the larger urban area. It is worth noting that most developments are quite small intrusions into existing areas and are the opposite of the older neighbourhood planning approach, for they appeal to the elderly, not young families, yet still attempt to incorporate some common facilities — albeit within a single building. The complexes vary in the extent to which the residents have common interaction patterns or cognitive identity.

Lifestyle Communities

The concept of a planned lifestyle community may overlap with some of the collaborative communities discussed earlier. Again, however, there are a variety of emerging forms. A rather unique example of a niche community based on a lifestyle can be found at Heliopolis near the historic port of Agdes, southern France. It is an example of a planned complex designed to cater for a lifestyle that is usually not accepted in western society, except in isolated and private spots: living without clothes. The area contains a large semi-circular apartment complex facing a large beach, with the interior comprising a series of tennis courts and interrelated swimming-pools graded for use by nudists of different ages. An adjacent hotel, shopping-centre and a caravan park for those unable to afford the rents completes the area. Non-nudists can enter although they are discouraged. Given the winds and temperatures in winter, it is not surprising that the area is seasonal in use with most vacationers staying only a few weeks at a time. Nevertheless, the adherence to a particular distinctive way of living means that it must be treated as representative of a different type of niche community. Additional examples may be found in the planned communities founded by various religions.

Conclusions

This discussion has traced the principal trends in the development of planned residential areas in cities and has shown how the concepts of designing community areas to produce some behavioural outcomes and to ensure the presence of desired services are far from dead. Although many studies have cast doubt on the importance of the influence of design on interaction, the ideas are still used, increasingly on designs that are supposed to influence the cognitive and affective domains to provide a better environment. In general terms the historic emphasis upon some focus for the planned community began with one for the settlement as a whole, and this has gradually diffused to a variety of designs for residential units within cities. However, there has been a recent revival of interest in the creation of a central open space to act as a gathering-place for the citizens of the city as a whole, after the lack of attention to the concept during the Industrial Revolution. The City Beautiful movement (Reps 1965; Hall 1988), stimulated by the Chicago Exhibition of 1892, led to a classical revival in the architecture of many cities, and a vigorous desire to improve the quality of city life by the addition of amenities such as parks, museums, theatres and open spaces. The concept of a central square, often outside the major municipal buildings, figured prominently in this movement. However, the commercialization of the central area, and the subsequently high land values were always a constraint upon the adoption of the idea, and it again fell into disrepute. From the 1960s onwards the concept of a city centre was revived as cities struggled to cope with the decline of the central area because of the suburbanization of many businesses. The concept of designing a people's place, a central open space, frequently outside a new town hall, was a typical feature of many city centre redevelopments.

Unfortunately the results were far from what was intended. Too many of the new commercial buildings internalized development in sterile, repetitive and homogenized malls, turning their back on the individualistic and often idiosyncratic streets. Pedestrianized malls often repelled, rather than attracted people. Too much emphasis was placed on large-scale inhuman projects full of blank walls and windy, dusty spaces. William Whyte (1988) in a devastating critique of the central areas of numerous American cities has documented many of these changes. He pointed the way back to designs that emphasize people and interaction, as well as to the need to create activity and spectacles in city centres. He seems to prefer a return to the multi-purpose character of the Greek agora, whereas it can be suggested that many of contemporary downtown civic spaces look more like the imposition of the centralized control of the Renaissance period — settings for buildings, not centres of lively interaction that contribute to civic pride. It is fascinating to note his concern for behaviour, particularly of an informal nature, in small spaces. From this he has suggested designs that encourage such interaction. In part, this is a return to one of the interests of neighbourhood unit planners in the past, although on another scale and in central city conflux points, not residential areas. Many cities now have planners whose responsibility is to improve the visibility and liveability of central areas. Unfortunately they are constantly thwarted by a common problem. Too few people live downtown to make them *people places* — especially at night — whilst there are the additional problems of congestion, crime and homeless people. In some ways this is the opposite of the community design problem in suburban areas, where there are too many low-density residences and not enough mixture of land uses and people of different types to create the vibrancy of the older, urban community experiences.

References

Alexander, C., Ishikawa, S. and Silverstein, M., 1977, *A pattern language*, Oxford University Press.

Bacon, E. N., 1974, *Design of cities*, revised edition, Penguin Books, New York.

Bell, C. and Bell, R., 1972, *City fathers: the early history of town planning in Britain*, Penguin, Harmondsworth, UK.

Bowlby, S., 1990, Women and the designed environment, Special Issue of *Built Environment*, 16.

Brown, R., 1991, Growing without pain, *Town and Country Planning*, 60, 59–60.

Carver, H., 1962, *Cities in the suburbs*, University of Toronto Press.

Cherry, G., 1974, *The evolution of town planning*, London.

Coleman, A., 1985, *Utopia on trial*, Hilary Shipman, London.

Creese, W. L., 1966, *The search for environment: the garden city before and after*, New Haven, Connecticut.

Elson, M., 1991, Managing community assets in new settlements, *Town and Country Planning*, 60, 2, 57–8.

Fitzgerald, F., 1987, *Cities on a hill*, Touchstone, Simon and Schuster, New York.

Fromm, D., 1991, *Collaborative communities*, Van Norstead, Reinhold, New York.

Gappert, G., 1987, *The future of winter cities*, Sage, California.

Gill, A., 1989, Experimenting with environmental design research in Canada's newest town, *Applied Geography*, 9, 171–95.

Hall, P., 1988, *Cities of tomorrow*, Basil Blackwell, Oxford, England.

HPR, 1987, Special Issue on high rises, *Housing and Planning Review*, 42, March.

Howard, E., 1902, *Garden cities of tomorrow* (originally published as *Tomorrow, a peaceful path to real reform*, 1898), London.

Jackson, F., 1985, *Sir Raymond Unwin*, A. Zwemmer, London.

Jarrett, D., 1978, *The English landscape garden*, Rizzoli International Publications.

Jacobs, J., 1961, *Death and life of great American cities*, Vintage, New York.

Johnston, D. L., 1990, *Frank Lloyd Wright versus America*, MIT Press, Cambridge, Mass.

Kropotkin, P., 1899, *Fields, factories and workshops*, in C. Ward (ed.), 1974 reprint, Allen and Unwin, London.

Le Corbusier, 1929, *City of tomorrow*, J. Rodker, London.

Le Corbusier, 1933, *The radiant city*, London (new edition, London, 1967).

McArthur, A. and Long, H. K., 1957, *No mean city*, Corgi, London.

Miller, M., 1990, *Letchworth: the first garden city*, Phillimore, Chichester, England.

Morgan, A., 1960, *Vitruvius*, Dover Publications, New York.

Mumford, L., 1961, *The city in history*, Martin Secker and Warburg, London.

Newman, O., 1972, *Defensible space*, Macmillan, New York.

O'Kelly, M. J., 1982, *New Grange: archaeology, art and legend*, London.

Perry, C., 1929, The neighbourhood unit, in Vol. 7, *Regional plan of New York and its environs*, Russell Sage Foundation, New York.

Perry, C., 1939, *Housing for the machine age*, Russell Sage, New York.

Purdom, C. B., 1963, *The Letchworth achievement*, London.

Reps, J. W., 1965, *The making of urban America*, Princeton University Press, New Jersey.

RUDAT, 1986, *Liveable winter cities*, Regional and Urban Design Team, Edmonton, Alberta.

Rohe, W. M. and Gates, L. B., 1985, *Planning with neighborhoods*, University of North Carolina Press, Chapel Hill.

Rose, E. A. and Bozeat, N. R., 1980, *Communal facilities in sheltered housing*, Saxon House, Farnborough, Hants, England.

Steeley, G., 1991, Green planning for new communities, *Town and Country Planning*, 60, March, 77–9.

Stein, C. S., 1951, *Toward new towns for America*, reprinted by Liverpool University Press.

Stren, R., White, R. and Whitney, J., 1992, *Sustainable cities*, Westview Press, Boulder, Colorado.

Summerson, J., 1962, *Georgian London*, Penguin, London.

Thompson, J., 1991, The spirit of the place, *Town and Country Planning*, 60, 36–7.

Vance, J., 1977, *This scene of man*, Harper's College Press, New York.

Vitruvius, 1511, *Ten books on architecture* (translated by M. H. Morgan, 1960), Dover Publications, New York.

Wheatley, P., 1971, *The pivot of the four quarters*, Aldine, Chicago.

Wheatley, P., 1975, Ancient Chinese city as a cosmological symbol, *Ekistics*, 232, 147–58.

Whyte, W., 1988, *Rediscovering the city centre*, Doubleday, New York.

Woodward, A., 1987, Public housing communes in Sweden, in W. Van Vliet et al. (eds), *Housing and neighbourhoods*, Greenwood Press, New York, 215–38.

9

Conclusions: Understanding Community

The community question is one which will continue to interest all those concerned with the realities of life in modern cities. It will also remain of central interest because it raises many of the conceptual issues which are linked with urbanization and urbanism. That the issue of definition is unresolved is in itself a pungent comment on the nature of the community question. Community as a concept is multi-dimensional and does mean different things to different people; its meaning will vary from time to time and from place to place, even within the lifetime of an individual. However, the present blurred areas in the study of community do not arise from a lack of research attention. As Keller (1988, 177) noted: 'Despite the hundreds even thousands of existing community studies, we do not have even the rudiments for a comprehensive classification — no periodic tables, no Leontieff chart. The legacy of past studies thus lies fallow'.

This is an unduly pessimistic statement. Although the many studies are difficult to inter-relate and may not have produced the perfect interpretation or typology, they have in a progressive way added to our understanding of a diffuse concept and an elusive reality. It has already been argued that communities are composed of very different elements and that their differences are the products of varying compositions and strengths of these individual features. Classification is an important objective for studies of community and a large amount of discussion has been devoted to it in this text, but it is no particular prize. Certainly, typologies improve our understanding, but they can never be more than an averaging of

subtle differences, at best an approximation; the more important objectives are those of understanding the processes entailed both in forming community and sustaining it in a particular form. In seeking to achieve these goals, four major strands of interest in the literature on communities can be recognized.

The first is that the various approaches towards the study of community reflect differences in both objectives and methodologies. The detailed descriptive statistics emerging from factorial ecologies clearly have something to offer and act as summaries of the social and demographic compositions of communities. Communities are not, however, identified only by measurable objective indicators, they are socially constructed, creations of mind and experiences which provide their inhabitants with distinctive senses of place. Similar contrasts can be observed in more applied forms of community study. For planners or administrators who need to partition the city into units of some meaning and of a manageable size in order to locate facilities or allocate resources, the quantitative methods of regionalization are appropriate. For social welfare agencies who are seeking to house problem individuals or those who need some form of caring and liveable community, more qualitative assessments become far more relevant. Some order can be given to these variations by suggesting that the literature on community spans three critical divides. The first is the **social science-humanities** dichotomy. Most social scientists aspire to measure and replicate the individual dimensions of community using systematic methodologies. Humanists by contrast seek to reveal the special character of places, emphasizing the different attitudes and experiences of people in communities. A second divide is that between **academics** and **practitioners**. For academics the community question is conceptual as well as empirical; for practitioners the central concerns are with the creation and empowerment of communities, with their efficiency in the delivery of services, and with the development of designs which aid social interaction and enhance the quality of life. The third divide can be stated as that between those who concentrate on particular case-studies in the real world and those who seek to generalize. This is the **empirical-generalist** divide which has assumed considerable importance in academic debates. The best studies are those which seek to integrate empirical and theoretical research and there are many good examples of this kind of approach. For some academics however, particularly those of the political economy school, the shift towards empiricism is one fraught with danger. Smith (1987, 60) argues: 'Where is the middle ground between the abyss of abstract theory on the one side and that of empiricism on the other ... between structure and agency, social and spatial ...?'

These arguments were conducted within the **locality** debate and have been discussed elsewhere in this text. These three divides are not easy to cross, let alone bridge. It must be remembered that the place communities we live in, and recognize, have diffuse and flexible boundaries that vary with individual and participant. There are signs of interaction among various approaches to community. It is worth noting that planners are increasingly using our knowledge of cognitive processes to design community boundaries and the attempts to achieve reconciliations between societal structures and locality are also positive moves. All these dichotomies, however, demonstrate the complexity of the community question: although it has issues particular to itself, it also touches upon some of the main generic issues of urban study.

A second recurrent theme in the discussion of community is that concerning the **loss** of community over time. It is commonplace to refer to the former strengths of communities with the full range of interdependence, support, shared values and territorial identity. The basic form of the community question with its debate over the relative merits of community lost, community found and community transformed, encapsulates this notion. Several strands exist as outcomes of research and study which throw some light on these issues. First, it is abundantly clear that urban society in the western world has changed. There are numerous and compelling reasons why many kinds of people are less dependent on local space and this is reflected in their attitudes and forms of behaviour. It is also evident however that the notion of **neighbourhood** or **community dependency** remains. Some groups have been described, notably the elderly, for whom local community is of great importance in modern cities. There is evidence that as the urban economies change and poverty becomes more localized, sections of the population are trapped in communities which show many of the hallmarks of both physical and social decline. Second, the distinction made by Wellman and his co-workers in Toronto (see Wellman and Leighton 1979) between personal network communities and local place communities, is one of considerable value in understanding this process of change in modern cities. The white, middle-class households in Toronto had a mobility and behaviour pattern which allowed them to range widely around the urban area and beyond in their pursuit of social interaction; for many of these local community was a convenient place of residence rather than a context for activities. It has been argued that the balance between personal network communities and local place communities will be variable and that the recognition of the former does not negate the latter, the concept of difference and its application has provided a powerful insight into the ways in which community has evolved.

A third major strand of importance in the study of the community question is that which was raised in an explicit form by Bell and Newby (1978). Their description of the concept of **communion** was based on the idea that community could exist in a latent or dormant form, with people of similar characteristics sharing a residential area, although this could be transformed into an active and socially-cohesive **communion** if an issue arose which threatened the area as a whole and united its residents in a sense of common purpose. Since this article was published the contexts in which **communion** may arise have widened. Longer-term objectives, recognized and stimulated by activists can lead to **communion** in similar ways as the notion of community-based protest or action has gained strength. Programmes such as Neighbourhood or Block Watch are most effective where they achieve **communion** and, in this example, unite all the residents in the fight against crime. The central idea here then is that communities can be mobilized and that there is a place of activities and informal organizations to pursue both spe-

cific and general issues which are neighbourhood-based. There are clear parallels here with Schmalenbach's (1977) argument for the role of conscious action in the development of communities.

A fourth strand to the community question relates directly to the discussion of communion and is based upon ideas of the 'rediscovery of community' in modern cities. Examples of the growth of neighbourhood and community associations have already been given and recent statistics from the Community Associations Institute of the United States, show that in 1989 there were 130,000 community associations helping to administer the lives of 30 million US citizens. Although many of these are condominium associations, this is still an impressive figure and as Figure 9.1 shows is expected to increase

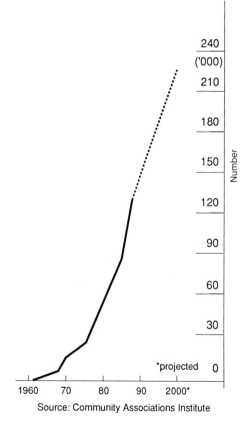

Source: Community Associations Institute

Figure 9.1 The growth of community associations in the United States

dramatically over the next decade. There is little doubt that many people, from the residents of troubled districts of downtown Los Angeles to those of comfortable suburbs, feel a need for collective locality-based action. A graphic example comes from a resident of Bristol's Hartcliffe estate, following several days of serious rioting in 1992. 'St Paul's (another Bristol estate) got plenty of money when they rioted. Let's see what we get now the trouble has started here. They will start throwing money at the place' (Musgrave, 1992, 2). This is clearly an exceptional example although not one which is unrealistic; the ways in which community action can and do take form gives the idea of **communion** a wider significance.

Despite some gloomy prognoses, it is clear that place communities still exist in western societies and several trends can be identified which suggest that they may play larger roles in the future. Although at many levels of society it has been possible to show a substitution of individualistic relationships and a retreat into home and immediate family, there is a clear awareness of the need for collective action where circumstances which justify it exist. There is less evidence to date that the range of influence of the new community organizations are increasing. In the obsolescent inner city areas, the level of physical and social dereliction is so high that only massive investment from public or private corporations can effect change. Yet local communities can provide an important grass-roots ingredient in the process of revitalization and Barke and Turnbull (1992) argue strongly for 'bottom–up' rather than 'top–down' policies using the example of the ineffectiveness of imposed youth training schemes in a problem estate in the north of England. In suburban areas, the successes are greatest in the protective and conservationist modes and reflect the greater articulacy, awareness of the need to organize and access to people in power of the middle-class residents. Again, in a negative vein, the attempts to use the notion of a caring community have been conspicuous failures. The mentally-ill and the elderly who are discharged from institutions into the community, do not

find the support and sustenance that they need. Beyond immediate kin and close friends, the local community *per se* has little to offer.

The big question for the future is the extent to which place communities will continue to be needed in cities. Most would regard the growth of community organizations and locality based action groups as some hope for the future since they seem to challenge, rather than accept the excesses of individualism. For example, Taylor (1991) argued that one should not simply criticize the self-indulgence of modern man and the fragmentation of society. He argued persuasively that 'authenticity' does not necessarily produce isolation and atomism. Taylor (1991, 33) lays a great deal of stress on the fact that human life is essentially dialogical. For example, although we may work on our own, much of our work only has value when it is used, or judged by, others: people who benefit from such actions. Today, of course, we need not follow such behaviour. There are no habitual societal or spiritual processes that force us into such action. However, if we do not engage in such dialogical activity, the world would be a poorer place. Although there is no really explicit call for a return to community in Taylor's work, the relevance of these ideas to our focus of concern must be clear. If we are to create a better society, there is a need to encourage new relationships among people. One of these ways — the stress must be on the word one — could be under the **place-community** banner, leading to increases in the interaction with, and commitment to, others. Contributors to a recent collection of essays on the philosophy of communities (Rouner 1991) have been more specific in their view that community action and participation represent an antidote to modern isolationism. For example, Deutsch (1992) argued that just as a person is an achievement, not a given, so a community is an achievement, not a given. Moreover, 'in the creation of a full community the skill is in orchestrating the necessary involvements of others in order to advance the welfare and dignity of all concerned' (Deutsch 1992, 25). This implies that revitalized communities should not be seen as some condition of totalitarian dependency to create some future world, or a retreat from society in the hope of ensuring one's place in a better one after death. Instead many advocate increased attention to our immediate environment. To achieve the fullest participation of individuals and the maximizing of individual identity in the future, there is a need to extend the contexts in which this sense of community through collaboration may be attained. Ideas such as grass-roots involvement and 'bottom–up' policies have a great deal to offer.

This book has examined the community question at a time when the idea of community has renewed prominence in modern thinking and policy. Both the historical roots of the community idea and its modern relevance have been reviewed together with its philosophical bases and its practicalities. This book expresses a belief in the value of the concept of **place** as part of the community question and it is that belief which offers unity to the text. As a topic, the concept of community has a large and diffuse literature and the particular foci chosen have certainly meant that some aspects have been too briefly analysed. The second statement of belief is that the study of community as a concept and as a reality remains of fundamental importance. There are now many established ways of looking at community — as place, as network, as image, as property, and as administrative unit — these all have something to offer individually and in association and deserve continuing attention. However, communities cannot be taken for granted, they have to be worked at and achieved. Perhaps the attitude should be positive and futuristic and less dependent upon a nostalgic memory of past neighbourhoods set in very different societal milieu and urban environments. New and vital place communities can help counteract some of the deficiencies of our contemporary society.

References

Barke, M. and Turnbull, G., 1992, *Meadowell: the biography of an estate with problems*, Avebury, Aldershot.

Bell, C. R. and Newby, H., 1978, Community, communion, class and community action: the social sources of the new urban politics, in D. T. Herbert and R. J. Johnston (eds), *Social areas in cities*, John Wiley, Chichester, 283–301.

Deutsch, E., 1992, Community as ritual participation, in L. S. Rouner (ed.) *On community*, Univ. of Notre Dame Press, Indiana, 15–26.

Keller, S., 1988, The American dream of community: an unfinished agenda, *Sociological Forum*, 3, 167–83.

Prestage, M., 1992, Riots mark of respect to dead local men, *The Independent*, July 18, p. 2.

Rouner, L. S., 1991, *On community*, University of Notre Dame Press, Indiana.

Schmalenbach, H., 1977, *On society and experience: selected essays*, translated and edited by G. Luschen and G. Stone, University of Chicago Press, Chicago.

Smith, N., 1987, Dangers of the empirical turn: some comments on the CURS initiative, *Antipode*, 19, 59–68.

Taylor, C., 1991, *The malaise of modernity*, Anansi, Concord, Ontario.

Wellman, B. and Leighton, B., 1979, Networks, neighbourhoods and communities, approaches to the study of the community question, *Urban Affairs Quarterly*, 14, 363–90.

Subject index

Name index